D1231538

Barneveldt Warned of His Danger

From drawings by Frederick Dielman

Barneveldt Warned of His Danger

From drawing by Frederick Dielman

The Complete Works of
John L. Motley

VOLUME XIV

The Life and Death of John of Barneveldt
Advocate of Holland

With a View of the Primary Causes and Movements
of the Thirty Years' War

Vol. III

The Jenson Society

New York

2975

CONTENTS

THE LIFE AND DEATH OF
JOHN OF BARNEVELDT

CHAPTER XVI

Maurice revolutionizes the provinces—Danckaerts's libelous pamphlet—Barneveldt's appeal to the prince—Barneveldt's Remonstrance to the states—The stadholder at Amsterdam—The treaty
of truce nearly expired—King of Spain and Archduke Albert—
Scheme for recovering the provinces—Secret plot to make Maurice
sovereign.

EARLY in the year (1618) Maurice set himself
about revolutionizing the provinces on which he
could not yet thoroughly rely. The town of Nimwegen, since its recovery from the Spaniards near the
close of the preceding century, had held its municipal
government, as it were, at the option of the prince.
During the war he had been, by the terms of surrender,
empowered to appoint and to change its magistracy at
will. No change had occurred for many years, but as
the government had of late fallen into the hands of the
Barneveldtians, and as Maurice considered the truce
to be a continuance of the war, he appeared suddenly
in the city at the head of a body of troops and surrounded by his life-guard. Summoning the whole

board of magistrates into the town house, he gave them all notice to quit, disbanding them like a company of mutinous soldiery, and immediately afterward appointed a fresh list of functionaries in their stead.[1]

This done, he proceeded to Arnheim, where the states of Gelderland were in session, appeared before that body, and made a brief announcement of the revolution which he had so succinctly effected in the most considerable town of their province. The assembly, which seems, like many other assemblies at precisely this epoch, to have had an extraordinary capacity for yielding to gentle violence, made but little resistance to the extreme measures now undertaken by the stadholder, and not only highly applauded the subjugation of Nimwegen, but listened with sympathy to his arguments against the wartgelders and in favor of the synod.

Having accomplished so much by a very brief visit to Gelderland, the prince proceeded to Overyssel, and had as little difficulty in bringing over the wavering minds of that province into orthodoxy and obedience. Thus there remained but two provinces out of seven that were still "wartgeldered" and refused to be "synodized."

It was rebellion against rebellion. Maurice and his adherents accused the states'-right party of mutiny against himself and the States-General. The states'-right party accused the Contra-Remonstrants in the cities of mutiny against the lawful sovereignty of each province.

The oath of the soldiery, since the foundation of the Republic, had been to maintain obedience and fidelity

[1] Wagenaer, x. 195 seq.   Van der Kemp, iv. 70, 71.

to the States-General, the stadholder, and the province in which they were garrisoned, and at whose expense they were paid. It was impossible to harmonize such conflicting duties and doctrines. Theory had done its best and its worst. The time was fast approaching, as it always must approach, when fact with its violent besom would brush away the fine-spun cobwebs which had been so long undisturbed.

"I will grind the advocate and all his party into fine meal,"[1] said the prince on one occasion.

A clever caricature of the time represented a pair of scales hung up in a great hall. In the one was a heap of parchments, gold chains, and magisterial robes, the whole bundle being marked the "holy right of each city." In the other lay a big, square, solid, iron-clasped volume, marked "Institutes of Calvin." Each scale was respectively watched by Gomarus and by Arminius. The judges, gowned, furred, and ruffed, were looking decorously on, when suddenly the stad-holder, in full military attire, was seen rushing into the apartment, and flinging his sword into the scale with the "Institutes."

The civic and legal trumpery was of course made to kick the beam.

Maurice had organized his campaign this year against the advocate and his party as deliberately as he had ever arranged the details of a series of battles and sieges against the Spaniard. And he was proving himself as consummate master in political strife as in the great science of war.

[1] Resol. Holl., May 21, 1618, bl. 122. Uytenb., 954, 951. Brandt, Hist. Ref., ii. 751. Wagenaer, x. 205. Van der Kemp, iv. 75.

He no longer made any secret of his conviction that Barneveldt was a traitor to his country, bought with Spanish gold. There was not the slightest proof for these suspicions, but he asserted them roundly. "The advocate is traveling straight to Spain," he said to Count Cuylenborg. "But we will see who has got the longest purse."[1]

And as if it had been a part of the campaign, a pre-arranged diversion to the more direct and general assault on the intrenchments of the states'-right party, a horrible personal onslaught was now made from many quarters upon the advocate. It was an age of pamphleteering, of venomous, virulent, unscrupulous libels. And never even in that age had there been anything to equal the savage attacks upon this great statesman. It moves the gall of an honest man, even after the lapse of two centuries and a half, to turn over those long-forgotten pages and mark the depths to which political and theological party spirit could descend. That human creatures can assimilate themselves so closely to the reptile, and to the subtle devil within the reptile, when a party end is to be gained, is enough to make the very name of man a term of reproach.

Day by day appeared pamphlets, each one more poisonous than its predecessor. There was hardly a crime that was not laid at the door of Barneveldt and all his kindred. The man who had borne a matchlock in early youth against the foreign tyrant, in days when unsuccessful rebellion meant martyrdom and torture; who had successfully guided the councils of the infant com-

---

[1] Wagenaer, x. 201. Van der Kemp, iv. 75. Uytenb. Leven, c. x. 172. Brandt, ii. 744.

monwealth at a period when most of his accusers were in their cradles, and when mistake was ruin to the Republic; he on whose strong arm the father of his country had leaned for support; the man who had organized a political system out of chaos; who had laid down the internal laws, negotiated the great indispensable alliances, directed the complicated foreign policy, established the system of national defense, presided over the successful financial administration of a state struggling out of mutiny into national existence; who had rocked the Republic in her cradle and ever borne her in his heart; who had made her name beloved at home and honored and dreaded abroad; who had been the first, when the great Taciturn had at last fallen a victim to the murderous tyrant of Spain, to place the youthful Maurice in his father's place, and to inspire the whole country with sublime courage to persist rather than falter in purpose after so deadly a blow; who was as truly the founder of the Republic as William had been the author of its independence,—was now denounced as a traitor, a pope, a tyrant, a venal huckster of his country's liberties. His family name, which had long been an ancient and knightly one, was defiled and its nobility disputed; his father and mother, sons and daughters, sisters and brothers, accused of every imaginable and unimaginable crime, of murder, incest, robbery, bastardy, fraud, forgery, blasphemy. He had received wagon-loads of Spanish pistoles; he had been paid one hundred and twenty thousand ducats by Spain for negotiating the truce; he was in secret treaty with Archduke Albert to bring eighteen thousand Spanish mercenaries across the border to defeat the machinations of Prince Maurice, destroy his life, or drive him from the country: all these foul and bitter charges and a thousand similar ones were rained almost daily upon that gray head.[1]

One day the loose sheets of a more than commonly libelous pamphlet were picked up in the streets of The Hague and placed in the advocate's hands. It was the work of the drunken notary Danckaerts already mentioned, then resident in Amsterdam, and among the papers thus found was a list of wealthy merchants of that city who had contributed to the expense of its publication.[2] The opposition of Barneveldt to the West India Corporation could never be forgiven. The advocate was notified in this production that he was soon to be summoned to answer for his crimes. The country was weary of him, he was told, and his life was forfeited.

Stung at last beyond endurance by the persistent malice of his enemies, he came before the states of Holland for redress. Upon his remonstrance the author of this vile libel was summoned to answer before the upper tribunal at The Hague for his crime. The city of Amsterdam covered him with the shield *de non evocando*, which had so often in cases of less consequence proved of no protective value, and the notary was never punished, but, on the contrary, after a brief lapse of time, rewarded as for a meritorious action.

Meantime the states of Holland, by formal act, took the name and honor of Barneveldt under their imme-

[1] Baudartius, **x**. 46. See especially the pamphlets entitled "Gulden Legende v. d. Nieuwen St. Jan," and the "Noodwendig Discours."

[2] Ibid. Wagenaer, x. 201. Van der Kemp, iv. 74–76. Van Rees and Brill, 787, 788 seq.

diate protection as a treasure belonging especially to
themselves.   Heavy penalties were denounced upon the
authors and printers of these libelous attacks, and large
rewards offered for their detection.[1]   Nothing came,
however, of such measures.

On the 24th April the advocate addressed a frank,
dignified, and conciliatory letter to the prince.[2]   The
rapid progress of calumny against him had at last
alarmed even his steadfast soul, and he thought it best
to make a last appeal to the justice and to the clear
intellect of William the Silent's son.

"GRACIOUS PRINCE," he said: "I observe to my
greatest sorrow an entire estrangement of your Excellency from me, and I fear lest what was said six
months since by certain clerical persons and afterward
by some politicians concerning your dissatisfaction
with me, which until now I have not been able to believe, must be true.   I declare nevertheless with a sincere heart to have never willingly given cause for any
such feeling, having always been your very faithful servant, and with God's help hoping as such to die.   Ten
years ago, during the negotiations for the truce, I

[1] Resol. Holl., June 20–25, 1618, bl. 154, 155, 199.   Groot Plak-
kaatboek, i. 457.   Wagenaer, x. 204.

The following are the names of a few among the swarm of
pamphlets of this year : " The Lamentations of Batavia " ; "Reve-
lation of Spanish and Jesuit Tricks " ; " A Joyful Drum-beat " ;
"The Arminian Road to Spain " ; "Declaration of the Golden Bellows " ; " The Arminian Dung-cart " ; " A Little Window, by peep-
ing through which one can see the Great Masters rolling down to
the Gates of Hell " ; " Golden Legend of the New St. John ; or,
Short Account of the Nobility, Virtues, and Actions of Master
John van Olden-Barneveldt " ; etc.

[2] Waaragtige Historie van Oldenbarneveld, 132 seq. (Rotterdam, Naeranus, 1670).

clearly observed the beginning of this estrangement, but your Excellency will be graciously pleased to remember that I declared to you at that time my upright and sincere intention in these negotiations to promote the service of the country and the interests of your Excellency, and that I nevertheless offered at the time not only to resign all my functions, but to leave the country rather than remain in office and in the country to the dissatisfaction of your Excellency.''

He then rapidly reviewed the causes which had produced the alienation of which he complained, and the melancholy divisions caused by the want of mutual religious toleration in the provinces; spoke of his efforts to foster a spirit of conciliation on the dread subject of predestination, and referred to the letter of the King of Great Britain deprecating discussion and schism on this subject, and urging that those favorable to the views of the Remonstrants ought not to be persecuted. Referring to the intimate relations which Uytenbogart had so long enjoyed with the prince, the advocate alluded to the difficulty he had in believing that his Excellency intended to act in opposition to the efforts of the states of Holland in the cause of mutual toleration, to the manifest detriment of the country and of many of its best and truest patriots and the greater number of the magistrates in all the cities.

He reminded the prince that all attempts to accommodate these fearful quarrels had been frustrated, and that on his departure the previous year to Utrecht on account of his health he had again offered to resign all his offices and to leave Holland altogether rather than find himself in perpetual opposition to his Excellency.

''I begged you in such case,'' he said, ''to lend your

hand to the procuring for me an honorable discharge from my lords the states; but your Excellency declared that you could in no wise approve such a step, and gave me hope that some means of accommodating the dissensions would yet be proposed.

"I went then to Vianen, being much indisposed; thence I repaired to Utrecht to consult my old friend Dr. Saulo Saul, in whose hands I remained six weeks, not being able, as I hoped, to pass my seventieth birthday on the 24th September last in my birthplace, the city of Amersfoort. All this time I heard not one single word or proposal of accommodation. On the contrary, it was determined by a majority vote, a thing never heard of before, that it was intended against the solemn resolves of the states of Holland, of Utrecht, and of Overyssel, to bring these religious differences before the assembly of my lords the States-General, a proceeding directly in the teeth of the Act of Union and other treaties, and before a synod which people called national, and that meantime every effort was making to discredit all those who stood up for the laws of these provinces and to make them odious and despicable in the eyes of the common people.

"Especially it was I that was thus made the object of hatred and contempt in their eyes. Hundreds of lies and calumnies, circulated in the form of libels, seditious pamphlets, and lampoons, compelled me to return from Utrecht to The Hague. Since that time I have repeatedly offered my services to your Excellency for the promotion of mutual accommodation and reconciliation of differences, but without success."

He then alluded to the publication with which the country was ringing, "The Necessary and Living Discourse of a Spanish Counselor,'' and which was attributed to his former confidential friend, now become his deadliest foe, ex-Ambassador Francis Aertsens, and warned the prince that if he chose, which God forbid, to follow the advice of that seditious libel, nothing but ruin to the beloved fatherland and its lovers, to the princely house of Orange-Nassau, and to the Christian religion could be the issue. ''The Spanish government could desire no better counsel,'' he said, ''than this which these fellows give you; to encourage distrust and estrangement between your Excellency and the nobles, the cities, and the magistrates of the land, and to propose high and haughty imaginings which are easy enough to write, but most difficult to practise, and which can only inure to the advantage of Spain. Therefore most respectfully I beg your Excellency not to believe these fellows, but to reject their counsels. . . . Among them are many malignant hypocrites and ambitious men who are seeking their own profit in these changes of government—many utterly ragged and beggarly fellows and many infamous traitors coming from the provinces which have remained under the dominion of the Spaniard, and who are filled with revenge, envy, and jealousy at the greater prosperity and bloom of these independent states than they find at home.

''I fear,'' he said in conclusion,''that I have troubled your Excellency too long, but to the fulfilment of my duty and discharge of my conscience I could not be more brief. It saddens me deeply that in recompense for my long and manifold services I am attacked by so many calumnious, lying, seditious, and fraudulent libels, and that these indecencies find their pretext and

their food in the evil disposition of your Excellency
toward me. And although for one-and-thirty years
long I have been able to live down such things with
silence, well-doing, and truth, still do I now find myself
compelled in this my advanced old age and infirmity
to make some utterances in defense of myself and
those belonging to me, however much against my heart
and inclinations.'' [1]

He ended by inclosing a copy of the solemn state
paper which he was about to lay before the states of
Holland in defense of his honor, and subscribed himself the lifelong and faithful servant of the prince.

The Remonstrance to the states contained a summary
review of the political events of his life, which was indeed nothing more nor less than the history of his
country and almost of Europe itself during that period, broadly and vividly sketched with the hand of a
master. It was published at once, and strengthened
the affection of his friends and the wrath of his enemies. It is not necessary to our purpose to reproduce
or even analyze the document, the main facts and
opinions contained in it being already familiar to the
reader.[2] The frankness, however, with which, in reply
to the charges so profusely brought against him,—of
having grown rich by extortion, treason, and corruption, of having gorged himself with plunder at home
and bribery from the enemy, of being the great pen-
sioner of Europe and the Marshal d'Ancre of the Netherlands,—he alluded to the exact condition of his pri-

[1] Waaragtige Historie van Oldenbarneveld, 132 seq. (Rotterdam, Naeranus, 1670).

[2] It is given in full in the Waaragtige Historie, 146 seq. It was
dated April 20, 1618.

vate affairs and the growth and sources of his revenue, giving, as it were, a kind of schedule of his property, has in it something half humorous, half touching in its simplicity.

He set forth the very slender salaries attached to his high offices of advocate of Holland, keeper of the seals, and other functions. He answered the charge that he always had at his disposition one hundred and twenty thousand florins to bribe foreign agents withal by saying that his whole allowance for extraordinary expenses and trouble in maintaining his diplomatic and internal correspondence was exactly five hundred florins yearly. He alluded to the slanders circulated as to his wealth and its sources by those who envied him for his position and hated him for his services.

"But I beg you to believe, my lords," he continued, "that my property is neither so great nor so small as some people represent it to be.

"In the year '75 I married my wife," he said. "I was pleased with her person. I was likewise pleased with the dowry which was promptly paid over to me, with firm expectation of increase and betterment. . . . I acknowledge that forty-three years ago my wife and myself had got together so much of real and personal property that we could live honorably upon it. I had at that time as good pay and practice as any advocate in the courts, which brought me in a good four thousand florins a year; there being but eight advocates practising at the time, of whom I was certainly not the least one employed. In the beginning of the year '77 I came into the service of the city of Rotterdam as pensionary. Upon my salary from that town I was enabled to support my family, having then

but two children.   Now, I can clearly prove that between the years 1577 and 1616, inclusive, I have inherited in my own right or that of my wife, from our
relatives, for ourselves and our children by lawful succession, more than four hundred Holland morgens of
land [about eight hundred acres], more than two thousand florins yearly of redeemable rents, a good house
in the city of Delft, some houses in the open country,
and several thousand florins in ready money.   I have
likewise reclaimed in the course of the past forty years
out of the water and swamps by diking more than an
equal number of acres to those inherited, and have
bought and sold property during the same period to the
value of eight hundred thousand florins, having sometimes bought one hundred thousand florins' worth and
sold sixty thousand of it for one hundred and sixty
thousand, and so on.''

It was evident that the thrifty advocate during his
long life had understood how to turn over his money,
and it was not necessary to imagine ''wagon-loads of
Spanish pistoles'' and bribes on a gigantic scale from
the hereditary enemy in order to account for a reasonable opulence on his part.

''I have had nothing to do with trade,'' he continued,
''it having been the custom of my ancestors to risk no
money except where the plow goes.   In the great East
India Company, however, which, with four years of
hard work, public and private, I have helped establish, in order to inflict damage on the Spaniards and
Portuguese, I have adventured somewhat more than
five thousand florins.   .   .   .   Now, even if my condition be reasonably good, I think no one has reason to
envy me.   Nevertheless, I have said it in your Lord-

ships' assembly, and I repeat it solemnly on this occasion, that I have pondered the state of my affairs during my recent illness, and found that in order to leave my children unencumbered estates I must sell property to the value of sixty or seventy thousand florins. This I would rather do than leave the charge to my children. That I should have got thus behindhand through bad management I beg your Highnesses not to believe. But I have inherited, with the succession of four persons whose only heir I was and with that of others to whom I was coheir, many burdens as well. I have bought property with encumbrances, and I have diked and bettered several estates with borrowed money. Now, should it please your Lordships to institute a census and valuation of the property of your subjects, I, for one, should be very well pleased. For I know full well that those who, in the estimates of capital in the year 1599, rated themselves at fifty or sixty thousand florins now may boast of having twice as much property as I have. Yet in that year out of patriotism I placed myself on the list of those liable for the very highest contributions, being assessed on a property of two hundred thousand florins.''

The advocate alluded with haughty contempt to the notorious lies circulated by his libelers in regard to his lineage, as if the vast services and unquestioned abilities of such a statesman would not have illustrated the obscurest origin. But as he happened to be of ancient and honorable descent, he chose to vindicate his position in that regard.

''I was born in the city of Amersfoort,'' he said, ''by the father's side an Olden-Barneveldt—an old and noble race, from generation to generation steadfast and true, who have been duly summoned for many hundred years to the assembly of the nobles of their province, as they are to this day. By my mother's side I am sprung from the ancient and knightly family of Amersfoort, which for three or four hundred years has been known as foremost among the nobles of Utrecht in all state affairs and as landed proprietors.''

It is only for the sake of opening these domestic and private lights upon an historical character whose life was so preëminently and almost exclusively a public one that we have drawn some attention to this stately defense made by the advocate of his birth, life, and services to the state. The public portions of the state paper belong exclusively to history, and have already been sufficiently detailed.

The letter to Prince Maurice was delivered into his hands by Cornelis van der Myle, son-in-law of Barneveldt.

No reply to it was ever sent, but several days afterward the stadholder called from his open window to Van der Myle, who happened to be passing by. He then informed him that he neither admitted the premises nor the conclusion of the advocate's letter, saying that many things set down in it were false. He furthermore told him a story of a certain old man who, having in his youth invented many things and told them often for truth, believed them when he came to old age to be actually true and was ever ready to stake his salvation upon them. Whereupon he shut the window and left Van der Myle to make such application of the parable as he thought proper, vouchsafing no further answer to Barneveldt's communication.[1]

[1] Carleton's Letters, 269.

Dudley Carleton related the anecdote to his government with much glee, but it may be doubted whether this bold way of giving the lie to a venerable statesman through his son-in-law would have been accounted as triumphant argumentation anywhere out of a barrack.

As for the Remonstrance to the states of Holland, although most respectfully received in that assembly except by the five opposition cities, its immediate effect on the public was to bring down a fresh "snow-storm" —to use the expression of a contemporary—of pamphlets, libels, caricatures, and broadsheets upon the head of the advocate. In every bookseller's and print-shop window in all the cities of the country the fallen statesman was represented in all possible ludicrous, contemptible, and hateful shapes, while hags and blind beggars about the streets screeched filthy and cursing ballads against him, even at his very doors.

The effect of energetic, uncompromising calumny has rarely been more strikingly illustrated than in the case of this statesman. Blackened daily all over by a thousand trowels, the purest and noblest character must have been defiled, and it is no wonder that the incrustation upon the advocate's fame should have lasted for two centuries and a half. It may perhaps endure for as many more. Not even the vile Marshal d'Ancre, who had so recently perished, was more the mark of obloquy in a country which he had dishonored, flouted, and picked to the bone than was Barneveldt in a commonwealth which he had almost created and had served faithfully from youth to old age. It was even the fashion to compare him with Concini [1] in order to

[1] Baudartius, x. 22–36.

heighten the wrath of the public, as if any parallel between the ignoble foreign paramour of a stupid and
sensual queen, and the great statesman, patriot, and
jurist of whom civilization will be always proud, could
ever enter any but an idiot's brain.

Meantime the stadholder, who had so successfully
handled the assembly of Gelderland and Overyssel, now
sailed across the Zuyder Zee from Kampen to Amsterdam. On his approach to the stately northern Venice,
standing full of life and commercial bustle upon its
vast submerged forest of Norwegian pines, he was met
by a fleet of yachts and escorted through the water-
gates of the Y into the city.[1]

Here an immense assemblage of vessels of every class,
from the humble gondola to the bulky East-Indiaman
and the first-rate ship of war, gaily bannered with the
Orange colors and thronged from deck to topmast by
enthusiastic multitudes, was waiting to receive their
beloved stadholder. A deafening cannonade saluted
him on his approach. The prince was escorted to the
Square, or Dam, where, on a high scaffolding covered
with blue velvet in front of the stately medieval town
hall, the burgomasters and board of magistrates, in
their robes of office, were waiting to receive him. The
strains of that most inspiriting and suggestive of national melodies, the "Wilhelmus van Nassouwen," rang
through the air, and when they were silent, the chief
magistrate poured forth a very eloquent and tedious
oration, and concluded by presenting him with a large
orange of solid gold, Maurice having succeeded to the
principality a few months before, on the death of his
half-brother Philip William.[2]

---

[1] Baudartius, x. 52, 53.   [2] Ibid., 32, 52, 53 seq.

The "Blooming in Love," as one of the chambers of "rhetoric" in which the hard-handed but half-artistic mechanics and shopkeepers of the Netherlands loved to disport themselves was called, then exhibited upon an opposite scaffold a magnificent representation of Jupiter astride upon an eagle and handing down to the stadholder as if from the clouds that same principality. Nothing could be neater or more mythological.

The prince and his escort, sitting in the windows of the town hall, the square beneath being covered with three or four thousand burgher militia in full uniform, with orange plumes in their hats and orange scarfs on their breasts, saw still other sights. A gorgeous procession set forth by the "Netherlandish Academy," another chamber of rhetoric, and filled with those emblematic impersonations so dear to the hearts of Netherlanders, had been sweeping through all the canals and along the splendid quays of the city. The Maid of Holland, twenty feet high, led the van, followed by the counterfeit presentment of each of her six sisters. An orange-tree full of flowers and fruit was conspicuous in one barge, while in another, strangely and lugubriously enough, lay the murdered William the Silent in the arms of his wife, and surrounded by his weeping sons and daughters, all attired in white satin.[1]

In the evening the Netherland Academy, to improve the general hilarity, and as if believing exhibitions of murder the most appropriate means of welcoming the prince, invited him to a scenic representation of the assassination of Count Florence V. of Holland by Gerrit van Velsen and other nobles. There seemed no especial reason for the selection, unless perhaps the

[1] Baudartius, x. 32, 52, 53 seq.

local one, one of the perpetrators of this crime against an ancient predecessor of William the Silent in the sovereignty of Holland having been a former lord proprietor of Amsterdam and the adjacent territories, Gysbrecht van Amstel.[1]

Maurice returned to The Hague. Five of the seven provinces were entirely his own. Utrecht, too, was already wavering, while there could be no doubt of the warm allegiance to himself of the important commercial metropolis of Holland, the only province in which Barneveldt's influence was still paramount.

Owing to the watchfulness and distrust of Barneveldt, which had never faltered, Spain had not secured the entire control of the disputed duchies, but she had at least secured the head of a venerated saint. "The bargain is completed for the head of the glorious St. Lawrence, which you know I so much desire," wrote Philip triumphantly to the Archduke Albert.[2] He had, however, not got it for nothing.

The Abbot of Glamart in Jülich, then in possession of that treasure, had stipulated before delivering it that if at any time the heretics or other enemies should destroy the monastery his Majesty would establish them in Spanish Flanders and give them the same revenues as they now enjoyed in Jülich. Count Hermann van den Berg was to give a guaranty to that effect.[3]

Meantime, the long controversy in the duchies having tacitly come to a standstill upon the basis of *uti possidetis*, the Spanish government had leisure, in the midst

[1] Baudartius, x. 32, 52, 53, seq.
[2] Philip III. to Archduke Albert, June 21, 1617, Belg. Arch. MS.
[3] Same to same.

of their preparation for the general crusade upon European heresy, to observe and enjoy the internal religious dissensions in their revolted provinces. Although they had concluded the convention with them as with countries over which they had no pretensions, they had never at heart allowed more virtue to the conjunction "as," which really contained the essence of the treaty, than grammatically belonged to it. Spain still chose to regard the independence of the seven provinces as a pleasant fiction to be dispelled when, the truce having expired by its own limitation, she should resume, as she fully meant to do, her sovereignty over all the seventeen Netherlands, the United as well as the obedient. Thus, at any rate, the question of state rights or central sovereignty would be settled by a very summary process. The Spanish ambassador was wroth, as may well be supposed, when the agent of the rebel provinces received in London the rank, title, and recognition of ambassador. Gondemar, at least, refused to acknowledge Noël de Caron as his diplomatic equal or even as his colleague, and was vehement in his protestations on the subject. But James, much as he dreaded the Spanish envoy and fawned upon his master, was not besotted enough to comply with these demands at the expense of his most powerful ally, the Republic of the Netherlands. The Spanish king, however, declared his ambassador's proceedings to be in exact accordance with his instructions. He was sorry, he said, if the affair had caused discontent to the King of Great Britain; he intended in all respects to maintain the treaty of truce, of which his Majesty had been one of the guarantors, but as that treaty had but a few more years to run, after which he should be reinstated in his former right of sovereignty over all the Netherlands, he entirely justified the conduct of Count Gondemar.[1]

It may well be conceived that, as the years passed by, as the period of the truce grew nearer and the religious disputes became every day more envenomed, the government at Madrid should look on the tumultuous scene with saturnine satisfaction. There was little doubt now, they thought, that the provinces, sick of their rebellion and that fancied independence which had led them into a whirlpool of political and religious misery, and convinced of their incompetence to govern themselves, would be only too happy to seek the forgiving arms of their lawful sovereign. Above all, they must have learned that their great heresy had carried its chastisement with it, that within something they called a Reformed Church other heresies had been developed which demanded condign punishment at the hands of that new church, and that there could be neither rest for them in this world nor salvation in the next except by returning to the bosom of their ancient mother.

Now was the time, so it was thought, to throw forward a strong force of Jesuits as skirmishers into the provinces, by whom the way would be opened for the reconquest of the whole territory.

"By the advices coming to us continually from thence," wrote the King of Spain to Archduke Albert, "we understand that the disquiets and differences continue in Holland on matters relating to their sects, and that from this has resulted the conversion of many to

[1] Langerac to States-General, March 11, 1615, Hague Archives MS.

the Catholic religion.   So it has been taken into consideration whether it would not be expedient that some fathers of the Company of Jesuits be sent secretly from Rome to Holland, who should negotiate concerning the conversion of that people.   Before taking a resolution, I have thought best to give an account of this matter to your Highness.   I should be glad if you would inform me what priests are going to Holland, what fruits they yield, and what can be done for the continuance of their labors.   Please to advise me very particularly, together with any suggestions that may occur to you in this matter." [1]

The archduke, who was nearer the scene, was not so sure that the old religion was making such progress as his royal nephew or those who spoke in his name believed.   At any rate, if it were not rapidly gaining ground, it would be neither for want of discord among the Protestants nor for lack of Jesuits to profit by it.

"I do not understand," said he, in reply, "nor is it generally considered certain, that from the differences and disturbances that the Hollanders are having among

[1] Philip III. to Archduke Albert, April 17, 1617, Belg. Arch. MS. : " SER^mo SEÑOR : Por los avisos que de ahí van veniendo se ha entendido que en Olanda se continuan las inquietudes y diferencias que traen alli sobre cosas tocantes á sus setas y que desto ha resultata el yrse convirtiendo muchos á la religion cattolica.   Y aunque se ha considerado seria conveniente que de Roma fuesen a Olanda con secreto algunos padres de la compañia que traten de la reduzion de aquella gente : Antes de tornar resolucion en ello ho querido dar cuenta de lo referido a V. A.   Y holgare ordene se sepa muy particularmente que religiosos andan en Olanda y el frute que hazen y que se podria hazer para la continuacion dellos y avisarme V. A. de todo muy particularmente con lo demas que se ofreciere en la materia."

themselves there has resulted the conversion of any of
them to our blessed Catholic faith, because their disputes are of certain points concerning which there are
different opinions within their sect.   There has always
been a goodly number of priests here, the greater part
of whom belong to the Company.   They are very dili-
gent and fervent, and the Catholics derive much comfort from them.   To send more of them would do more
harm than good.   It might be found out, and then they
would perhaps be driven out of Holland or even chastised.   So it seems better to leave things as they are
for the present."[1]

The Spanish government was not discouraged, however, but was pricking up its ears anew at strange communications it was receiving from the very bosom of
the council of state in the Netherlands.   This body, as
will be remembered, had been much opposed to Barneveldt and to the policy pursued under his leader-
ship by the states of Holland.   Some of its members
were secretly Catholic and still more secretly disposed
to effect a revolution in the government, the object of
which should be to fuse the United Provinces with the
obedient Netherlands in a single independent mon-
archy to be placed under the scepter of the son of
Philip III.

A paper containing the outlines of this scheme had
been sent to Spain, and the king at once forwarded it
in cipher to the archduke at Brussels for his opinion
and coöperation.

"You will see," he said, "the plan which a certain
person zealous for the public good has proposed for
reducing the Netherlanders to my obedience.   .   .   .

---

[1] Archduke Albert, May, 1617, Belg. Arch. MS.

You will please advise with Count Frederick van den Berg and let me know with much particularity and profound secrecy what is thought, what is occurring, and the form in which this matter ought to be negotiated, and the proper way to make it march."[1]

Unquestionably the paper was of grave importance.[2] It informed the King of Spain that some principal personages in the United Netherlands, members of the council of state, were of opinion that if his Majesty or Archduke Albert should propose peace, it could be accomplished at that moment more easily than ever before. They had arrived at the conviction that no assistance was to be obtained from the King of France, who was too much weakened by tumults and sedition at home, while nothing good could be expected from the King of England. The greater part of the province of Gelderland, they said, with all Friesland, Utrecht, Groningen, and Overyssel, were inclined to a permanent peace. Being all of them frontier provinces, they were constantly exposed to the brunt of hostilities. Besides this, the war expenses alone would now be more than three million florins a year. Thus the people were kept perpetually harassed, and although evil-intentioned persons approved these burdens under the pretense that such heavy taxation served to free them from the tyranny of Spain, those of sense and quality[3] reproved them and knew the contrary to be true. "Many here know," continued these traitors in the heart of the state council, "how good it would be for the people of the Netherlands to have a

1 Philip III. to Archduke Albert, June 21, 1617, Belg. Arch. MS.
2 "Puntos de lo que contiene el papel incluso."—Ibid.
3 " . . . entendimiento y calidad."

prince, and those having this desire, being on the frontier, are determined to accept the son of your Majesty
for their ruler.'' The conditions of the proposed arrangement were to be that the prince, with his successors who were thus to possess all the Netherlands, were
to be independent sovereigns, not subject in any way to
the crown of Spain, and that the great governments
and dignities of the country were to remain in the
hands then holding them.

This last condition was obviously inserted in the plan
for the special benefit of Prince Maurice and Count
Louis, although there is not an atom of evidence that
they had ever heard of the intrigue, or doubt that, if
they had, they would have signally chastised its guilty
authors.

It was further stated that the Catholics, having in
each town a church and free exercise of their religion,
would soon be in a great majority. Thus the political
and religious counter-revolution would be triumphantly
accomplished.

It was proposed that the management of the business
should be intrusted to some gentleman of the country
possessing property there, who, ''under pretext of the
public good, should make people comprehend what a
great thing it would be if they could obtain this favor
from the Spanish king, thus extricating themselves
from so many calamities and miseries, and obtaining
free traffic and a prince of their own.'' [1] It would be
necessary for the king and archduke to write many

---

[1] '' . . . el qual sobre pretesto del bien publico ha de proponer
les y darles á entender qual gran cosa seria conseguir esto de Su
Mᵈ para salir de tantas calamidades y miserias, tener el trafico
libre y un principe natural,'' etc.

letters and promise great rewards to persons who might otherwise embarrass the good work.

The plot was an ingenious one. There seemed in the opinion of these conspirators in the state council but one great obstacle to its success. It should be kept absolutely concealed from the states of Holland. The great stipendiary of Spain, John of Barneveldt, whose coffers were filled with Spanish pistoles, whose name and surname might be read by all men in the account-books at Brussels heading the register of mighty bribe-takers, the man who was howled at in a thousand lampoons as a traitor ever ready to sell his country, whom even Prince Maurice "partly believed" to be the pensionary of Philip, must not hear a whisper of this scheme to restore the Republic to Spanish control and place it under the scepter of a Spanish prince.

The states of Holland at that moment and so long as he was a member of the body were Barneveldt, and Barneveldt only, thinking his thoughts, speaking with his tongue, writing with his pen. Of this neither friend nor foe ever expressed a doubt. Indeed, it was one of the staple accusations against him.

Yet this paper in which the Spanish king in confidential cipher and profound secrecy communicated to Archduke Albert his hopes and his schemes for recovering the revolted provinces as a kingdom for his son contained these words of caution.

"The states of Holland and Zealand will be opposed to the plan," it said. "If the treaty come to the knowledge of the states and council of Holland before it has been acted upon by the five frontier provinces the whole plan will be demolished." [1]

[1] " . . . seria desbaratarlo."

Such was the opinion entertained by Philip himself of the man who was supposed to be his stipendiary. I am not aware that this paper has ever been alluded to in any document or treatise, private or public, from the day of its date to this hour. It certainly has never been published, but it lies deciphered in the Archives of the Kingdom at Brussels, and is alone sufficient to put to shame the slanderers of the advocate's loyalty.

Yet let it be remembered that in this very summer, exactly at the moment when these intrigues were going on between the King of Spain and the class of men most opposed to Barneveldt, the accusations against his fidelity were loudest and rifest.

Before the stadholder had so suddenly slipped down to Brielle in order to secure that important stronghold for the Contra-Remonstrant party, reports had been carefully strewn among the people that the advocate was about to deliver that place and other fortresses to Spain.

Brielle, Flushing, Rammekens, the very cautionary towns and keys to the country which he had so recently and in such masterly manner delivered from the grasp of the hereditary ally, he was now about to surrender to the ancient enemy.

The Spaniards were already on the sea, it was said. Had it not been for his Excellency's watchfulness and promptitude, they would already, under guidance of Barneveldt and his crew, have mastered the city of Brielle. Flushing, too, through Barneveldt's advice and connivance, was open at a particular point, in order that the Spaniards, who had their eye upon it, might conveniently enter and take possession of the place.[1]   The

[1] Brandt, Hist. Ref., ii. 631.   From Memoirs of J. Uytenbogart.

air was full of wild rumors to this effect, and already the humbler classes, who sided with the stadholder, saw in him the savior of the country from the treason of the advocate and the renewed tyranny of Spain.

. The prince made no such pretense, but simply took possession of the fortress in order to be beforehand with the wartgelders. The Contra-Remonstrants in Brielle had desired that "men should see who had the hardest fists,"[1] and it would certainly have been difficult to find harder ones than those of the hero of Nieuport.

Besides the Jesuits coming in so skilfully to triumph over the warring sects of Calvinists, there were other engineers on whom the Spanish government relied to effect the reconquest of the Netherlands. Especially it was an object to wreak vengeance on Holland, that head and front of the revolt, both for its persistence in rebellion and for the immense prosperity and progress by which that rebellion had been rewarded. Holland had grown fat and strong, while the obedient Netherlands were withered to the marrow of their bones. But there was a practical person then resident in Spain to whom the Netherlands were well known, to whom, indeed, everything was well known, who had laid before the king a magnificent scheme for destroying the commerce and with it the very existence of Holland, to the great advantage of the Spanish finances and of the Spanish Netherlands. Philip, of course, laid it before the archduke as usual, that he might ponder it well, and afterward, if approved, direct its execution.[2]

[1] Brandt, Hist. Ref., ii. 630.   From Memoirs of J. Uytenbogart.
[2] Philip III. to Archduke Albert, June 21, 1617, Belg. Arch. MS. The memoir was inclosed with the letter.

The practical person set forth in an elaborate memoir that the Hollanders were making rapid progress in commerce, arts, and manufactures, while the obedient provinces were sinking as swiftly into decay. The Spanish Netherlands were almost entirely shut off from the sea, the rivers Schelde and Meuse being hardly navigable for them on account of the control of those waters by Holland. The Dutch were attracting to their dominions all artisans, navigators, and traders. Despising all other nations and giving them the law, they had ruined the obedient provinces. Ostend, Nieuport, Dunkirk, were wasting away, and ought to be restored.

"I have profoundly studied forty years long the subjects of commerce and navigation," said the practical person, "and I have succeeded in penetrating the secrets and acquiring, as it were, universal knowledge—let me not be suspected of boasting—of the whole discovered world and of the ocean.[1] I have been assisted by study of the best works of geography and history, by my own labors, and by those of my late father, a man of illustrious genius and heroical conceptions, and very zealous in the Catholic faith."

The modest and practical son of an illustrious but anonymous father, then coming to the point, said it would be the easiest thing in the world to direct the course of the Schelde into an entirely new channel through Spanish Flanders to the sea. Thus the Dutch ports and forts which had been constructed with such magnificence and at such vast expense would be left

[1] " . . . y llegué á alcanzer los secretos y la noticia (no se me atribuye á jactancia) casi universal de todo el mundo descubierto y la mar," etc.

high and dry; the Spaniards would build new ones in Flanders, and thus control the whole navigation and deprive the Hollanders of that empire of the sea which they now so proudly arrogated. This scheme was much simpler to carry out than the vulgar might suppose, and, when accomplished, it would destroy the commerce, navigation, and fisheries of the Hollanders, throwing it all into the hands of the archdukes. This would cause such ruin, poverty, and tumults everywhere that all would be changed. The Republic of the United States would annihilate itself and fall to pieces; the religious dissensions, the war of one sect with another, and the jealousy of the house of Nassau, suspected of plans hostile to popular liberties, finishing the work of destruction. "Then the Republic," said the man of universal science, warming at sight of the picture he was painting, "laden with debt and steeped in poverty, will fall to the ground of its own weight, and, thus debilitated, will crawl humbly to place itself in the paternal hands of the illustrious house of Austria."

It would be better, he thought, to set about the work before the expiration of the truce. At any rate, the preparation for it, or the mere threat of it, would insure a renewal of that treaty on juster terms. It was most important, too, to begin at once the construction of a port on the coast of Flanders, looking to the north.

There was a position, he said, without naming it, in which whole navies could ride in safety, secure from all tempests, beyond the reach of the Hollanders, open at all times to traffic to and from England, France, Spain, Norway, Sweden, Russia—a perfectly free commerce, beyond the reach of any rights or duties claimed or levied by the insolent Republic. In this port would assemble all the navigators of the country, and it would become in time of war a terror to the Hollanders, English, and all Northern peoples. In order to attract, protect, and preserve these navigators and this commerce, many great public edifices must be built, together with splendid streets of houses and impregnable fortifications. It should be a walled and stately city, and its name should be Philippopolis. If these simple projects, so easy of execution, pleased his Majesty, the practical person was ready to explain them in all their details.

His Majesty was enchanted with the glowing picture, but before quite deciding on carrying the scheme into execution thought it best to consult the archduke.

The reply of Albert has not been preserved. It was probably not enthusiastic, and the man who, without boasting, had declared himself to know everything was never commissioned to convert his schemes into realities. That magnificent walled city, Philippopolis, with its gorgeous streets and bristling fortresses, remained unbuilt, the Schelde has placidly flowed through its old channel to the sea from that day to this, and the Republic remained in possession of the unexampled foreign trade with which rebellion had enriched it.

These various intrigues and projects show plainly enough, however, the encouragement given to the enemies of the United Provinces and of Protestantism everywhere by these disastrous internal dissensions. But yesterday and the Republic led by Barneveldt in council and Maurice of Nassau in the field stood at the head of the great army of resistance to the general crusade organized by Spain and Rome against all unbe-

lievers.   And now that the war was absolutely beginning in Bohemia, the Republic was falling upon its
own sword instead of smiting with it the universal foe.

It was not the King of Spain alone that cast longing
eyes on the fair territory of that commonwealth which
the unparalleled tyranny of his father had driven to
renounce his scepter.   But in the Netherlands and
France, among the extreme orthodox party, there were
secret schemes, to which Maurice was not privy, to raise
Maurice to the sovereignty of the provinces.   Other
conspirators, with a wider scope and more treasonable
design, were disposed to surrender their country to the
dominion of France, stipulating, of course, large rewards and offices for themselves, and the viceroyalty
of what should then be the French Netherlands to
Maurice.

The schemes were wild enough, perhaps, but their
very existence, which is undoubted, is another proof,
if more proof were wanted, of the lamentable tendency,
in times of civil and religious dissension, of political
passion to burn out the very first principles of patriotism.

It is also important, on account of the direct influence exerted by these intrigues upon subsequent events
of the gravest character, to throw a beam of light on
matters which were thought to have been shrouded for-
even in impenetrable darkness.

Langerac, the states' ambassador in Paris, was the
very reverse of his predecessor, the wily, unscrupulous,
and accomplished Francis Aertsens.   The envoys of
the Republic were rarely dull, but Langerac was a sim-
pleton.   They were renowned for political experience,
skill, familiarity with foreign languages, knowledge of

literature, history, and public law; but he was ignorant, spoke French very imperfectly, at a court where not a human being could address him in his own tongue, had never been employed in diplomacy or in high office of any kind, and could carry but small personal weight at a post where, of all others, the representative of the great Republic should have commanded deference both for his own qualities and for the majesty of his government. At a period when France was left without a master or a guide, the Dutch ambassador, under a becoming show of profound respect, might really have governed the country so far as regarded at least the all-important relations which bound the two nations together. But Langerac was a mere picker-up of trifles, a newsmonger who wrote a despatch to-day with information which a despatch was written on the morrow to contradict, while in itself conveying additional intelligence absolutely certain to be falsified soon afterward.[1] The Emperor of Germany had gone mad;[2] Prince Maurice had been assassinated [3] in The Hague, a fact which his correspondents, the States-General, might be supposed already to know, if it were one; there had been a revolution in the royal bedchamber;[4] the Spanish cook of the young queen had arrived from Madrid;[5] the Duke of Nevers was behaving very oddly at Vienna:[6] such communications, and others equally startling, were the staple of his correspondence.

[1] Mémoires de du Maurier, 382.

[2] Langerac to States-General, January 22, 1616, Hague Archives MS.

[3] Same to same, December 15, 1618, Hague Archives MS.

[4] Same to same, October 26, 1618, Hague Archives MS.

[5] Same to same.

[6] Same to same, January 22, 1619, Hague Archives MS.

Still, he was honest enough, very mild, perfectly docile to Barneveldt, dependent upon his guidance, and fervently attached to that statesman so long as his wheel was going up the hill. Moreover, his industry in obtaining information and his passion for imparting it made it probable that nothing very momentous would be neglected should it be laid before him, but that his masters, and especially the advocate, would be enabled to judge for themselves as to the attention due to it.

"With this you will be apprised of some very high and weighty matters," he wrote privately and in cipher to Barneveldt, "which you will make use of according to your great wisdom and forethought for the country's service."[1]

He requested that the matter might also be confided to M. van der Myle, that he might assist his father-in-law, so overburdened with business, in the task of deciphering the communication. He then stated that he had been "very earnestly informed three days before by M. du Agean"—member of the privy council of France—"that it had recently come to the king's ears, and his Majesty knew it to be authentic, that there was a secret and very dangerous conspiracy in Holland of persons belonging to the Reformed religion, in which others were also mixed. This party held very earnest and very secret correspondence with the factious portion of the Contra-Remonstrants both in the Netherlands and France, seeking under pretext of the religious dissensions or by means of them to confer the sovereignty upon Prince Maurice by general consent of the Contra-Remonstrants. Their object was also to strengthen and augment the force of the same religious

[1] Langerac to Barneveldt, May 19, 1618, Hague Archives MS.

party in France, to which end the Duc de Bouillon and
M. de Chatillon were very earnestly coöperating.''
Langerac had already been informed by Chatillon that
the Contra-Remonstrants had determined to make a
public declaration against the Remonstrants and come
to an open separation from them.

"Others propose, however," said the ambassador,
"that the king himself should use the occasion to seize
the sovereignty of the United Provinces for himself and
to appoint Prince Maurice viceroy, giving him in marriage Madame Henriette of France.'' The object of
this movement would be to frustrate the plots of the
Contra-Remonstrants, who were known to be passionately hostile to the king and to France, and who had
been constantly traversing the negotiations of M. du
Maurier. There was a disposition to send a special and
solemn embassy to the states, but it was feared that the
British king would at once do the same, to the immense
disadvantage of the Remonstrants. "M. de Barneveldt," said the envoy, "is deeply sympatinzed with
here and commiserated. The chancellor has repeatedly
requested me to present to you his very sincere and very
hearty respects, exhorting you to continue in your
manly steadfastness and courage.'' He also assured the
advocate that the French ambassador, M. du Maurier,
enjoyed the entire confidence of his government and of
the principal members of the council, and that the king,
although contemplating, as we have seen, the seizure
of the sovereignty of the country, was most amicably
disposed toward it, and so soon as the peace of Savoy
was settled "had something very good for it in his
mind.'' Whether the something very good was this
very design to deprive it of independence, the ambassa-

dor did not state. He, however, recommended the use
of sundry small presents at the French court,—especially to Madame de Luynes, wife of the new favorite
of Louis since the death of Concini, in which he had
aided, now rising rapidly to consideration, and to
Madame du Agean,—and asked to be supplied with
funds accordingly. By these means he thought it probable that at least the payment to the states of the long
arrears of the French subsidy might be secured.

Three weeks later, returning to the subject, the ambassador reported another conversation with M. du
Agean.[1] That politician assured him, "with high protestations," as a perfectly certain fact that a Frenchman duly qualified had arrived in Paris from Holland,
who had been in communication not only with him, but
with several of the most confidential members of the
privy council of France. This duly qualified gentleman had been secretly commissioned to say that, in
opinion of the conspirators already indicated, the occasion was exactly offered by these religious dissensions
in the Netherlands for bringing the whole country
under the obedience of the king. This would be done
with perfect ease if he would only be willing to favor
a little the one party, that of the Contra-Remonstrants,
and promise his Excellency "perfect and perpetual authority in the government, with other compensations."

The proposition, said Du Agean, had been rejected
by the privy councilors with a declaration that they
would not mix themselves up with any factions, nor
assist any party, but that they would gladly work with
the government for the accommodation of these difficulties and differences in the provinces.

[1] Langerac to Barneveldt, June 12, 1618, Hague Archives MS.

"I send you all this nakedly," concluded Langerac, "exactly as it has been communicated to me, having always answered according to my duty and with a view by negotiating with these persons to discover the intentions as well of one side as the other."

The advocate was not profoundly impressed by these revelations. He was too experienced a statesman to doubt that in times when civil and religious passion was running high there was never lack of fishers in troubled waters, and that if a body of conspirators could secure a handsome compensation by selling their country to a foreign prince, they would always be ready to do it.

But although believed by Maurice to be himself a stipendiary of Spain, he was above suspecting the prince of any share in the low and stupid intrigue which Du Agean had imagined or disclosed. That the stadholder was ambitious of greater power, he hardly doubted, but that he was seeking to acquire it by such corrupt and circuitous means, he did not dream. He confidentially communicated the plot, as in duty bound, to some members of the states, and had the prince been accused in any conversation or statement of being privy to the scheme, he would have thought himself bound to mention it to him. The story came to the ears of Maurice, however, and helped to feed his wrath against the advocate, as if he were responsible for a plot, if plot it were, which had been concocted by his own deadliest enemies. The prince wrote a letter alluding to this communication of Langerac and giving much alarm to that functionary. He thought his despatches must have been intercepted, and proposed in future to write always by special courier. Barneveldt thought that unnecessary except when there were more important

matters than those appeared to him to be and requiring
more haste.

"The letter of his Excellency," said he to the ambassador,[1] "is caused, in my opinion, by the fact that some
of the deputies to this assembly to whom I secretly
imparted your letter or its substance did not rightly
comprehend or report it. You did not say that his
Excellency had any such design or project, but that it
had been said that the Contra-Remonstrants were entertaining such a scheme. I would have shown the
letter to him myself, but I thought it not fair, for
good reasons, to make M. du Agean known as the informant. I do not think it amiss for you to write
yourself to his Excellency and tell him what is said,
but whether it would be proper to give up the name of
your author, I think doubtful. At all events, one must
consult about it. We live in a strange world, and one
knows not whom to trust."

He instructed the ambassador to inquire into the
foundation of these statements of Du Agean and send
advices by every occasion of this affair and others of
equal interest. He was, however, much more occupied
with securing the good will of the French government,
which he no more suspected of tampering in these
schemes against the independence of the Republic than
he did Maurice himself. He relied, and he had reason
to rely, on their steady good offices in the cause of
moderation and reconciliation. "We are not yet
brought to the necessary and much-desired unity," he
said, "but we do not despair, hoping that his Majesty's
efforts through M. du Maurier, both privately and publicly, will do much good. Be assured that they are

[1] Barneveldt to Langerac, June 2, 1618, Hague Archives MS.

very agreeable to all rightly disposed people. . . .
My trust is that God the Lord will give us a happy
issue and save this country from perdition." He approved of the presents to the two ladies, as suggested
by Langerac, if by so doing the payment of the arrear-
ages could be furthered. He was still hopeful and
confident in the justice of his cause and the purity of
his conscience. "Aertsens is crowing like a cock," he
said, "but the truth will surely prevail." [1]

[1] " . . . Aertsens maeckt stoutelyck den haen, maer de waer-
heyt sal wel die overhant winnen."

CHAPTER XVII

A deputation from Utrecht to Maurice—The fair at Utrecht—
Maurice and the states' deputies at Utrecht—Ogle refuses to act
in opposition to the states—The stadholder disbands the wartgelders—The prince appoints forty magistrates—The states
formally disband the wartgelders.

THE eventful midsummer had arrived. The lime-tree
blossoms were fragrant in the leafy bowers overshad-
owing the beautiful little rural capital of the commonwealth. The anniversary of the Nieuport victory,
July 2, had come and gone, and the stadholder was
known to be resolved that his political campaign this
year should be as victorious as that memorable military
one of eighteen years before.

Before the dog-days should begin to rage, the fierce
heats of theological and political passion were to wax
daily more and more intense.

The party at Utrecht in favor of a compromise and
in awe of the stadholder sent a deputation to The
Hague with the express but secret purpose of conferring with Maurice. They were eight in number, three
of whom, including Gillis van Ledenberg, lodged at
the house of Daniel Tressel, first clerk of the States-
General.[1]

[1] Wagenaer, x. 209–217. Van der Kemp, iv. 79. Baudartius,
x. 50 seq.

40

The leaders of the Barneveldt party, aware of the purport of this mission and determined to frustrate it, contrived a meeting between the Utrecht commissioners and Grotius, Hoogerbeets, De Haan, and De Lange at Tressel's house.

Grotius was spokesman. Maurice had accused the states of Holland of mutiny and rebellion, and the distinguished pensionary of Rotterdam now retorted the charges of mutiny, disobedience, and mischief-making upon those who, under the mask of religion, were attempting to violate the sovereignty of the states, the privileges and laws of the province, the authority of the magistrates, and to subject them to the power of others. To prevent such a catastrophe many cities had enlisted wartgelders. By this means they had held such mutineers to their duty, as had been seen at Leyden, Haarlem, and other places. The states of Utrecht had secured themselves in the same way. But the mischief-makers and the ill-disposed had been seeking everywhere to counteract these wholesome measures and to bring about a general disbanding of these troops. This it was necessary to resist with spirit. It was the very foundation of the provinces' sovereignty, to maintain which the public means must be employed. It was in vain to drive the foe out of the country if one could not remain in safety within one's own doors. They had heard with sorrow that Utrecht was thinking of cashiering its troops, and the speaker proceeded, therefore, to urge with all the eloquence he was master of the necessity of pausing before taking so fatal a step.[1]

The deputies of Utrecht answered by pleading the great pecuniary burden which the maintenance of the

---

[1] Authorities last cited.

mercenaries imposed upon that province, and complained that there was no one to come to their assistance, exposed as they were to a sudden and overwhelming attack from many quarters. The States-General had not only written but sent commissioners to Utrecht insisting on the disbandment. They could plainly see the displeasure of the prince. It was a very different affair in Holland, but the states of Utrecht found it necessary of two evils to choose the least. They had therefore instructed their commissioners to request the prince to remove the foreign garrison from their capital and to send the old companies of native militia in their place, to be in the pay of the episcopate. In this case the states would agree to disband the new levies.

Grotius, in reply, again warned the commissioners against communicating with Maurice according to their instructions, intimated that the native militia on which they were proposing to rely might have been debauched, and he held out hopes that perhaps the states of Utrecht might derive some relief from certain financial measures now contemplated in Holland.

The Utrechters resolved to wait at least several days before opening the subject of their mission to the prince. Meantime Ledenberg made a rough draft of a report of what had occurred between them and Grotius and his colleagues, which it was resolved to lay secretly before the states of Utrecht. The Hollanders hoped that they had at last persuaded the commissioners to maintain the wartgelders.[1]

The states of Holland now passed a solemn resolution to the effect that these new levies had been made to secure municipal order and maintain the laws from

[1] Authorities last cited.

subversion by civil tumults. If this object could be obtained by other means, if the stadholder were willing to remove garrisons of foreign mercenaries on whom there could be no reliance, and supply their place with native troops both in Holland and Utrecht, an arrangement could be made for disbanding the wartgelders.

Barneveldt, at the head of thirty deputies from the nobles and cities, waited upon Maurice and verbally communicated to him this resolution.[1] He made a cold and unsatisfactory reply, although it seems to have been understood that by according twenty companies of native troops he might have contented both Holland and Utrecht.

Ledenberg and his colleagues took their departure from The Hague without communicating their message to Maurice. Soon afterward the States-General appointed a commission to Utrecht, with the stadholder at the head of it.

The states of Holland appointed another, with Grotius as its chairman.

On the 25th July Grotius and Pensionary Hoogerbeets, with two colleagues, arrived in Utrecht.

Gillis van Ledenberg was there to receive them. A tall, handsome, bald-headed, well-featured, mild, gentlemanlike man was this secretary of the Utrecht assembly, and certainly not aware, while passing to and fro on such half-diplomatic missions between two sovereign assemblies, that he was committing high treason. He might well imagine, however, should Maurice discover that it was he who had prevented the commissioners

---

[1] Wagenaer, x. 218. Resol. Holl., July 11, 12, 1618, bl. 181–185. Grotius, Verantwoording, xix. 255.

from conferring with him as instructed, that it would go hard with him.

Ledenberg forthwith introduced Grotius and his committee to the assembly at Utrecht.[1]

While these great personages were thus holding solemn and secret council, another and still greater personage came upon the scene.

The stadholder, with the deputation from the States-General, arrived at Utrecht.[2]

Evidently the threads of this political drama were converging to a catastrophe, and it might prove a tragical one.

Meantime all looked merry enough in the old episcopal city. There were few towns in Lower or in Upper Germany more elegant and imposing than Utrecht. Situate on the slender and feeble channel of the ancient Rhine as it falters languidly to the sea, surrounded by trim gardens and orchards, and embowered in groves of beeches and lime-trees, with busy canals fringed with poplars, lined with solid quays, and crossed by innumerable bridges, with the stately brick tower of St. Martin's rising to a daring height above one of the most magnificent Gothic cathedrals in the Netherlands, this seat of the Anglo-Saxon Willibrord, who eight hundred years before had preached Christianity to the Frisians, and had founded that long line of hard-fighting, indomitable bishops, obstinately contesting for centuries the possession of the swamps and pastures about them with counts, kings, and emperors, was still worthy of its history and its position.

It was here, too, that, sixty-one years before, the famous Articles of Union were signed. By that funda-

[1] Wagenaer, Van der Kemp, Baudartius, ubi sup.   [2] Ibid.

mental treaty of the confederacy, the provinces agreed
to remain eternally united as if they were but one
province; to make no war nor peace save by unanimous
consent, while on lesser matters a majority should rule;
to admit both Catholics and Protestants to the Union
provided they obeyed its Articles and conducted themselves as good patriots; and expressly declared that no
province or city should interfere with another in the
matter of divine worship.[1]

From this memorable compact, so enduring a land-
mark in the history of human freedom, and distinguished by such breadth of view for the times both in
religion and politics, the city had gained the title of
"cradle of liberty"—*cunabula libertatis.*

Was it still to deserve the name? At that particular
moment the mass of the population was comparatively
indifferent to the terrible questions pending. It was
the kermess, or annual fair,[2] and all the world was
keeping holiday in Utrecht. The peddlers and itiner-
ant merchants from all the cities and provinces had
brought their wares,—jewelry and crockery, ribbons
and laces, plows and harrows, carriages and horses,
cows and sheep, cheeses and butter-firkins, doublets
and petticoats, guns and pistols, everything that could
serve the city and country-side for months to come,—
and displayed them in temporary booths or on the
ground, in every street and along every canal. The
town was one vast bazaar. The peasant women from
the country, with their gold and silver tiaras and the

[1] See Dutch Republic, vol. v. 111–113, and authorities there
cited.

[2] Van der Kemp, iv. 81. Deposition of Koningsvry, in MS. of
Van Voorst, kindly communicated by M. van Deventer.

year's rent of a comfortable farm in their ear-rings and necklaces, and the sturdy Frisian peasants, many of whom had borne their matchlocks in the great wars which had lasted through their own and their fathers' lifetime, trudged through the city, enjoying the blessings of peace. Bands of music and merry-go-rounds in all the open places and squares; open-air bakeries of pancakes and waffles; theatrical exhibitions, raree-shows, jugglers, and mountebanks at every corner—all these phenomena, which had been at every kermess for centuries, and were to repeat themselves for centuries afterward, now enlivened the atmosphere of the gray, episcopal city. Pasted against the walls of public edifices were the most recent placards and counter-placards of the States-General and the states of Utrecht on the great subject of religious schisms and popular tumults. In the shop-windows and on the book-stalls of Contra-Remonstrant tradesmen, now becoming more and more defiant as the last allies of Holland, the states of Utrecht, were gradually losing courage, were seen the freshest ballads and caricatures against the advocate. Here an engraving represented him seated at table with Grotius, Hoogerbeets, and others, discussing the national synod, while a flap of the picture being lifted put the head of the Duke of Alva on the legs of Barneveldt, his companions being transformed in similar manner into Spanish priests and cardinals assembled at the terrible Council of Blood, with rows of Protestant martyrs burning and hanging in the distance. Another print showed Prince Maurice and the States-General shaking the leading statesmen of the commonwealth in a mighty sieve through which came tumbling head foremost to perdition the hated advocate

and his abettors.   Another showed the Arminians as a
row of crestfallen cocks rained upon by the wrath of
the stadholder—Arminians, by a detestable pun, being
converted into "Arme haenen," or "Poor cocks." One
represented the pope and King of Spain blowing thousands of ducats out of a golden bellows into the lap
of the advocate, who was holding up his official robes
to receive them, or whole carriage-loads of Arminians
starting off bag and baggage on the road to Rome, with
Lucifer in the perspective waiting to give them a warm
welcome in his own dominions; and so on, and so on.
Moving through the throng, with iron casque on their
heads and halberd in hand, were groups of wartgelders, scowling fiercely at many popular demonstrations
such as they had been enlisted to suppress, but while
off duty concealing outward symptoms of wrath which
in many instances, perhaps, would have been far from
genuine.

For although these mercenaries knew that the states
of Holland, who were responsible for the pay of the
regular troops then in Utrecht, authorized them to
obey no orders save from the local authorities, yet it
was becoming a grave question for the wartgelders
whether their own wages were perfectly safe, a cir-
cumstance which made them susceptible to the atmosphere of Contra-Remonstrantism which was steadily
inwrapping the whole country.   A still graver question
was whether such resistance as they could offer to the
renowned stadholder, whose name was magic to every
soldier's heart not only in his own land but throughout Christendom, would not be like parrying a lance's
thrust with a bulrush.   In truth, the senior captain of
the wartgelders, Harteveld by name, had privately in-

formed the leaders of the Barneveldt party in Utrecht
that he would not draw his sword against Prince Maurice and the States-General. "Who asks you to do
so?" said some of the deputies, while Ledenberg, on the
other hand, flatly accused him of cowardice. For this
affront the captain had vowed revenge.[1]

And in the midst of this scene of jollity and confusion, that midsummer night, entered the stern stadholder with his fellow-commissioners, the feeble plans
for shutting the gates upon him not having been carried into effect.

"You hardly expected such a guest at your fair," [2]
said he to the magistrates, with a grim smile on his face
as who should say, "And what do you think of me now
I have come?"

Meantime the secret conference of Grotius and his
colleagues with the states of Utrecht proceeded. As a
provisional measure, Sir John Ogle, commander of the
forces paid by Holland, had been warned as to where
his obedience was due. It had likewise been intimated
that the guard should be doubled at the Amersfoort
gate, and a watch set on the river Lek above and below
the city in order to prevent fresh troops of the States-
General from being introduced by surprise.[3]

These precautions had been suggested a year before,
as we have seen, in a private autograph letter from
Barneveldt to Secretary Ledenberg.[4]

Sir John Ogle had flatly refused to act in opposition

[1] Wagenaer, x. 234, 199.

[2] Van der Kemp, iv. 81.

[3] Wagenaer, x. 222 [seq. Grotius, Verantwoording, xix. 267,
277.

[4] See vol. ii. 303.

to the stadholder and the States-General, whom he recognized as his lawful superiors and masters, and he
warned Ledenberg and his companions as to the perilous nature of the course which they were pursuing.
Great was the indignation of the Utrechters and the
Holland commissioners in consequence.[1]

Grotius in his speech enlarged on the possibility of
violence being used by the stadholder, while some of
the members of the assembly likewise thought it likely
that he would smite the gates open by force. Grotius,
when reproved afterward for such strong language
toward Prince Maurice, said that true Hollanders were
no courtiers, but were wont to call everything by its
right name.[2]

He stated in strong language the regret felt by Holland that a majority of the states of Utrecht had determined to disband the wartgelders, which had been constitutionally enlisted according to the right of each
province under the first article of the Union of Utrecht
to protect itself and its laws.

Next day there were conferences between Maurice [3]
and the states of Utrecht, and between him and the
Holland deputies. The stadholder calmly demanded
the disbandment and the synod. The Hollanders
spoke of securing first the persons and rights of the
magistracy.

"The magistrates are to be protected," said Maurice, "but we must first know how they are going to

[1] Baudartius, x. 56–59.

[2] Verantwoording, xix. 277.

[3] Maurice was accompanied by a committee of the States-General, namely, Voogd of Gelderland, Manmaker of Zealand, Swart-
senberg of Friesland.

govern. People have tried to introduce five false points into the divine worship. People have tried to turn me out of the stadholdership and to drive me from the country. But I have taken my measures. I know well what I am about. I have got five provinces on my side, and six cities of Holland will send deputies to Utrecht to sustain me here."[1]

The Hollanders protested that there was no design whatever, so far as they knew, against his princely dignity or person. All were ready to recognize his rank and services by every means in their power. But it was desirable by conciliation and compromise, not by stern decree, to arrange these religious and political differences.

The stadholder replied by again insisting on the synod. "As for the wartgelders," he continued, "they are worse than Spanish fortresses. They must away."

After a little further conversation in this vein the prince grew more excited.

"Everything is the fault of the advocate," he cried.

"If Barneveldt were dead," replied Grotius, "all the rest of us would still deem ourselves bound to maintain the laws. People seem to despise Holland and to wish to subject it to the other provinces."

"On the contrary," cried the prince, "it is the advocate who wishes to make Holland the States-General."[2]

Maurice was tired of argument. There had been much ale-house talk some three months before, by a certain blusterous gentleman called Van Ostrum, about the necessity of keeping the stadholder in check. "If the prince should undertake," said this pot-valiant

[1] K. Brandt, Leven van de Groot, 126 (from MS. notes of Grotius).   [2] Ibid.

hero, "to attack any of the cities of Utrecht or Holland with the hard hand, it is settled to station eight or ten thousand soldiers in convenient places. Then we shall say to the prince, if you don't leave us alone, we shall make an arrangement with the Archduke of Austria and resume obedience to him. We can make such a treaty with him as will give us religious freedom and save us from tyranny of any kind. I don't say this for myself, but have heard it on good authority from very eminent persons." [1]

This talk had floated through the air to the stadholder.

What evidence could be more conclusive of a deep design on the part of Barneveldt to sell the Republic to the archduke and drive Maurice into exile? Had not Esquire van Ostrum solemnly declared it at a tavern table? And although he had mentioned no names, could the "eminent personages" thus cited at second-hand be anybody but the advocate?

Three nights after his last conference with the Hollanders, Maurice quietly ordered a force of regular troops in Utrecht to be under arms at half-past three o'clock next morning. About one thousand infantry, including companies of Ernest of Nassau's command at Arnheim and of Brederode's from Vianen, besides a portion of the regular garrison of the place, had accordingly been assembled without beat of drum, before half-past three in the morning, and were now drawn up on the market-place, or Neu. At break of day the prince himself appeared on horseback, surrounded by his staff, on the Neu or Neude, a large, long, irregular square into which the seven or eight principal streets

[1] Wagenaer, x. 261, 262. Van der Kemp, iv. 83, 84.

and thoroughfares of the town emptied themselves. It was adorned by public buildings and other handsome edifices, and the tall steeple of St. Martin's, with its beautiful openwork spire, lighted with the first rays of the midsummer sun, looked tranquilly down upon the scene.

Each of the entrances to the square had been securely guarded by Maurice's orders, and cannon planted to command all the streets. A single company of the famous wartgelders was stationed in the Neu or near it. The prince rode calmly toward them and ordered them to lay down their arms. They obeyed without a murmur. He then sent through the city to summon all the other companies of wartgelders to the Neu. This was done with perfect promptness, and in a short space of time the whole body of mercenaries, nearly one thousand in number, had laid down their arms at the feet of the prince.[1]

The snaphances and halberds being then neatly stacked in the square, the stadholder went home to his early breakfast. There was an end to those mercenaries thenceforth and forever. The faint and sickly resistance to the authority of Maurice offered at Utrecht was attempted nowhere else.

For days there had been vague but fearful expectations of a "blood-bath," of street battles, rioting, and plunder. Yet the stadholder, with the consummate art which characterized all his military manœuvers, had so admirably carried out his measure that not a shot was fired, not a blow given, not a single burgher disturbed in his peaceful slumbers. When the population had

[1] Baudartius, x. 50–59. Van Rees and Brill, 829 seq. Wagenaer, x. 232, 233.

taken off their nightcaps, they woke to find the awful
bugbear removed which had so long been appalling
them. The wartgelders were numbered with the terrors of the past, and not a cat had mewed at their
disappearance.

Charter-books, parchments, thirteenth articles, Barneveldt's teeth, Arminian forts, flowery orations of
Grotius, tavern talk of Van Ostrum, city immunities,
states' rights, provincial laws, wartgelders and all—
the martial stadholder, with the orange plume in his
hat and the sword of Nieuport on his thigh, strode
through them as easily as through the whirligigs and
mountebanks, the waffles and fritters, encumbering the
streets of Utrecht on the night of his arrival.

Secretary Ledenberg and other leading members of
the states had escaped the night before. Grotius and
his colleagues also took a precipitate departure. As
they drove out of town in the twilight, they met the
deputies of the six opposition cities of Holland just
arriving in their coach from The Hague. Had they
tarried an hour longer, they would have found themselves safely in prison.[1]

Four days afterward the stadholder, at the head of
his body-guard, appeared at the town house. His halberdmen tramped up the broad staircase, heralding his
arrival to the assembled magistracy. He announced
his intention of changing the whole board then and
there. The process was summary. The forty members
were required to supply forty other names, and the
prince added twenty more. From the hundred candidates thus furnished the prince appointed forty magistrates such as suited himself. It is needless to say

[1] Authorities last cited.

that but few of the old bench remained, and that those
few were devoted to the synod, the States-General, and
the stadholder.[1]   He furthermore announced that these
new magistrates were to hold office for life, whereas
the board had previously been changed every year.
The cathedral church was at once assigned for the use
of the Contra-Remonstrants.

This process was soon to be repeated throughout the
two insubordinate provinces Utrecht and Holland.

The prince was accused of aiming at the sovereignty
of the whole country, and one of his griefs against the
advocate was that he had begged the princess widow,
Louise de Coligny, to warn her son-in-law of the dangers of such ambition.   But so long as an individual,
sword in hand, could exercise such unlimited sway over
the whole municipal and provincial organization of
the commonwealth, it mattered but little whether he
was called king or kaiser, doge or stadholder.   Sovereign he was for the time being at least, while
courteously acknowledging the States-General as his
sovereign.

Less than three weeks afterward the States-General
issued a decree formally disbanding the wartgelders—
an almost superfluous edict, as they had almost ceased
to exist, and there were none to resist the measure.[2]
Grotius recommended complete acquiescence.   Barneveldt's soul could no longer animate with courage a
whole people.

The invitations which had already in the month of
June been prepared for the synod to meet in the city

[1] Baudartius, x. 50–59. Van Rees and Brill, 829 seq. Wagenaer, x. 232, 233. Van der Kemp, iv. 85–88. Brandt, ii. 826–830.
[2] Brandt, ii. 826–830.

of Dort, or Dordrecht, were now issued. The states of
Holland sent back the notification unopened, deeming
it an unwarrantable invasion of their rights that an
assembly resisted by a large majority of their body
should be convoked in a city on their own territory.
But this was before the disbandment of the wartgelders and the general change of magistracies had been
effected.

Earnest consultations were now held as to the possibility of devising some means of compromise, of providing that the decisions of the synod should not be
considered binding until after having been ratified by
the separate states.[1] In the opinion of Barneveldt,
they were within a few hours' work of a favorable result when their deliberations were interrupted by a
startling event.

[1] Brandt, Hist. Ref., ii. 841. Uytenb., 1204. Wagenaer, x.
240 seq.

Besides the printed authorities already cited for these proceedings at Utrecht, I have read a mass of unpublished papers in the
archives of the realm, especially a packet marked "AA, 61," in
which all the papers exchanged between the commissioners of the
States-General and the authorities of Utrecht, and containing the
elaborate controversy on the respective claims of provincial sovereignty and the central authority, are preserved, together with a
mass of notes and drafts of Barneveldt, the brief out of which
the states'-right argument was formed.

In a MS. collection of extracts from the state papers of Utrecht,
kindly lent me by M. de Jonghe, and belonging to his late father,
the archivist and historian, are many interesting passages which I
have also used in preparing the narrative.

The MS. of Van Voorst, and other unpublished documents
which I owe to M. van Deventer, contain many important deposi-
tions and statements.

CHAPTER XVIII

Fruitless interview between Barneveldt and Maurice—The advocate, warned of his danger, resolves to remain at The Hague—Arrest of Barneveldt, of Grotius, and of Hoogerbeets—The States-General assume the responsibility in a "billet"—The states of Holland protest—The advocate's letter to his family—Audience of Boississe—Mischief-making of Aertsens—The French ambassadors intercede for Barneveldt—The King of England opposes their efforts—Langerac's treachery to the advocate—Maurice continues his changes in the magistracy throughout the country—Vote of thanks by the states of Holland.

THE advocate, having done what he believed to be his duty, and exhausted himself in efforts to defend ancient law and to procure moderation and mutual toleration in religion, was disposed to acquiesce in the inevitable. His letters giving official and private information of those grave events were neither vindictive nor vehement.

"I send you the last declaration of my lords of Holland," he said to Caron,[1] "in regard to the national synod, with the counter-declaration of Dordrecht and the other five cities. Yesterday was begun the debate about cashiering the enrolled soldiers called wartgelders. To-day the late M. van Kereburg was buried."

Nothing could be calmer than his tone. After the wartgelders had been disbanded, Utrecht revolutionized

[1] Barneveldt to Caron, July 8, 1618, Hague Archives MS.

by main force, the national synod decided upon, and
the process of changing the municipal magistracies
everywhere in the interest of Contra-Remonstrants
begun, be continued to urge moderation and respect
for law. Even now, although discouraged, he was not
despondent, and was disposed to make the best even of
the synod.

He wished at this supreme moment to have a personal interview with the prince in order to devise some
means for calming the universal agitation and effecting, if possible, a reconciliation among conflicting passions and warring sects. He had stood at the side of
Maurice and of Maurice's great father in darker hours
even than these. They had turned to him on all trying
and tragical occasions, and had never found his courage wavering or his judgment at fault. "Not a friend
to the house of Nassau, but a father," thus had Maurice with his own lips described the advocate to the
widow of William the Silent. Incapable of an unpa-
triotic thought, animated by sincere desire to avert
evil and procure moderate action, Barneveldt saw no
reason whatever why, despite all that had been said
and done, he should not once more hold counsel with
the prince. He had a conversation accordingly with
Count Louis, who had always honored the advocate,
while differing with him on the religious question. The
stadholder of Friesland, one of the foremost men of
his day in military and scientific affairs, in adminis-
trative ability and philanthropic instincts, and, in a
family perhaps the most renowned in Europe for heroic
qualities and achievements, hardly second to any who
had borne the name, was in favor of the proposed interview, spoke immediately to Prince Maurice about it,

but was not hopeful as to its results. He knew his cousin well, and felt that he was at that moment resentful, perhaps implacably so, against the whole Remonstrant party, and especially against their great leader.

Count Louis was small of stature, but dignified, not to say pompous, in demeanor. His style of writing to one of lower social rank than himself was lofty, almost regal, and full of old-world formality.

"NOBLE, SEVERE, RIGHT WORSHIPFUL, HIGHLY LEARNED AND DISCREET, SPECIAL GOOD FRIEND," he wrote to Barneveldt:[1] "We have spoken to his Excellency concerning the expediency of what you requested of us this forenoon. We find, however, that his Excellency is not to be moved to entertain any other measure than the national synod, which he has himself proposed in person to all the provinces, to the furtherance of which he has made so many exertions, and which has already been announced by the States-General.

"We will see by what opportunity his Excellency will appoint the interview, and so far as lies in us you may rely on our good offices. We could not answer sooner, as the French ambassadors had audience of us this forenoon and we were visiting his Excellency in the afternoon. Wishing your worship good evening, we are your very good friend."

Next day Count William wrote again.[2] "We have taken occasion," he said, "to inform his Excellency that you were inclined to enter into communication with him in regard to an accommodation of the reli-

[1] Count Louis William to Barneveldt, August 4 (14), 1618, Hague Archives MS.

[2] Same to same, August 5 (15), 1618, Hague Archives MS.

gious difficulties and to the cashiering of the wartgelders. He answered that he could accept no change in
the matter of the national synod, but nevertheless
would be at your disposal whenever your Worship
should be pleased to come to him.'' [1]

Two days afterward [2] Barneveldt made his appearance at the apartments of the stadholder. The two
great men on whom the fabric of the Republic had so
long rested stood face to face once more.

The advocate, with long gray beard and stern blue
eye, haggard with illness and anxiety, tall but bent
with age, leaning on his staff and wrapped in black
velvet cloak, an imposing, magisterial figure; the florid,
plethoric prince, in brown doublet, big russet boots,
narrow ruff, and shabby felt hat with its string of dia-
monds, with hand clutched on sword-hilt, and eyes full
of angry menace, the very type of the high-born, imperious soldier—thus they surveyed each other as men,
once friends, between whom a gulf had opened.

Barneveldt sought to convince the prince that in the
proceedings at Utrecht, founded as they were on strict
adherence to the laws and traditions of the provinces,
no disrespect had been intended to him, no invasion of
his constitutional rights, and that, on his part, his lifelong devotion to the house of Nassau had suffered no
change. He repeated his usual incontrovertible arguments against the synod as illegal and directly tending
to subject the magistracy to the priesthood, a course

[1] I find no allusion to these letters of Count William among
Barneveldt's papers or elsewhere. The learned Groen v. Prinsterer
does not give them, and they have never been printed, so far as I
know. As they are short, I give them entire in the Appendix.

[2] August 17, 1618.

of things which eight-and-twenty years before had nearly brought destruction on the country and led both the prince and himself to captivity in a foreign land.

The prince sternly replied in very few words that the national synod was a settled matter, that he would never draw back from his position, and could not do so without singular disservice to the country, and to his own disreputation. He expressed his displeasure at the particular oath exacted from the wartgelders. It diminished his lawful authority and the respect due to him, and might be used *per indirectum* to the oppression of those of the religion which he had sworn to maintain. His brow grew black when he spoke of the proceedings at Utrecht, which he denounced as a conspiracy against his own person and the constitution of the country.

Barneveldt used in vain the powers of argument by which he had guided kings and republics, cabinets and assemblies, during so many years. His eloquence fell powerless upon the iron taciturnity of the stadholder. Maurice had expressed his determination, and had no other argument to sustain it but his usual exasperating silence.

The interview ended as hopelessly as Count Louis William had anticipated, and the prince and the advocate separated to meet no more on earth.[1]

[1] I find no allusion to this interview in Barneveldt's papers, nor in contemporary historians. The two letters of Louis William prove that it must have taken place, and Ouvré, writing from Du Maurier's unpublished despatches (p. 284), briefly alludes to it, characterizes it, and gives its date. Departing from my uniform rule in this single case, I have ventured slightly to indicate the course of a conversation of which no minute exists, because Count William wrote two letters to the advocate expressly to state what

"You have doubtless heard already," wrote Barneveldt to the ambassador in London,[1] "of all that has
been passing here and in Utrecht. One must pray to
God that everything may prosper to his honor and the
welfare of the country. They are resolved to go
through with the national synod, the government of
Utrecht, after the change made in it, having consented
with the rest. I hope that his Majesty, according to
your statement, will send some good, learned, and
peace-loving personages here, giving them wholesome
instructions to help bring our affairs into Christian
unity, accommodation, and love, by which his Majesty
and these provinces would be best served."

Were these the words of a baffled conspirator and
traitor? Were they uttered to produce an effect upon
public opinion and avert a merited condemnation by
all good men? There is not in them a syllable of reproach, of anger, of despair. And let it be remembered that they were not written for the public at all.
They were never known to the public, hardly heard of
either by the advocate's enemies or friends, save the one
to whom they were addressed and the monarch to whom
that friend was accredited. They were not contained
in official despatches, but in private, confidential out-
pourings to a trusted political and personal associate
of many years. From the day they were written until
this hour they have never been printed, and for centuries perhaps not read.

He proceeded to explain what he considered to be the

Maurice had just said to him, and meant to say to Barneveldt. I
have used those very words, and there can be little doubt that the
prince did say them.

[1] Barneveldt to Caron, August 18, 1618, Hague Archives MS.

law in the Netherlands with regard to military allegiance. It is not probable that there was in the country a more competent expounder of it; and defective and even absurd as such a system was, it had carried the provinces successfully through a great war, and a better method for changing it might have been found among so law-loving and conservative a people as the Netherlanders than brute force.

"Information has apparently been sent to England," he said, "that my lords of Holland through their commissioners in Utrecht dictated to the soldiery standing at their charges something that was unreasonable. The truth is that the states of Holland, as many of them as were assembled, understanding that great haste was made to send his Excellency and some deputies from the other provinces to Utrecht, while the members of the Utrecht assembly were gone to report these difficulties to their constituents and get fresh instructions from them, wishing that the return of those members should be waited for and that the assembly of Holland might also be complete,—a request which was refused, —sent a committee to Utrecht, as the matter brooked no delay, to give information to the states of that province of what was passing here and to offer their good offices.

"They sent letters also to his Excellency to move him to reasonable accommodation without taking extreme measures in opposition to those resolutions of the states of Utrecht which his Excellency had promised to conform with and to cause to be maintained by all officers and soldiers. Should his Excellency make difficulty in this, the commissioners were instructed to declare to him that they were ordered to warn the colonels and

captains standing in the payment of Holland, by letter
and word of mouth, that they were bound by oath to
obey the states of Holland as their paymasters and
likewise to carry out the orders of the provincial and
municipal magistrates in the places where they were
employed. The soldiery was not to act or permit anything to be done against those resolutions, but help to
carry them out, his Excellency himself and the troops
paid by the states of Holland being indisputably bound
by oath and duty so to do.''

Doubtless a more convenient arrangement from a
military point of view might be imagined than a system of quotas by which each province in a confederacy
claimed allegiance and exacted obedience from the
troops paid by itself in what was, after all, a general
army. Still, this was the logical and inevitable result
of state rights pushed to the extreme, and indeed had
been the indisputable theory and practice in the Netherlands ever since their revolt from Spain. To pretend that the proceedings and the oath were new because they were embarrassing was absurd. It was only
because the dominant party saw the extreme inconvenience of the system, now that it was turned against
itself, that individuals contemptuous of law and ignorant of history denounced it as a novelty.

But the strong and beneficent principle that lay at
the bottom of the advocate's conduct was his unflag-
ging resolve to maintain the civil authority over the
military in time of peace. What liberal or healthy
government would be possible otherwise? Exactly as
he opposed the subjection of the magistracy by the
priesthood or the mob, so he now defended it against
the power of the sword. There was no justification

whatever for a claim on the part of Maurice to exact obedience from all the armies of the Republic, especially in time of peace. He was himself by oath sworn to obey the states of Holland, of Utrecht, and of the three other provinces of which he was governor. He was not commander-in-chief. In two of the seven provinces he had no functions whatever, military or civil. They had another governor.

Yet the exposition of the law, as it stood, by the advocate, and his claim that both troops and stadholder should be held to their oaths, was accounted a crime. He had invented a new oath, it was said, and sought to diminish the power of the prince. These were charges, unjust as they were, which might one day be used with deadly effect.

"We live in a world where everything is interpreted to the worst," he said.[1] "My physical weakness continues, and is increased by this affliction. I place my trust in God the Lord and in my upright and conscientious determination to serve the country, his Excellency, and the religion in which, through God's grace, I hope to continue to the end."

On the 28th August of a warm afternoon, Barneveldt was seated on a porcelain seat in an arbor in his garden. Councilor Berkhout, accompanied by a friend, called to see him, and after a brief conversation gave him solemn warning that danger was impending, that there was even a rumor of an intention to arrest him.

The advocate answered gravely, "Yes, there are wicked men about."

Presently he lifted his hat courteously and said, "I thank you, gentlemen, for the warning."[2]

[1] Letter to Caron last cited.   [2] Wagenaer, x. 240 seq.

It seems scarcely to have occurred to him that he had been engaged in anything beyond a constitutional party struggle in which he had defended what in his view was the side of law and order. He never dreamed of seeking safety in flight. Some weeks before, he had been warmly advised to do as both he and Maurice had done in former times in order to escape the stratagems of Leicester, to take refuge in some strong city devoted to his interests rather than remain at The Hague. But he had declined the counsel. "I will await the issue of this business," he said, "in The Hague, where my home is, and where I have faithfully served my masters. I had rather for the sake of the fatherland suffer what God chooses to send me for having served well than that through me and on my account any city should fall into trouble and difficulties."[1]

Next morning, Wednesday, at seven o'clock, Uytenbogart paid him a visit. He wished to consult him concerning a certain statement in regard to the synod which he desired him to lay before the states of Holland. The preacher did not find his friend busily occupied at his desk, as usual, with writing and other work. The advocate had pushed his chair away from the table encumbered with books and papers, and sat with his back leaning against it, lost in thought. His stern, stoical face was like that of a lion at bay.

Uytenbogart tried to arouse him from his gloom, consoling him by reflections on the innumerable instances, in all countries and ages, of patriotic statesmen who for faithful service had reaped nothing but ingratitude.

Soon afterward he took his leave, feeling a presentiment of evil within him which it was impossible for

[1] Brandt, Hist. Ref., ii. 841.

him to shake off as he pressed Barneveldt's hand at parting.[1]

Two hours later the advocate went in his coach to the session of the states of Holland. The place of the assembly, as well as that of the States-General, was within what was called the Binnenhof, or Inner Court, the large quadrangle inclosing the ancient hall once the residence of the sovereign counts of Holland. The apartments of the stadholder composed the southwestern portion of the large series of buildings surrounding this court. Passing by these lodgings on his way to the assembly, he was accosted by a chamberlain of the prince and informed that his Highness desired to speak with him. He followed him toward the room where such interviews were usually held, but in the antechamber was met by Lieutenant Nythof, of the prince's body-guard. This officer told him that he had been ordered to arrest him in the name of the States-General. The advocate demanded an interview with the prince. It was absolutely refused. Physical resistance on the part of a man of seventy-two, stooping with age and leaning on a staff, to military force, of which Nythof was the representative, was impossible. Barneveldt put a cheerful face on the matter, and was even inclined to converse. He was at once carried off a prisoner and locked up in a room belonging to Maurice's apartments.[2]

Soon afterward Grotius, on his way to the States-General, was invited in precisely the same manner to go to the prince, with whom, as he was informed, the advo-

[1] Uytenb., 1204.

[2] Waaragt. Hist., 223, 224 seq. Wagenaer, x. 252–255. Baudartius, x. 50–62. Carleton's Letters, 281.

cate was at that moment conferring. As soon as he had
ascended the stairs, however, he was arrested by Captain van der Meulen in the name of the States-General,
and taken to a chamber in the same apartments, where
he was guarded by two halberdmen. In the evening he
was removed to another chamber, where the window-
shutters were barred, and where he remained three
days and nights. He was much cast down and silent.
Pensionary Hoogerbeets was made prisoner in precisely
the same manner. Thus the three statesmen, culprits
as they were considered by their enemies, were secured
without noise or disturbance, each without knowing
the fate that had befallen the other. Nothing could
have been more neatly done. In the same quiet way
orders were sent to secure Secretary Ledenberg, who
had returned to Utrecht, and who now, after a short
confinement in that city, was brought to The Hague
and imprisoned in the Hof.[1]

At the very moment of the advocate's arrest his son-
in-law, Van der Myle, happened to be paying a visit to
Sir Dudley Carleton, who had arrived very late the
night before from England. It was some hours before
he or any other member of the family learned what
had befallen.

The ambassador reported to his sovereign that the
deed was highly applauded by the well-disposed as the
only means left for the security of the state. "The
Arminians," he said, "condemn it as violent and in-
sufferable in a free republic."

Impartial persons, he thought, considered it a superfluous proceeding now that the synod had been voted
and the wartgelders disbanded.

[1] Authorities last cited. K. Brandt, Leven van de Groot, 135,

While he was writing his despatch, the stadholder came to call upon him, attended by his cousin Count Louis William. The crowd of citizens following at a little distance, excited by the news with which the city was now ringing, mingled with Maurice's gentlemen and body-guards, and surged up almost into the ambassador's doors.

Carleton informed his guests, in the course of conversation, as to the general opinion of indifferent judges of these events. Maurice replied that he had disbanded the wartgelders, but it had now become necessary to deal with their colonel and the chief captains, meaning thereby Barneveldt and the two other prisoners.[1]

The news of this arrest was soon carried to the house of Barneveldt, and filled his aged wife, his son, and sons-in-law with grief and indignation. His eldest son, William, commonly called the Seignior van Groeneveld, accompanied by his two brothers-in-law, Veenhuizen, president of the upper council, and Van der Myle, obtained an interview with the stadholder that same afternoon.

They earnestly requested that the advocate, in consideration of his advanced age, might, on giving proper bail, be kept prisoner in his own house.

The prince received them at first with courtesy. "It is the work of the States-General," he said. "No harm shall come to your father any more than to myself."

Veenhuizen sought to excuse the opposition which the advocate had made to the Cloister Church.

The word was scarcely out of his mouth when the

[1] Carleton's Letters, 281.

prince fiercely interrupted him. "Any man who says a word against the Cloister Church," he cried in a rage, "his feet shall not carry him from this place."[1]

The interview gave them, on the whole, but little satisfaction. Very soon afterward two gentlemen, Asperen and Schagen, belonging to the Chamber of Nobles, and great adherents of Barneveldt, who had procured their enrolment in that branch, forced their way into the stadholder's apartments and penetrated to the door of the room where the advocate was imprisoned. According to Carleton, they were filled with wine as well as rage, and made a great disturbance, loudly demanding their patron's liberation. Maurice came out of his own cabinet on hearing the noise in the corridor, and ordered them to be disarmed and placed under arrest. In the evening, however, they were released.[2]

Soon afterward Van der Myle fled to Paris, where he endeavored to make influence with the government in favor of the advocate. His departure without leave, being, as he was, a member of the Chamber of Nobles and of the council of state, was accounted a great offense. Uytenbogart also made his escape, as did Taurinus, author of "The Balance," Van Moersbergen of Utrecht, and many others more or less implicated in these commotions.[3]

There was profound silence in the states of Holland when the arrest of Barneveldt was announced. The majority sat like men distraught. At last Mathenesse

[1] Brandt, Hist. Ref., ii. 842, who cites Uytenbogart's Journal, dated August 29, 1618, from Van der Myle's own lips; but see Van der Kemp, iv. 94, 284.

[2] Brandt, ii. 842. Van der Kemp, iv. 90. Carleton's Letters, 279.

[3] Carleton's Letters, 279. Wagenaer, x. 259.

said: "You have taken from us our head, our tongue, and our hand; henceforth we can only sit still and look on." [1]

The States-General now took the responsibility of the arrest, which eight individuals calling themselves the States-General had authorized by secret resolution the day before (28th August). On the 29th, accordingly, the following "billet," as it was entitled, was read to the assembly and ordered to be printed and circulated among the community. It was without date or signature.

"Whereas, in the course of the changes within the city of Utrecht and in other places brought about by the high and mighty lords the States-General of the United Netherlands, through his Excellency and their Lordships' committee to him adjoined, sundry things have been discovered of which previously there had been great suspicion, tending to the great prejudice of the provinces in general and of each province in particular, not without apparent danger to the state of the country, and that thereby not only the city of Utrecht, but various other cities of the United Provinces would have fallen into a blood-bath; and whereas the chief ringleaders in these things are considered to be John van Barneveldt, advocate of Holland, Rombout Hoogerbeets, and Hugo Grotius, whereof hereafter shall declaration and announcement be made, therefore their High Mightinesses, in order to prevent these and similar inconveniences, to place the country in security, and to bring the good burghers of all the cities into friendly unity again, have resolved to arrest those three persons, in order that out of their imprisonment

[1] Carleton's Letters. Wagenaer.

pieces in the streets. Men feared to defend him lest
they, too, should be accused of being stipendiaries of
Spain. It was a piteous spectacle; not for the venerable statesman sitting alone there in his prison, but
for the Republic in its lunacy, for human nature in its
meanness and shame. He whom Count Louis, although
opposed to his politics, had so lately called one of the
two columns on which the whole fabric of the states
reposed,[1] Prince Maurice being the other, now lay pros-
trate in the dust and reviled of all men.

"Many who had been promoted by him to high
places," said a contemporary, "and were wont to worship him as a god, in hope that he would lift them up
still higher, now deserted him, and ridiculed him, and
joined the rest of the world in heaping dirt upon
him."[2]

On the third day of his imprisonment the advocate
wrote this letter to his family:

"My very dear Wife, Children, Children-in-law,
and Grandchildren: I know that you are sorrowful
for the troubles which have come upon me, but I beg
you to seek consolation from God the Almighty and to
comfort each other. I know before the Lord God of
having given no single lawful reason for the misfortunes which have come upon me, and I will with patience await from his divine hand and from my lawful
superiors a happy issue, knowing well that you and
my other well-wishers will with your prayers and good
offices do all that you can to that end.

"And so, very dear wife, children, children-in-law,

[1] Wagenaer, x. 244.   Uytenbog. Leven, x. 157.
[2] Baudartius, ubi sup.

and grandchildren, I commend you to God's holy keeping.

"I have been thus far well and honorably treated and accommodated, for which I thank his princely Excellency.

"From the chamber of arrest, last of August, anno 1618.

"Your dear husband, father, father-in-law, and grandfather,   JOHN OF BARNEVELDT."[1]

On the margin was written:

"From the first I have requested and have at last obtained materials for writing."

A fortnight before the arrest, but while great troubles were known to be impending, the French ambassador extraordinary, De Boississe, had audience before the assembly of the States-General. He entreated them to maintain the cause of unity and peace as the foundation of their state—"that state," he said, "which lifts its head so high that it equals or surpasses the mightiest republics that ever existed, and which could not have risen to such a height of honor and grandeur in so short a time but through harmony and union of all the provinces, through the valor of his Excellency, and through your own wise counsels, both sustained by our great king, whose aid is continued by his son."[2] "The king my master," he continued, "knows not the cause of your disturbances; you have not communicated them to him; but their most apparent cause is a difference of opinion, born in the schools, thence brought before the public, upon a point of theology.

---

[1] Waaragt. Hist. v. Oldenb., 234.

[2] Baudartius, x. 60, 61. Brandt, Hist. Ref., ii. 821 seq.

That point has long been deemed by many to be so hard and so high that the best advice to give about it is to follow what God's Word teaches touching God's secrets, to wit, that one should use moderation and modesty therein and should not rashly press too far into that which he wishes to be covered with the veil of reverence and wonder. That is a wise ignorance to keep one's eyes from that which God chooses to conceal. He calls us not to eternal life through subtle and perplexing questions."

And further exhorting them to conciliation and compromise, he enlarged on the effect of their internal dissensions on their exterior relations. "What joy, what rapture, you are preparing for your neighbors by your quarrels! How they will scorn you! How they will laugh! What a hope do you give them of revenging themselves upon you without danger to themselves! Let me implore you to baffle their malice, to turn their joy into mourning, to unite yourselves to confound them."[1]

He spoke much more in the same vein, expressing wise and moderate sentiments. He might as well have gone down to the neighboring beach when a southwest gale was blowing and talked of moderation to the waves of the German Ocean. The tempest of passion and prejudice had risen in its might and was sweeping all before it. Yet the speech, like other speeches and intercessions made at this epoch by De Boississe and by the regular French ambassador, Du Maurier, was statesmanlike and reasonable. It is superfluous to say that it was in unison with the opinions of Barneveldt, for Barneveldt had probably furnished the text of the

[1] Brandt, Hist. Ref., ii. 821 seq.

oration. Even as he had a few years before supplied the letters which King James had signed and subsequently had struggled so desperately to disavow, so now the advocate's imperious intellect had swayed the docile and amiable minds of the royal envoys into complete sympathy with his policy. He usually dictated their general instructions. But an end had come to such triumphs. Dudley Carleton had returned from his leave of absence in England, where he had found his sovereign hating the advocate as doctors hate who have been worsted in theological arguments and despots who have been baffled in their imperious designs. Who shall measure the influence on the destiny of this statesman caused by the French-Spanish marriages, the sermons of James through the mouth of Carleton, and the mutual jealousy of France and England?

But the advocate was in prison, and the earth seemed to have closed over him. Hardly a ripple of indignation was perceptible on the calm surface of affairs, although in the States-General, as in the states of Holland, his absence seemed to have reduced both bodies to paralysis.

They were the more easily handled by the prudent, skilful, and determined Maurice.

The arrest of the four gentlemen had been communicated to the Kings of France and Great Britain and the Elector Palatine in an identical letter from the States-General. It is noticeable that on this occasion the central government spoke of giving orders to the Prince of Orange, over whom they would seem to have had no legitimate authority, while, on the other hand, he had expressed indignation on more than one occasion that the respective states of the five provinces where he was

governor and to whom he had sworn obedience should
presume to issue commands to him.[1]

In France, where the advocate was honored and beloved, the intelligence excited profound sorrow. A few
weeks previously the government of that country had,
as we have seen, sent a special ambassador to the states,
M. de Boississe, to aid the resident envoy, Du Maurier,
in his efforts to bring about a reconciliation of parties
and a termination of the religious feud. Their exertions were sincere and unceasing. They were as steadily countermined by Francis Aertsens, for the aim of
that diplomatist was to bring about a state of bad feeling, even at cost of rupture, between the Republic and

[1] States-General to King of France, August 29, 1618, Hague
Archives MS.

"Since the change in the government of the city of Utrecht,"
said the States-General, "effected by the order which we gave on
the subject to the Prince of Orange and to some of our deputies,
many affairs and practices have been discovered concerning which
we had some distrust and doubtful knowledge before, tending to
the great disturbance of the repose not only of Utrecht but of
several other of the United Provinces, out of which might have
come a great effusion of blood. The care we owe to the protection
of concord and the security of this state has given us just occasion
to seize the persons of Messrs. J. of Barneveldt, Rombout Hoogerbeets, and Hugo de Groot, held to be principal authors of those
dangerous practices, in order to break up and prevent all ulterior
progress and explosion of these and other intrigues which during
several years past have been troubling this state, notwithstanding
all the care and diligence which we have brought to cause them to
cease by gentleness and moderation; and as this important action,
necessary to the conservation of our authority and public peace,
could be variously interpreted, we have chosen to give a true account to your Majesty, and accordingly, as we get to the bottom
of this affair, we shall give more information thereof to your
Majesty."

France, because France was friendly to the man he most hated and whose ruin he had sworn.

During the summer a bitter personal controversy had been going on, sufficiently vulgar in tone, between Aertsens and another diplomatist, Barneveldt's son-in-law, Cornelis van der Myle.[1] It related to the recall of Aertsens from the French embassy, of which enough has already been laid before the reader. Van der Myle, by the production of the secret letters of the queen dowager and her councilors, had proved beyond dispute that it was at the express wish of the French government that the ambassador had retired, and that indeed they had distinctly refused to receive him, should he return. Foul words, resulting in propositions for a hostile meeting on the frontier, which, however, came to nothing, were interchanged,[2] and Aertsens, in the course of his altercation with his son-in-law, had found ample opportunity for venting his spleen upon his former patron, the now fallen statesman.

Four days after the arrest of Barneveldt he brought the whole matter before the States-General,[3] and the intention with which he thus raked up the old quarrel with France after the death of Henry, and his charges in regard to the Spanish marriages, was as obvious as it was deliberate.

[1] AA, 22, Loket Kastje No. 1. "Stukken rakende den Twist tusschen Aertsens ende v. d. Myle, anno 1618," Hague Archives MS.

[2] "Extracten uit de Registers der Resolut. v. d. Raad v. State betreffende de Waartgelders te Utrecht, Oldenbarneveld, Van der Myle, etc., annis 1617, 1618, 1619."

[3] Aertsens to States-General, September 2, 1618, Hague Archives MS.

The French ambassadors were furious. Boississe had arrived not simply as friend of the advocate, but to assure the states of the strong desire entertained by the French government to cultivate warmest relations with them.[1] It had been desired by the Contra-Remonstrant party that deputies from the Protestant churches of France should participate in the synod, and the French king had been much assailed by the Catholic powers for listening to those suggestions. The papal nuncius, the Spanish ambassador, the envoy of the archduke, had made a great disturbance at court concerning the mission of Boississe. They urged with earnestness that his Majesty was acting against the sentiments of Spain, Rome, and the whole Catholic Church, and that he ought not to assist with his counsel those heretics who were quarreling among themselves over points in their heretical religion and wishing to destroy each other.[2]

Notwithstanding this outcry, the weather was smooth enough until the proceedings of Aertsens came to stir up a tempest at the French court. A special courier come from Boississe, a meeting of the whole council, although it was Sunday, was instantly called, and the reply of the States-General to the remonstrance of the ambassador in the Aertsens affair was pronounced to be so great an affront to the king that, but for overpowering reasons, diplomatic intercourse would have at once been suspended.[3] ''Now instead of friendship there is great anger here,'' said Langerac. The king forbade under vigorous penalties the departure of any French

[1] Langerac to States-General, July 22, 1618, Hague Archives MS.   [2] Ibid.

[3] Same to same, October 26, 1618, Hague Archives MS.

theologians to take part in the synod, although the royal consent had nearly been given. The government complained that no justice was done in the Netherlands to the French nation, that leading personages there openly expressed contempt for the French alliance, denouncing the country as "Hispaniolized," and declaring that all the council were regularly pensioned by Spain for the express purpose of keeping up the civil dissensions in the United Provinces.

Aertsens had publicly and officially declared that a majority of the French council since the death of Henry had declared the crown in its temporal as well as spiritual essence to be dependent on the pope, and that the Spanish marriages had been made under express condition of the renunciation of the friendship and alliance of the states.

Such were among the first-fruits of the fall of Barneveldt and the triumph of Aertsens, for it was he in reality who had won the victory, and he had gained it over both stadholder and advocate. Who was to profit by the estrangement between the Republic and its powerful ally at a moment, too, when that great kingdom was at last beginning to emerge from the darkness and nothingness of many years, with the faint, glimmering dawn of a new great policy?

Barneveldt, whose masterful statesmanship, following out the traditions of William the Silent, had ever maintained through good and ill report cordial and beneficent relations between the two countries, had always comprehended, even as a great cardinal-minister was ere long to teach the world, that the permanent identification of France with Spain and the Roman League was unnatural and impossible.

Meantime Barneveldt sat in his solitary prison, knowing not what was passing on that great stage where he had so long been the chief actor, while small intriguers now attempted to control events.

It was the intention of Aertsens to return to the embassy in Paris, whence he had been driven, in his own opinion, so unjustly. To render himself indispensable, he had begun by making himself provisionally formidable to the king's government. Later there would be other deeds to do before the prize was within his grasp.

Thus the very moment when France was disposed to cultivate the most earnest friendship with the Republic had been seized for fastening an insult upon her. The Twelve Years' Truce with Spain was running to its close, the relations between France and Spain were unusually cold, and her friendship therefore more valuable than ever.

On the other hand, the British king was drawing closer his relations with Spain, and his alliance was demonstrably of small account. The phantom of the Spanish bride had become more real to his excited vision than ever, so that early in the year, in order to please Gondemar, he had been willing to offer an affront to the French ambassador.

The Prince of Wales had given a splendid masquerade at court, to which the envoy of his Most Catholic Majesty was bidden. Much to his amazement, the representative of the Most Christian King received no invitation, notwithstanding that he had taken great pains to procure one.[1] M. de la Boderie was very angry, and

---

[1] Caron to States-General, January 31, 1618, Hague Archives MS.: " . . . niettegenstaende den voors. ambassadeur daertoe veel debvoir gedaen hadde om genoyt te werden," etc.

went about complaining to the states' ambassador and his other colleagues of the slight, and darkened the lives of the court functionaries having charge of such matters with his vengeance and despair. It was represented to him that he had himself been asked to a festival the year before when Count Gondemar was left out. It was hinted to him that the king had good reasons for what he did, as the marriage with the daughter of Spain was now in train, and it was desirable that the Spanish ambassador should be able to observe the prince's disposition and make a more correct report of it to his government.[1] It was in vain. M. de la Boderie refused to be comforted, and asserted that one had no right to leave the French ambassador uninvited to any "festival or triumph" at court. There was an endless disturbance. De la Boderie sent his secretary off to Paris to complain to the king that his ambassador was of no account in London, while much favor was heaped upon the Spaniard. The secretary returned with instructions from Louis that the ambassador was to come home immediately, and he went off accordingly in dudgeon. "I could see that he was in the highest degree indignant," said Caron, who saw him before he left, "and I doubt not that his departure will increase and keep up the former jealousy between the governments."

The ill humor created by this event lasted a long time, serving to neutralize, or at least perceptibly diminish, the Spanish influence produced in France by

[1] " . . . meenende daertoe goede redenen te hebben doordien het huwelyk met de dochter van Spagne nu in treinne is, ende dat den ambassadeur's princen dispositie soude connen mercken ende daervan in Spagnen beter rapport senden."

the Spanish marriages. In the autumn Secretary de
Puysieux, by command of the king, ordered every
Spaniard to leave the French court. All the "Spanish
ladies and gentlemen, great and small," who had accompanied the queen from Madrid were included in
this expulsion, with the exception of four individuals—
her Majesty's father confessor, physician, apothecary,
and cook.

The fair young queen was much vexed, and shed
bitter tears at this calamity, which, as she spoke nothing but Spanish, left her isolated at the court; but she
was a little consoled by the promise that thenceforth
the king would share her couch. It had not yet occurred to him that he was married.[1]

The French envoys at The Hague exhausted themselves in efforts, both private and public, in favor of
the prisoners, but it was a thankless task. Now that
the great man and his chief pupils and adherents were
out of sight, a war of shameless calumny was begun
upon him, such as has scarcely a parallel in political
history.

It was as if a whole tribe of noxious and obscene
reptiles were swarming out of the earth which had
suddenly swallowed him. But it was not alone the
obscure or the anonymous who now triumphantly vili-
fied him. Men in high places who had partaken of his
patronage, who had caressed him and groveled before
him, who had grown great through his tuition and rich

[1] Langerac to States-General, October 26, 1618: "Waerover
H. M. seer bedroeft synde ende bitterlyk schreyende, daerna we-
derom een weynig vertrost is geworden door de hoope ende be-
loftenisse, soo men techt, van dat de Coninck nu by haer slapen
soude."

through his bounty, now rejoiced in his ruin or hastened at least to save themselves from being involved in it. Not a man of them all but fell away from him like water. Even the great soldier forgot whose respectful but powerful hand it was which, at the most tragical moment, had lifted him from the high school at Leyden into the post of greatest power and responsibility, and had guided his first faltering footsteps by the light of his genius and experience. Francis Aertsens, master of the field, had now become the political tutor of the mature stadholder. Step by step we have been studying the inmost thoughts of the advocate as revealed in his secret and confidential correspondence, and the reader has been enabled to judge of the wantonness of the calumny which converted the determined antagonist into the secret friend of Spain. Yet it had produced its effect upon Maurice.

He told the French ambassadors [1] a month after the arrest that Barneveldt had been endeavoring, during and since the truce negotiations, to bring back the provinces, especially Holland, if not under the dominion of, at least under some kind of vassalage to, Spain. Persons had been feeling the public pulse as to the possibility of securing permanent peace by paying tribute to Spain, and this secret plan of Barneveldt had so alienated him from the prince as to cause him to attempt every possible means of diminishing or destroying altogether his authority. He had spread through many cities that Maurice wished to make himself master of the state by using the religious dissensions to keep the people weakened and divided.

[1] Despatches of Boississe and Du Maurier, September 27, 1618, in Ouvré, 289.

There is not a particle of evidence, and no attempt was ever made to produce any, that the advocate had such plans, but certainly, if ever man had made himself master of a state, that man was Maurice. He continued, however, to place himself before the world as the servant of the States-General, which he never was, either theoretically or in fact.

The French ambassadors became every day more indignant and more discouraged. It was obvious that Aertsens, their avowed enemy, was controlling the public policy of the government. Not only was there no satisfaction to be had for the offensive manner in which he had filled the country with his ancient grievances and his nearly forgotten charges against the queen dowager and those who had assisted her in the regency, but they were repulsed at every turn when, by order of their sovereign, they attempted to use his good offices in favor of the man who had ever been the steady friend of France.

The stadholder also professed friendship for that country, and referred to Colonel-General Chatillon, who had for a long time commanded the French regiments in the Netherlands, for confirmation of his uniform affection for those troops and attachment to their sovereign.

He would do wonders, he said, if Louis would declare war upon Spain by land and sea.

"Such fruits are not ripe," said Boississe, "nor has your love for France been very manifest in recent events."

"Barneveldt," replied the prince, "has personally offended me, and has boasted that he would drive me out of the country like Leicester. He is accused of having wished to trouble the country in order to bring it back under the yoke of Spain. Justice will decide. The states only are sovereign to judge this question. You must address yourself to them."

"The states," replied the ambassadors, "will require to be aided by your counsels."

The prince made no reply and remained chill and "impregnable." [1] The ambassadors continued their intercessions in behalf of the prisoners both by public address to the assembly [2] and by private appeals to the stadholder and his influential friends. In virtue of the intimate alliance and mutual guaranties existing between their government and the Republic, they claimed the acceptance of their good offices. They insisted upon a regular trial of the prisoners according to the laws of the land, that is to say, by the High Court of Holland, which alone had jurisdiction in the premises. If they had been guilty of high treason, they should be duly arraigned. In the name of the signal services of Barneveldt and of the constant friendship of that great magistrate for France, the king demanded clemency or proof of his crimes. His Majesty complained through his ambassadors of the little respect shown for his counsels and for his friendship. "In times past you found ever prompt and favorable action in your time of need." [3]

"This discourse," said Maurice to Chatillon, "proceeds from evil intention."

[1] Despatches of Boississe and Du Maurier, in Ouvré, 291.

[2] "Proposition des Ambassadeurs de France faite aux États-Généraux, 28 nov., 1618." "Proposition des Ambassadeurs, 23 et 24 mars, 1619." "Réponse des États-Généraux aux Ambassadeurs, 29 mars, 1619." Hague Archives MSS.

[3] Ouvré, 295.

Thus the prisoners had disappeared from human sight, and their enemies ran riot in slandering them. Yet thus far no public charges had been made.

"Nothing appears against them," said Du Maurier, "and people are beginning to open their mouths with incredible freedom. While waiting for the condemnation of the prisoners, one is determined to dishonor them."[1]

The French ambassadors were instructed to intercede to the last, but they were steadily repulsed; while the King of Great Britain, anxious to gain favor with Spain by aiding in the ruin of one whom he knew and Spain knew to be her determined foe, did all he could through his ambassador to frustrate their efforts and bring on a catastrophe.[2] The States-General and Maurice were now on as confidential terms with Carleton as they were cold and repellent to Boississe and Du Maurier.

"To recall to them the benefits of the king," said Du Maurier, "is to beat the air. And then Aertsens bewitches them, and they imagine that after having played runaway horses his Majesty will be only too happy to receive them back, caress them, and, in order to have their friendship, approve everything they have been doing, right or wrong."

Aertsens had it all his own way, and the States-Gen-

[1] Despatch, December 24, 1618, in Ouvré, 294.

[2] "El Rey de Inglaterra que es en quien ahora se fian mas los Estados aprieta paraque executen á Barneveld pero los Franceses hazen diligᵃ en su favor . . . como tiene el Conde Mauricio de su parte al Ingles se entiende que dentro pocas dias se pronunciara la sentencia á Barneveld," etc.—Eman₁ Sueyro (confidential agent of King of Spain in the Netherlands) to ——, Antwerp, December 29, 1618, Arch. de Simancas MS.

eral had just paid him twelve thousand francs in cash on the ground that Langerac's salary was larger than his had been when at the head of the same embassy many years before.

His elevation into the body of nobles, which Maurice had just stocked with five other of his partizans, was accounted an additional affront to France, while, on the other hand, the queen mother, having through Epergnon's assistance made her escape from Blois, where she had been kept in durance since the death of Concini, now enumerated among other grievances for which she was willing to take up arms against her son that the king's government had favored Barneveldt.[1]

It was strange that all the devotees of Spain—Mary de' Medici and Epergnon, as well as James I. and his courtiers—should be thus embittered against the man who had sold the Netherlands to Spain.

At last the prince told the French ambassadors that the "people of the provinces considered their persistent intercessions an invasion of their sovereignty."[2] Few would have anything to say to them. "No one listens to us, no one replies to us," said Du Maurier, "every one visiting us is observed, and it is conceived a reproach here to speak to the ambassadors of France."[3]

Certainly the days were changed since Henry IV. leaned on the arm of Barneveldt, and consulted with him, and with him only among all the statesmen of Europe, on his great schemes for regenerating Christendom and averting that general war which, now that

[1] Ouvré, 299.
[2] Despatches, January 21 and 27, 1619.   Ouvré, 296.
[3] Ouvré, 298.   Despatches, February 1 and 12, 1619.

the great king had been murdered and the advocate imprisoned, had already begun to ravage Europe.

Van der Myle had gone to Paris to make such exertions as he could among the leading members of the council in favor of his father-in-law.[1] Langerac, the states' ambassador there, who but yesterday had been turning at every moment to the advocate for light and warmth as to the sun, now hastened to disavow all respect or regard for him. He scoffed at the slender sympathy Van der Myle was finding in the bleak political atmosphere. He had done his best to find out what he had been negotiating with the members of the council, and was glad to say that it was so inconsiderable as to be not worth reporting. He had not spoken with or seen the king. Jeannin, his own and his father-in-law's principal and most confidential friend, had only spoken with him half an hour and then departed for Burgundy, although promising to confer with him sympathetically on his return. "I am very displeased at his coming here," said Langerac, ". . . but he has found little friendship or confidence, and is full of woe and apprehension."

The ambassador's labors were now confined to personally soliciting the king's permission for deputations from the Reformed churches of France to go to the synod,[2] now opened (13th November) at Dordrecht, and to clearing his own skirts with the prince and States-General of any suspicion of sympathy with Barneveldt.

---

[1] Langerac to States-General, October 29, 1618, Hague Archives MS.

[2] Same to same, July 22 and October 9, 1618. Same to the king, October 6 and 31, 1618. Same to States-General, October 26, November 2 and 23, 1618. Hague Archives MSS.

In the first object he was unsuccessful, the king telling him at last "with clear and significant words that this was impossible, on account of his conscience, his respect for the Catholic religion, and many other reasons." [1]

In regard to the second point he acted with great promptness.

He received a summons in January, 1619, from the States-General and the prince to send them all letters that he had ever received from Barneveldt. He crawled at once to Maurice on his knees, with the letters in his hand.

"Most illustrious, high-born Prince, most gracious Lord," he said : [2] "Obeying the commands which it has pleased the states and your princely Grace to give me, I send back the letters of Advocate Barneveldt. If your princely Grace should find anything in them showing that the said advocate had any confidence in me, I most humbly beg your princely Grace to believe that I never entertained any affection for him, except only in respect to and so far as he was in credit and good authority with the government, and according to the upright zeal which I thought I could see in him for the service of my high and puissant lords the States-General and your princely Grace."

Greater humbleness could be expected of no ambassador. Most nobly did the devoted friend and pupil of the great statesman remember his duty to the illustrious prince and their High Mightinesses. Most

[1] Despatch of November 23 last cited.

[2] Langerac to Prince Maurice, January 29, 1619, Hague Archives MS.

promptly did he abjure his patron now that he had
fallen into the abyss.

"Nor will it be found," he continued, "that I have
had any sympathy or communication with the said
advocate, except alone in things concerning my service.
The great trust I had in him as the foremost and oldest councilor of the state, as the one who so confidentially instructed me on my departure for France, and
who had obtained for himself so great authority that
all the most important affairs of the country were intrusted to him, was the cause that I simply and sincerely wrote to him all that people were in the habit
of saying at this court.

"If I had known in the least or suspected that he
was not what he ought to be in the service of my lords
the states and of your princely Grace, and for the welfare and tranquillity of the land, I should have been
well on my guard against letting myself in the least
into any kind of communication with him whatever."

The reader has seen how steadily and frankly the
advocate had kept Langerac as well as Caron informed
of passing events, and how little concealment he made
of his views in regard to the synod, the wartgelders,
and the respective authority of the States-General and
States-Provincial. Not only had Langerac no reason
to suspect that Barneveldt was not what he ought to
be, but he absolutely knew the contrary from that most
confidential correspondence with him which he was
now so abjectly repudiating. The advocate, in a protracted constitutional controversy, had made no secret
of his views either officially or privately. Whether
his positions were tenable or flimsy, they had been
openly taken.

"What is more," proceeded the ambassador, "had I thought that any account ought to be made of what I wrote to him concerning the sovereignty of the provinces, I should for a certainty not have failed to advise your Grace of it above all."

He then, after profuse and maudlin protestations of his most dutiful zeal all the days of his life for "the service, honor, reputation, and contentment of your princely Grace," observed that he had not thought it necessary to give him notice of such idle and unfounded matters, as being likely to give the prince annoyance and displeasure. He had, however, always kept within himself the resolution duly to notify him in case he found that any belief was attached to the reports in Paris. "But the reports," he said, "were popular and calumnious inventions of which no man had ever been willing or able to name to him the authors."

The ambassador's memory was treacherous, and he had doubtless neglected to read over the minutes, if he had kept them, of his wonderful disclosures on the subject of the sovereignty before thus exculpating himself. It will be remembered that he had narrated the story of the plot for conferring sovereignty upon Maurice not as a popular calumny flying about Paris with no man to father it, but he had given it to Barneveldt on the authority of a privy councilor of France and of the king himself. "His Majesty knows it to be authentic," he had said in his letter. That letter was a pompous one, full of mystery, and so secretly ciphered that he had desired that his friend Van der Myle, whom he was now deriding for his efforts in Paris to save his father-in-law from his fate, might assist the advocate in unraveling its contents. He had now discovered

that it had been idle gossip not worthy of a moment's
attention.

The reader will remember, too, that Barneveldt, without attaching much importance to the tale, had distinctly pointed out to Langerac that the prince himself
was not implicated in the plot, and had instructed the
ambassador to communicate the story to Maurice.[1]
This advice had not been taken, but he had kept the
perilous stuff upon his breast. He now sought to lay
the blame, if it were possible to do so, upon the man
to whom he had communicated it and who had not believed it.

The business of the States-General, led by the advocate's enemies this winter, was to accumulate all kinds
of tales, reports, and accusations to his discredit on
which to form something like a bill of indictment.
They had demanded all his private and confidential
correspondence with Caron and Langerac. The ambassador in Paris had been served, moreover, with a
string of nine interrogatories which he was ordered to
answer on oath and honor.   This he did, and appended
the reply to his letter.

The nine questions had simply for their object to
discover what Barneveldt had been secretly writing to
the ambassador concerning the synod, the enlisted
troops, and the supposed projects of Maurice concerning the sovereignty.[2] Langerac was obliged to admit

[1] Antea, p. 38, vol. iii.
[2] "Poincten waerop Zyne Excellentie by goetvinden v. d. H.
M. St. Gen[l] begeert dat de H. van Langerac, Ambassadeur, etc.,
aen Zyne Ex[tie] zal geven contentement ende doen zyne verclaer-
inge op zyn eere ende eet," etc., in ten articles, with the answers
appended, Hague Archives MS.

in his replies that nothing had been written except the regular correspondence which he indorsed, and of which the reader has been able to see the sum and substance in the copious extracts which have been given.

He stated also that he had never received any secret instructions save the marginal notes to the list of questions addressed by him, when about leaving for Paris in 1614, to Barneveldt. Most of these were of a trivial and commonplace nature.

They had, however, a direct bearing on the process to be instituted against the advocate, and the letter, too, which we have been examining will prove to be of much importance. Certainly pains enough were taken to detect the least trace of treason in a very loyal correspondence. Langerac concluded by inclosing the Barneveldt correspondence since the beginning of the year 1614, protesting that not a single letter had been kept back or destroyed. "Once more I recommend myself to mercy, if not to favor," he added, "as the most faithful, most obedient, most zealous servant of their High Mightinesses and your princely Grace, to whom I have devoted and sacrificed my honor and life in most humble service; and am now and forever the most humble, most obedient, most faithful servant of my most serene, most illustrious, most highly born Prince, most gracious Lord and princeliest Grace."

The former adherent of plain Advocate Barneveldt could hardly find superlatives enough to bestow upon the man whose displeasure that prisoner had incurred.

Directly after the arrest the stadholder had resumed his tour through the provinces in order to change the governments. Sliding over any opposition which recent events had rendered idle, his course in every city

was nearly the same. A regiment or two and a train
of eighty or a hundred wagons coming through the
city gate, preceded by the prince and his body-guard
of three hundred, a tramp of halberdmen up the great
staircase of the town hall, a jingle of spurs in the
assembly-room, and the whole board of magistrates
were summoned into the presence of the stadholder.
They were then informed that the world had no further
need of their services, and were allowed to bow themselves out of the presence. A new list was then announced, prepared beforehand by Maurice on the
suggestion of those on whom he could rely. A faint resistance was here and there attempted by magistrates
and burghers who could not forget in a moment the
rights of self-government and the code of laws which
had been enjoyed for centuries. At Hoorn, for instance, there was deep indignation among the citizens.
An imprudent word or two from the authorities might
have brought about a blood-bath.

The burgomaster ventured, indeed, to expostulate.
They requested the prince not to change the magistracy.
"This is against our privileges," they said, "which it
is our duty to uphold. You will see what deep displeasure will seize the burghers, and how much disturbance and tumult will follow. If any faults have been
committed by any member of the government, let him
be accused, and let him answer for them. Let your
Excellency not only dismiss but punish such as cannot
properly justify themselves." [1]

But his Excellency summoned them all to the town
house, and, as usual, deposed them all. A regiment

[1] Wagenaer, x. 272 seq. Van der Kemp, iv. 99, 100. Brandt,
Hist. Ref., ii. 853 seq. Baudartius, x. 69 seq.

was drawn up in half-moon on the square beneath the windows. To the magistrates asking why they were deposed, he briefly replied: "The quiet of the land requires it. It is necessary to have unanimous resolutions in the States-General at The Hague. This cannot be accomplished without these preliminary changes. I believe that you had good intentions and have been faithful servants of the fatherland. But this time it must be so." [1]

And so the faithful servants of the fatherland were dismissed into space. Otherwise how could there be unanimous voting in parliament? It must be regarded perhaps as fortunate that the force of character, undaunted courage, and quiet decision of Maurice enabled him to effect this violent series of revolutions with such masterly simplicity. It is questionable whether the stadholder's commission technically empowered him thus to trample on municipal law; it is certain that, if it did, the boasted liberties of the Netherlands were a dream; but it is equally true that, in the circumstances then existing, a vulgar, cowardly, or incompetent personage might have marked his pathway with massacres without restoring tranquillity.

Sometimes there was even a comic aspect to these strokes of state. The lists of new magistrates being hurriedly furnished by the prince's adherents to supply the place of those evicted, it often happened that men not qualified by property, residence, or other attributes were appointed to the government, so that many became magistrates before they were citizens.

1 Wagenaer, x. 272 seq. Van der Kemp, iv. 99, 100. Brandt, Hist. Ref., ii. 853 seq. Baudartius, x. 69 seq. Brandt, 856. Vel. Hoornsche Chron., 385.

On being respectfully asked sometimes who such a magistrate might be whose face and name were equally unknown to his colleagues and to the townsmen in general, "Do I know the fellows?"[1] he would say, with a cheerful laugh. And indeed they might have all been dead men, those new functionaries, for aught he did know. And so on through Medemblik and Alkmaar, Brielle, Delft, Monnickendam, and many other cities, progressed the prince, sowing new municipalities broadcast as he passed along. At The Hague, on his return, a vote of thanks to the prince was passed by the nobles and most of the cities for the trouble he had taken in this reforming process. But the unanimous vote had not yet been secured, the strongholds of Arminianism, as it was the fashion to call them, not being yet reduced.

The prince, in reply to the vote of thanks, said that "in what he had done and was going to do his intention sincerely and uprightly had been no other than to promote the interests and tranquillity of the country, without admixture of anything personal and without prejudice to the general commonwealth or the laws and privileges of the cities." He desired further that "note might be taken of this declaration as record of his good and upright intentions."[2]

But the sincerest and most upright intentions may be refracted by party atmosphere from their aim, and the purest gold from the mint elude the direct grasp through the clearest fluid in existence. At any rate, it would have been difficult to convince the host of deposed magistrates hurled from office, although recog-

---

[1] Brandt, ii. 853–857. Van der Kemp, iv. 100.

[2] Brandt, 859, 860. Wagenaer, x. 271, 272. Resol. Holl., October 12 and 19, 1618, bl. 295, 307.

nized as faithful servants of the fatherland, that such violent removal had taken place without detriment to the laws and privileges.

And the stadholder went to the few cities where some of the leaven still lingered.

He arrived at Leyden on the 22d October, "accompanied by a great suite of colonels, ritmeesters, and captains," having sent on his body-guard to the town, strengthened by other troops. He was received by the magistrates at the "Prince's Court" with great reverence, and entertained by them in the evening at a magnificent banquet.[1]

Next morning he summoned the whole forty of them to the town house, disbanded them all, and appointed new ones in their stead, some of the old members, however, who could be relied upon being admitted to the revolutionized board.

The populace, mainly of the stadholder's party, made themselves merry over the discomfited "Arminians." They hung wisps of straw as derisive wreaths of triumph over the dismantled pallisade lately encircling the town hall, disposed of the famous "Olden-Barneveldt's teeth" at auction in the public square,[2] and chased many a poor cock and hen, with their feathers completely plucked from their bodies, about the street, crying, "Arme haenen, arme haenen,"—Arminians, or poor fowls,—according to the practical witticism much esteemed at that period.[3] Certainly the unfortunate Barneveldtians or Arminians, or however the Remonstrants might be designated, had been sufficiently stripped of their plumes.

[1] Brandt, 860, 861.   [2] Baudartius, x. 59.
[3] Carleton's Letters, 295.

The prince, after having made proclamation from the town house enjoining "modesty upon the mob" and a general abstention from "perverseness and petulance," went his way to Haarlem,[1] where he dismissed the magistrates and appointed new ones, and then proceeded to Rotterdam, to Gouda, and to Amsterdam.

It seemed scarcely necessary to carry out the process in the commercial capital, the abode of Peter Plancius, the seat of the West India Company, the headquarters of all most opposed to the advocate, most devoted to the stadholder. But although the majority of the city government was an overwhelming one, there was still a respectable minority who, it was thought possible, might under a change of circumstances effect much mischief and even grow into a majority.

The prince therefore summoned the board before him according to his usual style of proceeding and dismissed them all. They submitted without a word of remonstrance.

Ex-Burgomaster Hoofd, a man of seventy-two,—father of the illustrious Pieter Corneliszoon Hoofd, one of the greatest historians of the Netherlands or of any country, then a man of thirty-seven,—shocked at the humiliating silence, asked his colleagues if they had none of them a word to say in defense of their laws and privileges.

They answered with one accord, "No."

The old man, a personal friend of Barneveldt and born the same year, then got on his feet and addressed the stadholder. He spoke manfully and well, characterizing the summary deposition of the magistracy as illegal and unnecessary, recalling to the memory of

[1] Baudartius, ubi sup.

those who heard him that he had been thirty-six years long a member of the government and always a warm friend of the house of Nassau, and respectfully submitting that the small minority in the municipal government, while differing from their colleagues and from the greater number of the States-General, had limited their opposition to strictly constitutional means, never resorting to acts of violence or to secret conspiracy.[1]

Nothing could be more truly respectable than the appearance of this ancient magistrate, in long black robe with fur edgings, high ruff around his thin, pointed face, and decent skullcap covering his bald old head, quavering forth to unsympathetic ears a temperate and unanswerable defense of things which in all ages the noblest minds have deemed most valuable.

His harangue was not very long. Maurice's reply was very short.

"Grandpapa," he said, "it must be so this time. Necessity and the service of the country require it."[2]

With that he dismissed the thirty-six magistrates, and next day appointed a new board, who were duly sworn to fidelity to the States-General. Of course a large proportion of the old members were renominated.

Scarcely had the echo of the prince's footsteps ceased to resound through the country as he tramped from one city to another, molding each to his will, when the states of Holland, now thoroughly reorganized, passed a solemn vote of thanks to him for all that he had done.

[1] Brandt, Hist. Ref., ii. 867, 868, and C. P. Hoofd's own notes. Wagenaer, x. 280. Van der Kemp, iv. 105.
[2] Ibid.

The six cities of the minority had now become the majority, and there was unanimity at The Hague.   The seven provinces, States-General and States-Provincial, were as one, and the synod was secured.   Whether the prize was worth the sacrifices which it had cost and was still to cost might at least be considered doubtful.

CHAPTER XIX

Rancor between the politico-religious parties—Spanish intrigues
—Inconsistency of James—Brewster and Robinson's congregation
at Leyden—They decide to leave for America—Robinson's farewell sermon and prayer at parting.

DURING this dark and mournful winter the internal dissensions and, as a matter of course, the foreign intrigues had become more dangerous than ever. While
the man who for a whole generation had guided the
policy of the Republic and had been its virtual chief
magistrate lay hidden from all men's sight, the troubles which he had sought to avert were not diminished
by his removal from the scene. The extreme or Go-
marist party, which had taken a pride in secret con-
venticles where they were in a minority, determined,
as they said, to separate Christ from Belial, and, medi-
tating the triumph which they had at last secured, now
drove the Arminians from the great churches. Very
soon it was impossible for these heretics to enjoy the
rights of public worship anywhere. But they were not
dismayed. The canons of Dordrecht had not yet been
fulminated. They avowed themselves ready to sacrifice worldly goods and life itself in defense of the Five
Points. In Rotterdam, notwithstanding a garrison of
fifteen companies, more than a thousand Remonstrants
assembled on Christmas day in the Exchange, for want

of a more appropriate place of meeting, and sang the
One Hundred and Twelfth Psalm in mighty chorus.
A clergyman of their persuasion, accidentally passing
through the street, was forcibly laid hands upon and
obliged to preach to them, which he did with great
unction.[1] The magistracy, where now the Contra-Remonstrants had the control, forbade, under severe penalties, a repetition of such scenes. It was impossible
not to be reminded of the days half a century before,
when the early Reformers had met in the open fields
or among the dunes, armed to the teeth, and with out-
lying pickets to warn the congregation of the approach
of Red Rod and the functionaries of the Holy Inquisition.

In Schoonhoven the authorities attempted one Sunday by main force to induct a Contra-Remonstrant into
the pulpit from which a Remonstrant had just been
expelled. The women of the place turned out with
their distaffs and beat them from the field. The garrison was called out, and there was a pitched battle in
the streets between soldiers, police officers, and women,
not much to the edification certainly of the Sabbath-
loving community on either side,[2] the victory remaining with the ladies.

In short, it would be impossible to exaggerate the
rancor felt between the different politico-religious parties. All heed for the great war now raging in the
outside world between the hostile elements of Catholicism and Protestantism, embattled over an enormous
space, was lost in the din of conflict among the respective supporters of conditional and unconditional dam-

[1] Eman¹ Sueyro to ——, January 14, 1619, Arch. de Simancas
MS.   [2] Ibid.

nation within the pale of the Reformed Church. The earthquake shaking Europe rolled unheeded, as it was of old said to have done at Cannæ, amid the fierce shock of mortal foes in that narrow field.

The respect for authority which had so long been the distinguishing characteristic of the Netherlanders seemed to have disappeared. It was difficult, now that the time-honored laws and privileges in defense of which, and of liberty of worship included in them, the provinces had made war forty years long had been trampled upon by military force, for those not warmed by the fire of Gomarus to feel their ancient respect for the magistracy. The magistracy at that moment seemed to mean the sword.

The Spanish government was inevitably encouraged by the spectacle thus presented. We have seen the strong hopes entertained by the council at Madrid, two years before the crisis now existing had occurred. We have witnessed the eagerness with which the king indulged the dream of recovering the sovereignty which his father had lost, and the vast schemes which he nourished toward that purpose, founded on the internal divisions which were reducing the Republic to impotence.[1] Subsequent events had naturally made him more sanguine than ever. There was now a web of intrigue stretching through the provinces to bring them all back under the scepter of Spain. The imprisonment of the great stipendiary, the great conspirator, the man who had sold himself and was on the point of selling his country, had not terminated those plots. Where was the supposed center of that intrigue? In the council of state of the Netherlands, ever fiercely

[1] Vide antea, pp. 21–31.

opposed to Barneveldt and stuffed full of his mortal
enemies. Whose name was most familiar on the lips
of the Spanish partizans engaged in these secret
schemes? That of Adrian Manmaker, president of the
council, representative of Prince Maurice as first noble
of Zealand in the States-General, chairman of the committee sent by that body [1] to Utrecht to frustrate the
designs of the advocate, and one of the twenty-four
commissioners soon to be appointed to sit in judgment
upon him.

The tale seems too monstrous for belief, nor is it to
be admitted with certainty, that Manmaker and the
other councilors implicated had actually given their
adhesion to the plot, because the Spanish emissaries in
their correspondence with the king assured him of the
fact. But if such a foundation for suspicion could
have been found against Barneveldt and his friends,
the world would not have heard the last of it from that
hour to this.

It is superfluous to say that the prince was entirely
foreign to these plans. He had never been mentioned
as privy to the little arrangements of Councilor du
Agean and others, although he was to benefit by them.
In the Spanish schemes he seems to have been considered as an impediment, although indirectly they might
tend to advance him.

"We have managed now, I hope, that his Majesty
will be recognized as sovereign of the country," wrote
the confidential agent of the King of Spain in the
Netherlands, Emanuel Sueyro, to the government of
Madrid.[2] "The English will oppose it with all their

---

[1] Vide antea, pp. 21–31.
[2] Eman¹ Sueyro to——,'January 21, 1619, Arch. de Simancas MS.

strength. But they can do nothing except by making
Count Maurice sovereign of Holland and Duke of
Jülich and Cleves. Maurice will also contrive to make
himself master of Wesel, so it is necessary for the archduke to be beforehand with him and make sure of the
place. It is also needful that his Majesty should induce the French government to talk with the Netherlanders and convince them that it is time to prolong
the truce.''

This was soon afterward accomplished. The French
minister at Brussels informed Archduke Albert that
Du Maurier had been instructed to propose the pro-
longation, and that he had been conferring with the
Prince of Orange and the States-General on the subject. At first the prince had expressed disinclination,
but at the last interview both he and the states had
shown a desire for it, and the French king had requested from the archduke a declaration whether the
Spanish government would be willing to treat for it.
In such case Louis would offer himself as mediator and
do his best to bring about a successful result.[1]

But it was not the intention of the conspirators in
the Netherlands that the truce should be prolonged.
On the contrary, the negotiation for it was merely to
furnish the occasion for fully developing their plot.
''The states, and especially those of Zealand, will reply
that they no longer wish the truce,'' continued Sueyro,
''and that they would prefer war to such a truce.
They desire to put ships on the coast of Flanders, to
which the Hollanders are opposed because it would be
disagreeable to the French. So the Zealanders will be
the first to say that the Netherlanders must come back

[1] Archduke Albert to Philip III., April 5, 1619, Brussels Arch. MS.

to his Majesty. *This their President Manmaker has sworn.* The states of Overyssel will likewise give their hand to this, because they say they will be the first to feel the shock of the war. Thus we shall very easily carry out our design, and as we shall concede to the Zealanders their demands in regard to the navigation, they at least will place themselves under the dominion of his Majesty, as will be the case with Friesland as well as Overyssel.''

It will be observed that in this secret arrangement for selling the Republic to its ancient master it was precisely the provinces and the politicians most steadily opposed to Barneveldt that took the lead. Zealand, Friesland, Overyssel, were in the plot, but not a word was said of Utrecht. As for Holland itself, hopes were founded on the places where hatred to the advocate was fiercest.

''Between ourselves,'' continued the agent, ''we are ten here in the government of Holland to support the plan, but we must not discover ourselves, for fear of suffering what has happened to Barneveldt.''

He added that the time for action had not yet come, and that if movements were made before the synod had finished its labors, ''the Gomarists would say that they were all sold.'' He implored the government at Madrid to keep the whole matter for the present profoundly secret, because ''Prince Maurice and the Gomarists had the forces of the country at their disposition.'' In case the plot was sprung too suddenly, therefore, he feared that with the assistance of England Maurice might, at the head of the Gomarists and the army, make himself sovereign of Holland and Duke of Cleves, while he and the rest of the Spanish partizans might be in prison with Barneveldt for trying to accomplish what Barneveldt had been trying to prevent.

The opinions and utterances of such a man as James I. would be of little worth to our history had he not happened to occupy the place he did. But he was a leading actor in the mournful drama which filled up the whole period of the Twelve Years' Truce. His words had a direct influence on great events. He was a man of unquestionable erudition, of powers of mind above the average, while the absolute deformity of his moral constitution made him incapable of thinking, feeling, or acting rightly on any vital subject, by any accident or on any occasion. If there were one thing that he thoroughly hated in the world, it was the Reformed religion. If in his thought there were one term of reproach more loathsome than another to be applied to a human creature, it was the word "Puritan." In the word was subversion of all established authority in church and state—revolution, republicanism, anarchy. "There are degrees in heaven," he was wont to say, "there are degrees in hell: there must be degrees on earth."

He forbade the Calvinist churches of Scotland to hold their customary synod in 1610, passionately reviling them and their belief, and declaring "their aim to be nothing else than to deprive kings and princes of their sovereignty, and to reduce the whole world to a popular form of government where everybody would be master." [1]

[1] Lois de Groote, agent of Archduke Albert at the court of King James, to the archduke, October 14, 1610, "Négotiat. d'Anglet.," Belg. Arch. MS.

When the Prince of Neuburg embraced Catholicism, thus complicating matters in the duchies and strengthening the hand of Spain and the emperor in the debatable land, he seized the occasion to assure the agent of the archduke in London, Councilor Boissetot, of his warm Catholic sympathies. "They say that I am the greatest heretic in the world," he exclaimed; "but I will never deny that the true religion is that of Rome, even if corrupted." [1] He expressed his belief in the real presence, and his surprise that the Roman Catholics did not take the chalice for the blood of Christ.[2] The English bishops, he averred, drew their consecration, through the bishops in Mary Tudor's time, from the pope.[3]

As Philip II., and Ferdinand II. echoing the sentiments of his illustrious uncle, had both sworn they would rather reign in a wilderness than tolerate a single heretic in their dominions, so James had said "he would rather be a hermit in a forest than a king over such people as the pack of Puritans were who overruled the lower house." [4]

For the Netherlanders he had an especial hatred, both as rebels and Puritans. Soon after coming to the English throne he declared that their revolt, which had been going on all his lifetime and of which he never expected to see the end, had begun by petition for matters of religion. "His mother and he from their cradles," he said, "had been haunted with a

---

[1] Boissetot to Archduke Albert, July 10, 1614, Belg. Arch. MS.
[2] " . . . no tomassen el calis por sangre de Cristo."—Ibid.
[3] Ibid.
[4] Hallam, Const. Hist., i. 408–424. Bancroft, Hist. United States, i. 298.

Puritan devil, which he feared would not leave him to
his grave. And he would hazard his crown but he
would suppress those malicious spirits."[1] It seemed
a strange caprice of destiny that assigned to this hater
of Netherlanders, of Puritans, and of the Reformed
religion the decision of disputed points between Puritans and anti-Puritans in the Reformed Church of the
Netherlands.

It seemed stranger that his opinions should be hotly
on the side of the Puritans.

Barneveldt, who often used the expression in later
years, as we have seen in his correspondence, was opposed to the Dutch Puritans because they had more
than once attempted subversion of the government on
pretext of religion, especially at the memorable epoch
of Leicester's government.

The business of stirring up these religious conspira-
cies against the magistracy he was apt to call "Flan-
derizing," in allusion to those disastrous days and to
the origin of the ringleaders in those tumults. But his
main object, as we have seen, was to effect compromises
and restore good feeling between members of the one
church, reserving the right of disposing over religious
matters to the government of the respective provinces.

But James had remedied his audacious inconsistency
by discovering that Puritanism in England and in the
Netherlands resembled each other no more than certain
letters transposed into totally different words meant
one and the same thing.[2] The anagrammatic argu-

---

[1] Peck's Desiderata Curiosa, lib. v. 44. I borrow the quotation
from Mr. Charles Deane's excellent edition of Governor Bradford's
invaluable and long-lost History of the Plymouth Plantation,
9, note †.   [2] Belknap, Robinson, 278 (ed. 1841).

ment had been neatly put by Sir Dudley Carleton, convincing no man. Puritanism in England "denied the right of human invention or imposition in religious matters." Puritanism in the Netherlands denied the right of the legal government to impose its authority in religious matters. This was the great matter of debate in the provinces. In England the argument had been settled very summarily against the Puritans by sheriffs' officers, bishops' pursuivants, and county jails.

As the political tendencies, so, too, the religious creed and observances of the English Puritans were identical with those of the Contra-Remonstrants, whom King James had helped to their great triumph. This was not very difficult to prove. It so happened that there were some English Puritans living at that moment in Leyden. They formed an independent society by themselves, which they called a Congregational church, and in which were some three hundred communicants. The length of their residence there was almost exactly coeval with the Twelve Years' Truce. They knew before leaving England that many relics of the Roman ceremonial, with which they were dissatisfied, and for the discontinuance of which they had in vain petitioned the crown,—the ring, the sign of the cross, white surplices, and the like,—besides the whole hierarchical system, had been disused in the Reformed churches of France, Switzerland, and the United Provinces, where the forms of worship, in their view, had been brought more nearly to the early apostolic model.[1] They admitted for truth the doctrinal articles of the Dutch Reformed churches. They had not come to the Netherlands without cause. At an early period of King

[1] Van Meteren, b. xxv. f. 490.

James's reign this congregation of seceders from the establishment had been wont to hold meetings at Scrooby in Nottinghamshire, once a manor of the Archbishop of York, but then the residence of one William Brewster. This was a gentleman of some fortune, educated at Cambridge, a good scholar, who in Queen Elizabeth's time had been in the service of William Davison when secretary of state.[1] He seemed to have been a confidential private secretary of that excellent and unlucky statesman, who found him so discreet and faithful as to deserve employment before all others in matters of trust and secrecy.[2] He was esteemed by Davison "rather as a son than a servant," and he repaid his confidence by doing him many faithful offices in the time of his troubles. He had, however, long since retired from connection with public affairs, living a retired life, devoted to study, meditation, and practical exertion to promote the cause of religion, and in acts of benevolence sometimes beyond his means.

The pastor of the Scrooby church, one John Robinson, a graduate of Cambridge,[3] who had been a beneficed clergyman in Norfolk, was a man of learning, eloquence, and lofty intellect. But what were such good gifts in the possession of rebels, seceders, and Puritans? It is needless to say that Brewster and Robinson were baited, persecuted, watched day and night, some of the congregation often clapped into prison, others into the stocks, deprived of the means of livelihood, outlawed, famished, banned. Plainly their country was no place for them. After a few years of such work they resolved to establish themselves in Hol-

[1] Bradford's History, 409 (ed. Deane).   [2] Ibid.
[3] Probably. Belknap, in voce.

land, where at least they hoped to find refuge and toleration.

But it proved as difficult for them to quit the country as to remain in it. Watched and hunted like gangs of coiners, forgers, or other felons attempting to flee from justice, set upon by troopers armed with "bills and guns and other weapons," seized when about to embark, pillaged and stripped by catchpoles, exhibited as a show to grinning country folk, the women and children dealt with like drunken tramps, led before magistrates, committed to jail,—Mr. Brewster and six other of the principal ones being kept in prison and bound over to the assizes,—they were only able after attempts lasting through two years' time to effect their escape to Amsterdam. After remaining there a year they had removed to Leyden, which they thought "a fair and beautiful city, and of a sweet situation." [1]

They settled in Leyden in the very year in which Arminius was buried beneath the pavement of St. Peter's Church in that town. It was the year, too, in which the truce was signed. They were a singularly tranquil and brotherly community. Their pastor, who was endowed with remarkable gentleness and tact in dealing with his congregation, settled amicably all their occasional disputes. The authorities of the place held them up as a model. To a Walloon congregation in which there were many troublesome and litigious members, they said: "These English have lived among us ten years, and yet we never had any suit or accusation against any of them, but your quarrels are continual." [2]

Although many of them were poor, finding it difficult to earn their living in a foreign land, among people

[1] Bradford, 13.   [2] Ibid., 20.

speaking a strange tongue, and with manners and habits differing from their own, and where they were obliged to learn new trades, having most of them come out of an agricultural population, yet they enjoyed a singular reputation for probity. Bakers and butchers and the like willingly gave credit to the poorest of these English, and sought their custom if known to be of the congregation.[1] Mr. Brewster, who had been reduced almost to poverty by his charities and munificent aid to his struggling brethren, earned his living by giving lessons in English, having first composed a grammar according to the Latin model for the use of his pupils. He also set up a printing establishment, publishing many controversial works prohibited in England, a proceeding which roused the wrath of Carleton, impelling him to do his best to have him thrown into prison.[2]

It was not the first time that this plain, mechanical, devout Englishman, now past middle age, had visited the Netherlands. More than twenty-five years before he had accompanied William Davison on his famous embassy to the states, as private secretary.[3] When the keys of Flushing, one of the cautionary towns, were committed to the ambassador, he confided them to the care of Brewster, who slept with them under his pillow. The gold chain which Davison received as a present from the provincial government on leaving the country was likewise placed in his keeping, with orders to wear it around his neck until they should appear before the queen. To a youth of ease and affluence, familiar with

---

[1] Bradford, 20.   [2] Ibid.   Carleton's Letters.
[3] Bradford, 408–412. See Hist. United Netherlands, i. 102 seq., 404.

ambassadors and statesmen and not unknown at courts, had succeeded a mature age of obscurity, deep study, and poverty. No human creature would have heard of him had his career ended with his official life. Two centuries and a half have passed away, and the name of the outlawed Puritan of Scrooby and Leyden is still familiar to millions of the English race.

All these Englishmen were not poor. Many of them occupied houses of fair value and were admitted to the freedom of the city. The pastor, with three of his congregation, lived in a comfortable mansion, which they had purchased for the considerable sum of eight thousand florins, and on the garden of which they subsequently erected twenty-one lesser tenements for the use of the poorer brethren.[1]

Mr. Robinson was himself chosen a member of the famous university and admitted to its privileges. During his long residence in Leyden, besides the daily care of his congregation, spiritual and temporal, he wrote many learned works. Thus the little community, which grew gradually larger by emigration from England, passed many years of tranquillity. Their footsteps were not dogged by constables and pursuivants, they were not dragged daily before the magistrates, they were not thrown into the town jails, they were not hunted from place to place with bows and bills and mounted musketeers. They gave offense to none, and were respected by all. "Such was their single-heartedness and sincere affection one toward another," says their historian and magistrate, "that they came as near the primitive pattern of the first churches as

---

[1] Information kindly communicated to me by the Rev. H. M. Dexter.

any other church of these later times has done, according to their rank and quality.''

Here certainly were English Puritans more competent than any men else in the world to judge if it were a slander upon the English government to identify them with Dutch Puritans. Did they sympathize with the party in Holland which the king, who had so scourged and trampled upon themselves in England, was so anxious to crush, the hated Arminians? Did they abhor the Contra-Remonstrants, whom James and his ambassador Carleton doted upon, and whom Barneveldt called ''Double Puritans'' and ''Flanderizers''?

Their pastor may answer for himself and his brethren.

''We profess before God and men,'' said Robinson in his ''Apologia,'' ''that we agree so entirely with the Reformed Dutch churches in the matter of religion as to be ready to subscribe to all and each of their articles exactly as they are set forth in the Netherland Confession. We acknowledge those Reformed Churches as true and genuine, we profess and cultivate communion with them as much as in us lies. Those of us who understand the Dutch language attend public worship under their pastors. We administer the Holy Supper to such of their members as, known to us, appear at our meetings.'' [1] This was the position of the Puritans—absolute, unqualified accordance with the Contra-Remonstrants.

[1] Neal's Puritans, ii. 49 (8vo). Belknap, 277. ''Profitemur coram Deo et hominibus adeo nobis convenire cum ecclesiis reformatis Belgicis in re religionis, ut omnibus et singulis earundem ecclesiarum fidei articulis, prout habentur in harmonia confessionum fidei, parati sumus subscribere. Ecclesias reformatas pro veris et genuinis habemus, cum iisdem in sacris Dei communionem

As the controversy grew hot in the university between the Arminians and their adversaries, Mr. Robinson, in the language of his friend Bradford, became "terrible to the Arminians, . . . who so greatly molested the whole state, and that city in particular."

When Episcopius, the Arminian professor of theology, set forth sundry theses challenging all the world to the onset, it was thought that "none was fitter to buckle with them" than Robinson. The orthodox professor Polyander so importuned the English Puritan to enter the lists on behalf of the Contra-Remonstrants that at last he consented, and overthrew the challenger, horse and man, in three successive encounters. Such, at least, was the account given by his friend and admirer the historian.[1] "The Lord did so help him to

profitemur et quantum in nobis est colimus. Conciones publicas ab illarum pastoribus habitas ex nostris qui norunt linguam Belgicam frequentant. Sacram coenam earum membris si qua forte nostris coetibus intersint nobis cognita participamus."

[1] Bradford, 20, 21. I have searched in vain, both in unpublished documents and printed books, for any confirmation of or allusion to this scene. In a careful life of Simon Episcopius by Ph. van Limborch, published fifty years after the professor's death, there are many notices of Polyander, but there is no mention of any public disputation between them, or between Episcopius and Robinson. There is an elaborate account given of a supper-party in Leyden on Whitsunday (May 22, 1616), at which both Episcopius and Polyander, with other divines of the conflicting persuasions, were present, in which the convivialities were for a time unpleasantly interrupted. The conversation turned on the Reformation and the reasons why the doctrine of Luther had made such progress. Episcopius thought among the chief causes were the rigidity of the pope and his adherents in refusing all concession, and the enthusiasm excited by the theses of Luther.

Polyander began to mutter half to himself: "They who seek to make any change here are rogues and rascals, aye, a pack of

defend the truth and foil this adversary as he put him
to an apparent nonplus in this great and public audience.   And the like he did a second or third time upon
such like occasions,'' said Bradford, adding that, if it
had not been for fear of offending the English government, the university would have bestowed preferments
and honors upon the champion.[1]

We are concerned with this ancient and exhausted
controversy only for the intense light it threw, when
burning, on the history which occupies us.

Of the extinct volcano itself which once caused such
devastation, and in which a great commonwealth was
well-nigh swallowed up, little is left but slag and cin-
ders.   The past was made black and barren with them.
Let us disturb them as little as possible.

The little English congregation remained at Leyden
till toward the end of the truce, thriving, orderly, respected, happy.   They were witnesses to the tumultuous, disastrous, and tragical events which darkened the
Republic in those later years, themselves unobserved

---

knaves," and soon afterward repeated the expression so loudly that
Episcopius was forced to remonstrate.   "Why use words, O my
colleague," he said, "which can only serve to injure and irritate?"
"What I said I will stand to," thundered Polyander; "those
who are seeking a change of doctrine are rogues, rascals, knaves."

The other divines flew to the conflict, taking sides according to
their respective views of predestination, and for a season after it
seemed that a game of fisticuffs might succeed to the keen encounter of wits and to the circulation of the cheerful Rhine wine.   The
more pacific of the party, however, succeeded at last in restoring
harmony, and the company finished their Whitsunday supper in
comparative tranquillity.   (Ph. v. Limborch, Lev. v. Episcopius,
67, 68, Amsterdam, 1693.)   The name of Robinson is not mentioned with those of the other revelers on this occasion.

[1] Bradford, 20, 21.

and unmolested. Not a syllable seems to remain on record of the views or emotions which may have been excited by those scenes in their minds, nor is there a trace left on the national records of the Netherlands of their protracted residence on the soil.

They got their living as best they might by weaving, printing, spinning, and other humble trades; they borrowed money on mortgages, they built houses, they made wills, and such births, deaths, and marriages as occurred among them were registered by the town clerk.

And at last for a variety of reasons they resolved to leave the Netherlands. Perhaps the solution of the problem between church and state in that country by the temporary subjection of state to church may have encouraged them to realize a more complete theocracy, if a sphere of action could be found where the experiment might be tried without a severe battle against time-hallowed institutions and vested rights. Perhaps they were appalled by the excesses into which men of their own religious sentiments had been carried by theological and political passion. At any rate, depart they would, the larger half of the congregation remaining behind, however, till the pioneers should have broken the way and, in their own language, "laid the stepping-stones." [1]

[1] I have looked in vain through the Archives at The Hague during the whole period of the truce—almost exactly coeval, as often observed, with their residence in Leyden—for some notice of this congregation. It is superfluous to say with what delight I should have hailed the slightest trace of them, and the pleasure it would have given me to record it in these pages. The information in Bradford, with the excellent notes and introduction of the editor, Mr. Deane, the tracts of the Rev. Joseph Hunter, and of the late Mr. George Sumner, brother of the illustrious senator, and

They had thought of the lands beneath the equator, Raleigh having recently excited enthusiasm by his poetical descriptions of Guiana. But the tropical scheme was soon abandoned. They had opened negotiations with the stadholder and the States-General through Amsterdam merchants in regard to settling in New Amsterdam, and offered to colonize that country if assured of the protection of the United Provinces. Their petition had been rejected.[1] They had then turned their faces to their old master and their own country, applying to the Virginia Company for a land patent, which they were only too happy to promise, and to the king for liberty of religion in the wilderness confirmed under his broad seal, which his Majesty of course refused. It was hinted, however, that James would connive at them and not molest them if they carried themselves peaceably. So they resolved to go without the seal, for, said their magistrate very wisely, "if there should be a purpose or desire to wrong them, a seal would not serve their turn though it were as broad as the house floor." [2]

of Hon. H. C. Murphy, with the well-known works of Morton, Belknap, Prince, and others, to say nothing of the investigations of the great national historians Bancroft and Palfrey, interesting as all this is, only increases the desire to learn more.

It is especially tantalizing to read in Bradford of "the several passages that befell these people whilst they lived in the Low Countries, which might worthily require a treatise of itself" (p. 19).

All lovers of New England will receive with interest the results of the personal researches of the Rev. Henry Martyn Dexter in Holland, and especially at Leyden, who has been devoting himself to the task of reproducing the life of the Pilgrims in Holland with an assiduity which may insure our knowledge of all that remains to be known of them.

[1] Brodhead, Hist. New York, 123–126.   [2] Bradford, 30.

Before they left Leyden, their pastor preached to them a farewell sermon, which for loftiness of spirit and breadth of vision has hardly a parallel in that age of intolerance. He laid down the principle that criticism of the Scriptures had not been exhausted merely because it had been begun; that the human conscience was of too subtle a nature to be imprisoned forever in formulas, however ingeniously devised; that the religious reformation begun a century ago was not completed; and that the Creator had not necessarily concluded all his revelations to mankind.

The words have long been familiar to students of history, but they can hardly be too often laid to heart.[1]

[1] Belknap, in voce.

"Brethren," he said, "we are now quickly to part from one another, and whether I may ever live to see your face on earth any more, the God of heaven only knows. But whether the Lord hath appointed that or not, I charge you before God and his blessed angels that you follow me no further than you have seen me follow the Lord Jesus Christ. If God reveal anything to you by any other instrument of his, be as ready to receive it as ever you were to receive any truth by my ministry; for I am verily persuaded that the Lord has more truth yet to break forth out of his Holy Word. For my part, I cannot sufficiently bewail the condition of the Reformed churches, who are come to a period in religion, and will go at present no further than the instruments of their reformation. The Lutherans cannot be drawn to go beyond what Luther saw. Whatever part of his will our good God has revealed to Calvin, they will rather die than embrace it. And the Calvinists, you see, stick fast where they were left by that great man of God, who yet saw not all things.

"This is a misery much to be lamented; for though they were burning and shining lights, yet they penetrated not into the whole counsel of God, but, were they now living, would be as willing to embrace further light as that which they first received. I beseech you to remember it is an article of your church covenant 'that you be ready to receive whatever truth shall be made

Noble words, worthy to have been inscribed over the altar of the first church to be erected by the departing brethren, words to bear fruit after centuries should go by. Had not the deeply injured and misunderstood Grotius already said, "If the trees we plant do not shade us, they will yet serve for our descendants"? [1]

Yet it is passing strange that the preacher of that sermon should be the recent champion of the Contra-Remonstrants in the great controversy, the man who had made himself so terrible to the pupils of the gentle and tolerant Arminius.[2]

known to you from the written Word of God.' But I must here-withal exhort you to take heed what you receive as truth. Examine it, consider it, and compare it with other scriptures of truth before you receive it, for it is not possible that the Christian world should come so lately out of such thick antichristian darkness, and that perfection of knowledge should break forth at once."

[1] Reply to Sil. Lubbertz's letter to Archbishop of Canterbury. Op. Grot., ii. 1, liv. 99. Hug. Grot., Epist., 7, 15. Ouvré, 258.

[2] I cannot resist adding in this note a brief extract from the judicious letter, breathing the very spirit of common sense in po-litical matters, which the pastor addressed to the little democracy which was so soon to put forth in the *Mayflower* :

"Whereas you are to become a body politic, using amongst yourselves civil government, and are not furnished with any per-sons of special eminence above the rest to be chosen by you into office of government, let your wisdom and godliness appear not only in choosing such persons as do entirely love and will promote the common good, but also in yielding unto them all honor and obedience in their lawful administrations; not beholding in them the ordinariness of their persons, but God's ordinance for your good, not being like the foolish multitude who more honor the gay coat than either the virtuous mind of the man or glorious ordinance of the Lord. But you know better things, and that the image of the Lord's power and authority which the magistrate beareth is honorable in how mean persons whatever. And this duty you both may the more willingly perform because you are, at

And thus half of that English congregation went down to Delfshaven, attended by the other half, who were to follow at a later period with their beloved pastor. There was a pathetic leave-taking. Even many of the Hollanders, mere casual spectators, were in tears.

Robinson, kneeling on the deck of the little vessel, offered a prayer and a farewell. Who could dream that this departure of an almost nameless band of emigrants to the wilderness was an epoch in the world's history? Yet these were the Pilgrim Fathers of New England, the founders of what was to be the mightiest republic of modern history, mighty and stable because it had been founded upon an idea.

They were not in search of material comfort and the chances of elevating their condition, by removing from an overpeopled country to an organized commonwealth, offering a wide field for pauper laborers. Some of them were of good social rank and highest education, most of them in decent circumstances, none of them in absolute poverty. And a few years later they were to be joined by a far larger company, with leaders and many brethren of ancient birth and landed possessions, men of "education, figure, and estate," all ready to convert property into cash and to place it in joint-stock, not as the basis of promising speculation, but as the foundation of a church.

least for the present, to have only them for your ordinary governors which yourselves shall make choice of for that work," etc. —Bradford, 67.

Grotius or Barneveldt could not have spoken more soundly on the rights and duties of magistracy and the people. Such words as these reflect more honor on the famous pastor than all the hot rhetoric which he poured forth upon Episcopius at the desire of Polyander, and which has left no trace behind.

It signifies not how much or how little one may sympathize with their dogma or their discipline now.   To
the fact that the early settlement of that wilderness
was by self-sacrificing men of earnestness and faith,
who were bent on "advancing the gospel of Christ in
remote parts of the world,"[1] in the midst of savage
beasts, more savage men, and unimaginable difficulties and dangers, there can be little doubt that the
highest forms of Western civilization are due.   Through
their provisional theocracy, the result of the independent church system was to establish the true purport
of the Reformation, absolute religious equality.   Civil
and political equality followed as a matter of course.

Two centuries and a half have passed away.

There are now some seventy or eighty millions of the
English-speaking race on both sides the Atlantic, almost equally divided between the United Kingdom and
the United Republic, and the departure of those out-
casts of James has interest and significance for them all.

Most fitly then, as a distinguished American statesman has remarked,[2] does that scene on board the little
English vessel, with the English pastor uttering his
farewell blessing to a handful of English exiles for
conscience' sake, depicted on canvas by eminent artists,
now adorn the halls of the American Congress and of
the British Parliament.   Sympathy with all that is
lofty and heroic in our common race is one of the many
imperishable bonds of union between the two great and
scarcely divided peoples.

We return to Barneveldt in his solitary prison.

[1] Bradford, 24.
[2] Hon. R. C. Winthrop, in his eloquent discourse at Plymouth
on the Two Hundred and Fiftieth Anniversary of the Landing of
the Pilgrim Fathers (Boston, 1871).

CHAPTER XX

THE advocate had been removed within a few days
after the arrest from the chamber in Maurice's apartments where he had originally been confined, and was
now in another building.

It was not a dungeon nor a jail. Indeed, the commonplace and domestic character of the scenery in
which these great events were transacted has in it something pathetic. There was and still remains a two-
storied structure, then of modern date, immediately
behind the antique hall of the old counts within the
Binnenhof. On the first floor was a court-room of
considerable extent, the seat of one of the chief tribunals of justice. The story above was divided into three
chambers, with a narrow corridor on each side. The
first chamber, on the northeastern side, was appropriated for the judges when the state prisoners should be
tried. In the next Hugo Grotius was imprisoned. In
the third was Barneveldt. There was a tower at the
northeast angle of the building, within which a wind-

ing and narrow staircase of stone led up to the corridor and so to the prisoners' apartments. Rombout Hoogerbeets was confined in another building.

As the advocate, bent with age and a life of hard work, and leaning on his staff, entered the room appropriated to him, after toiling up the steep staircase, he observed:

"This is the admiral of Aragon's apartment."

It was true. Eighteen years before, the conqueror of Nieuport had assigned this lodging to the chief prisoner of war in that memorable victory over the Spaniards, and now Maurice's faithful and trusted counselor at that epoch was placed in durance here, as the result of the less glorious series of victories which had just been achieved.

It was a room of moderate dimensions, some twenty-five feet square, with a high vaulted roof and decently furnished. Below and around him in the courtyard were the scenes of the advocate's lifelong and triumphant public services. There in the opposite building were the windows of the beautiful "Hall of Truce," with its sumptuous carvings and gildings, its sculptures and portraits, where he had negotiated with the representatives of all the great powers of Christendom the famous treaty which had suspended the war of forty years, and where he was wont almost daily to give audience to the envoys of the greatest sovereigns or the least significant states of Europe and Asia, all of whom had been ever solicitous of his approbation and support. Farther along in the same building was the assembly-room of the States-General, where some of the most important affairs of the Republic and of Europe had for years been conducted, and where he had been so indispensable that, in the words of a contemporary who loved him not, "absolutely nothing could be transacted in his absence, all great affairs going through him alone." [1]

There were two dull windows, closely barred, looking northward over an irregular assemblage of tile-roofed houses and chimney-stacks, while within a stone's throw to the west, but unseen, was his own elegant mansion on the Voorhout, surrounded by flower-gardens and shady pleasure-grounds, where now sat his aged wife and her children, all plunged in deep affliction.

He was allowed the attendance of a faithful servant, John Franken by name, and a sentinel stood constantly before his door. His papers had been taken from him, and at first he was deprived of writing-materials.

He had small connection with the outward world. The news of the municipal revolution which had been effected by the stadholder had not penetrated to his solitude. But his wife was allowed to send him fruit from their garden. One day a basket of fine saffron pears was brought to him. On slicing one with a knife he found a portion of a quill inside it. Within the quill was a letter on thinnest paper, in minutest handwriting in Latin. It was to this effect:

"Don't rely upon the states of Holland, for the Prince of Orange has changed the magistracies in many cities. Dudley Carleton is not your friend." [2]

A sergeant of the guard, however, before bringing in these pears, had put a couple of them in his pocket to take home to his wife. The letter, copies of which, perhaps, had been inserted for safety in several of

---

[1] Baudartius, x. 52.

[2] Wagenaer, x. 287.   Baudartius, x. 70.

them, was thus discovered and the use of this ingenious device prevented for the future.[1]

Secretary Ledenberg, who had been brought to The Hague in the early days of September, was the first of the prisoners subjected to examination. He was much depressed at the beginning of it, and is said to have exclaimed, with many sighs, "O Barneveldt, Barneveldt, what have you brought us to!"[2]

He confessed that the wartgelders at Utrecht had been enlisted on notification by the Utrecht deputies in The Hague, with knowledge of Barneveldt, and in consequence of a resolution of the states, in order to prevent internal tumults. He said that the advocate had advised in the previous month of March a request to the prince not to come to Utrecht; that the communication of the message, in regard to disbanding the wartgelders, to his Excellency had been postponed after the deputies of the states of Holland had proposed a delay in that disbandment; that those deputies had come to Utrecht of their own accord; . . . that they had judged it possible to keep everything in proper order in Utrecht if the garrison in the city, paid by Holland, were kept quiet, and if the states of Utrecht gave similar orders to the wartgelders, for they did not believe that his Excellency would bring in troops from the outside. He said that he knew nothing of a new oath to be demanded of the garrison. He stated that the advocate, when at Utrecht, had exhorted the states, according to his wont, to maintain their liberties and privileges, representing to them that the right to decide on the synod and the wartgelders belonged to them. Lastly, he denied knowing who was

---

[1] Wagenaer, x. 287. Baudartius, x. 70.   [2] Ibid., 64.

the author of "The Balance," except by common report.[1]

Now, these statements hardly amounted to a confession of abominable and unpardonable crimes by Ledenberg, nor did they establish a charge of high treason and corrupt correspondence with the enemy against Barneveldt. It is certain that the extent of the revelations seemed far from satisfactory to the accusers, and that some pressure would be necessary in order to extract anything more conclusive. Lieutenant Nythof told Grotius that Ledenberg had accordingly been threatened with torture, and that the executioner had even handled him for that purpose. This was, however, denied by the judges of instruction who had been charged with the preliminary examination.[2]

That examination took place on the 27th September. After it had been concluded, Ledenberg prayed long and earnestly on returning to prison. He then intrusted a paper written in French to his son Joost, a boy of eighteen, who did not understand that language. The youth had been allowed to keep his father company in his confinement, and slept in the same room.

The next night but one, at two o'clock, Joost heard his father utter a deep groan. He was startled, groped in the darkness toward his bed, and felt his arm, which was stone-cold. He spoke to him and received no answer. He gave the alarm, the watch came in with lights, and it was found that Ledenberg had given himself two mortal wounds in the abdomen with a penknife and then cut his throat with a table-knife which he had secreted, some days before, among some papers.

[1] Wagenaer, x. 289, 290 seq.
[2] Baudartius, x. 56.

The paper in French given to his son was found to be to this effect:

"I know that there is an inclination to set an example in my person, to confront me with my best friends, to torture me, afterward to convict me of contradictions and falsehoods, as they say, and then to found an ignominious sentence upon points and trifles, for this it will be necessary to do in order to justify the arrest and imprisonment. To escape all this I am going to God by the shortest road. Against a dead man there can be pronounced no sentence of confiscation of property. Done 17th September (O. S.), 1618." [1]

The family of the unhappy gentleman begged his body for decent burial. The request was refused. It was determined to keep the dead secretary aboveground and in custody until he could be tried, and, if possible, convicted and punished. [2] It was to be seen whether it were so easy to baffle the power of the States-General, the synod, and the stadholder, and whether "going to God by the shortest road" was to save a culprit's carcass from ignominy, and his property from confiscation.

The French ambassadors, who had been unwearied in their endeavor to restore harmony to the distracted commonwealth before the arrest of the prisoners, now exerted themselves to throw the shield of their sovereign's friendship around the illustrious statesman and his fellow-sufferers.

"It is with deepest sorrow," said De Boississe, "that I have witnessed the late hateful commotions. Espe-

---

[1] Wagenaer, x. 292. Brandt, ii. 875.
[2] Ibid. Baudartius, ubi sup.

cially from my heart I grieve for the arrest of the
Seignior Barneveldt, who with his discretion and wise
administration for the past thirty years has so drawn
the hearts of all neighboring princes to himself, especially that of the king my master, that on taking up
my pen to apprise him of these events I am gravely
embarrassed, fearing to infringe on the great respect
due to your Mightinesses or against the honor and
merits of the Seignior Barneveldt. . . .   My lords,
take heed to your situation, for a great discontent is
smoldering among your citizens.   Until now, the Union
has been the chief source of your strength.   And I now
fear that the king my master, the adviser of your renowned commonwealth, may be offended that you have
taken this resolution after consulting with others, and
without communicating your intention to his ambassador. . . .   It is but a few days that an open edict
was issued testifying to the fidelity of Barneveldt, and
can it be possible that within so short a time you have
discovered that you have been deceived?   I summon
you once more in the name of the king to lay aside all
passion, to judge these affairs without partiality, and
to inform me what I am to say to the king.   Such very
conflicting accounts are given of these transactions that
I must beg you to confide to me the secret of the affair.
The wisest in the land speak so strongly of these proceedings that it will be no wonder if the king my master should give me orders to take the Seignior Barneveldt under his protection.   Should this prove to be
the case, your Lordships will excuse my course. . . .
I beg you earnestly in your wisdom not to give cause
of offense to neighboring princes, especially to my sovereign, who wishes from his heart to maintain your dig-

nity and interests and to assure you of his friendship." [1]

The language was vigorous and sincere, but the ambassador forgot that the France of to-day was not the France of yesterday; that Louis XIII. was not Henry IV.; that it was but a cheerful fiction to call the present king the guide and counselor of the Republic, and that, distraught as she was by the present commotions, her condition was strength and tranquillity compared with the apparently decomposing and helpless state of the once great kingdom of France. De Boississe took little by his demonstration.

On the 12th December both De Boississe and Du Maurier came before the States-General once more, and urged a speedy and impartial trial for the illustrious prisoners. If they had committed acts of treason and rebellion, they deserved exemplary punishment, but the ambassadors warned the States-General with great earnestness against the dangerous doctrine of constructive treason, and of confounding acts dictated by violence of party spirit at an excited period with the crime of high treason against the sovereignty of the state.

"Barneveldt, so honorable," they said, "for his immense and long-continued services, has both this Republic and all princes and commonwealths for his witnesses. It is most difficult to believe that he has attempted the destruction of his fatherland, for which you know that he has toiled so faithfully."

They admitted that so grave charges ought now to be investigated. "To this end," said the ambassadors, "you ought to give him judges who are neither suspected nor impassioned, and who will decide according

[1] Brandt, Hist. Ref., ii. 876, 877.

interest at that time in the works of the Hague poet.
Constant efforts made to attract his attention to those
poems, however, excited suspicion among his keepers,
and the scheme was discovered before the Leyden pensionary had found the means to profit by it.[1]

The allusions to the trial of the advocate referred to
the preliminary examination which took place, like the
first interrogatories of Grotius and Hoogerbeets, in the
months of November and December.

The thorough manner in which Maurice had reformed the states of Holland has been described.
There was one department of that body, however, which
still required attention. The order of knights, small
in number but potential in influence, which always
voted first on great occasions, was still, through a majority of its members, inclined to Barneveldt. Both
his sons-in-law had seats in that college. The stadholder had long believed in a spirit of hostility on the
part of those nobles toward himself. He knew that a
short time before this epoch there had been a scheme
for introducing his young brother, Frederick Henry,
into the Chamber of Knights. The count had become
proprietor of the barony of Naaldwyk, a property
which he had purchased of the counts of Aremberg,
and which carried with it the hereditary dignity of
Great Equery of the Counts of Holland.[2] As the
counts of Holland had ceased to exist, although their
sovereignty had nearly been revived and conferred
upon William the Silent, the office of their chief of the
stables might be deemed a sinecure. But the jealousy
of Maurice was easily awakened, especially by any
movement made or favored by the advocate. He be-

[1] Wagenaer, x. 245, 246.   [2] Ibid.

lieved that in the election of Frederick Henry as a member of the college of knights a plan lay concealed to thrust him into power and to push his elder brother from his place. The scheme, if scheme it were, was never accomplished, but the prince's rancor remained.

He now informed the nobles that they must receive into their body Francis Aertsens, who had lately purchased the barony of Sommelsdyk, and Daniel de Hartaing, Seignior of Marquette. With the presence of this deadly enemy of Barneveldt and another gentleman equally devoted to the stadholder's interest it seemed probable that the refractory majority of the board of nobles would be overcome. But there were grave objections to the admission of these new candidates. They were not eligible. The constitution of the states and of the college of nobles prescribed that Hollanders only of ancient and noble race and possessing estates in the province could sit in that body. Neither Aertsens nor Hartaing was born in Holland or possessed of the other needful qualifications. Nevertheless, the prince, who had just remodeled all the municipalities throughout the Union which offered resistance to his authority, was not to be checked by so trifling an impediment as the statutes of the House of Nobles. He employed very much the same arguments which he had used to "good papa" Hoofd: "This time it must be so." Another time it might not be necessary. So, after a controversy which ended as controversies are apt to do when one party has a sword in his hand and the other is seated at a green-baize-covered table, Sommelsdyk and Marquette took their seats among the knights.[1] Of course there was a spir-

1 Wagenaer, x. 332–339.

ited protest. Nothing was easier for the stadholder than to concede the principle while trampling it with his boot-heels in practice.

"Whereas it is not competent for the said two gentlemen to be admitted to our board," said the nobles in brief, "as not being constitutionally eligible, nevertheless, considering the strong desire of his Excellency the Prince of Orange, we, the nobles and knights of Holland, admit them with the firm promise to each other by noble and knightly faith ever in future for ourselves and descendants to maintain the privileges of our order now violated, and never again to let them be directly or indirectly infringed." [1]

And so Aertsens, the unscrupulous plotter, and dire foe of the advocate and all his house, burning with bitter revenge for all the favors he had received from him during many years, and the author of the venomous pamphlets and diatribes which had done so much of late to blacken the character of the great statesman before the public, now associated himself officially with his other enemies, while the preliminary proceedings for the state trials went forward.

Meantime the synod had met at Dordrecht. The great John Bogerman, with fierce, handsome face, beak and eye of a bird of prey, and a deluge of curly brown beard reaching to his waist, took his seat as president. Short work was made with the Arminians. They and their Five Points were soon thrust out into outer darkness.

It was established beyond all gainsaying that two forms of divine worship in one country were forbidden by God's Word, and that thenceforth by Netherland

[1] Wagenaer, x. 332–339.

law there could be but one religion, namely, the Reformed or Calvinistic creed.

It was settled that one portion of the Netherlanders and of the rest of the human race had been expressly created by the Deity to be forever damned, and another portion to be eternally blessed. But this history has little to do with that infallible council save in the political effect of its decrees on the fate of Barneveldt. It was said that the canons of Dordrecht were likely to shoot off the head of the advocate.[1] Their sessions and the trial of the advocate were simultaneous, but not technically related to each other. The conclusions of both courts were preordained, for the issue of the great duel between priesthood and state had been decided when the military chieftain threw his sword into the scale of the church.

There had been purposely a delay, before coming to a decision as to the fate of the state prisoners, until the work of the synod should have approached completion.

It was thought good that the condemnation of the opinions of the Arminians and the chastisement of their leaders should go hand in hand.

On the 23d April, 1619, the canons were signed by all the members of the synod.[2] Arminians were pronounced heretics, schismatics, teachers of false doctrines. They were declared incapable of filling any clerical or academical post.[3] No man thenceforth was to teach children, lecture to adolescents, or preach to the mature, unless a subscriber to the doctrines of the unchanged, unchangeable, orthodox church. On the 30th April and 1st May the Netherland Confession and

[1] Du Maurier.   [2] Van Rees and Brill, 193–195.
[3] Carleton, 361.

the Heidelberg Catechism were declared to be infallible. No change was to be possible in either formulary.

Schools and pulpits were inexorably bound to the only true religion.

On the 6th May there was a great festival at Dordrecht in honor of the conclusion of the synod.[1] The canons, the sentence, and long prayers and orations in Latin by President Bogerman gladdened the souls of an immense multitude, which were further enlivened by the decree that both Creed and Catechism had stood the test of several criticisms and come out unchanged by a single hair. Nor did the orator of the occasion forget to render thanks "to the most magnanimous King James of Great Britain, through whose godly zeal, fiery sympathy, and truly royal labor God had so often refreshed the weary synod in the midst of their toil." [2]

The synod held one hundred and eighty sessions be-

[1] Carleton, 361.

[2] Van Rees and Brill, 198. Acta Syn. Nat., 383–391. Brandt, iii. 599–603.

Six years later (July 5, 1625) all the Synodal Acts, including the original decree condemning the Five Points, with the signatures of all the theologians annexed, were placed in a coffer provided with eight locks, one key of which was deposited with the States-General and one with the states of each province. It was decreed that the coffer should remain in the custody of the States-General in The Hague, and be opened every three years in order to preserve them from worms.

One hundred and sixty-nine years later (Tuesday, May 23, 1794) a committee appointed to examine the coffer reported that they had solemnly done so, and found no defects or marks of worms in the documents. The eight locks were then fastened again, and the keys handed to Mr. Greffier Fagel.

"Extract uit het Register der Resolutien v. d. H. M. H. St. Gl. d. Ver. Ned," MS. extract-book of Mr. Archivist de Jonghe.

tween the 13th November, 1618, and 29th May, 1619,[1] all the doings of which have been recorded in chronicles innumerable. There need be no further mention of them here.

Barneveldt and the companions of his fate remained in prison.

On the 7th March the trial of the great advocate began. He had sat in prison since the 18th of the preceding August. For nearly seven months he had been deprived of all communication with the outward world save such atoms of intelligence as could be secretly conveyed to him in the inside of a quill concealed in a pear and by other devices. The man who had governed one of the most important commonwealths of the world for nearly a generation long, during the same period almost controlling the politics of Europe, had now been kept in ignorance of the most insignificant every-day events. During the long summer heat of the dog-days immediately succeeding his arrest, and the long, foggy, snowy, icy winter of Holland which ensued, he had been confined in that dreary garret room to which he had been brought when he left his temporary imprisonment in the apartments of Prince Maurice.

There was nothing squalid in the chamber, nothing specially cruel or repulsive in the arrangements of his captivity. He was not in fetters, nor fed upon bread and water. He was not put upon the rack, nor even threatened with it as Ledenberg had been. He was kept in a mean, commonplace, meagerly furnished, tolerably spacious room, and he was allowed the services of his faithful domestic servant John Franken. A sentinel paced day and night up the narrow corridor

---

[1] Wagenaer, x. 312, 329.

JOHN OF BARNEVELDT

before his door.   As spring advanced, the notes of the
nightingale came through the prison window from the
neighboring thicket.   One day John Franken, opening
the window that his master might the better enjoy its
song, exchanged greeting with a fellow-servant in the
Barneveldt mansion who happened to be crossing the
courtyard.   Instantly workmen were sent to close and
barricade the windows, and it was only after earnest
remonstrances and pledges that this resolve to consign
the advocate to darkness was abandoned.[1]

He was not permitted the help of lawyer, clerk, or
man of business.   Alone and from his chamber of
bondage, suffering from bodily infirmities and from
the weakness of advancing age, he was compelled to
prepare his defense against a vague, heterogeneous collection of charges, to meet which required constant reference not only to the statutes, privileges, and customs
of the country and to the Roman law, but to a thousand minute incidents out of which the history of the
provinces during the past dozen years or more had
been compounded.[2]

It is true that no man could be more familiar with
the science and practice of the law than he was, while
of contemporary history he was himself the central
figure.   His biography was the chronicle of his country.   Nevertheless, it was a fearful disadvantage for
him day by day to confront two dozen hostile judges
comfortably seated at a great table piled with papers,
surrounded by clerks with bags full of documents and
with a library of authorities and precedents duly
marked and dog's-eared and ready to their hands, while

[1] Leven en Sterven, 178.

[2] Wagenaer, x. 342 seq.   Waaragt. Hist., 235 seq.

his only library and chronicle lay in his brain.   From day to day, with frequent intermissions, he was led down through the narrow turret stairs to a wide chamber on the floor immediately below his prison, where a temporary tribunal had been arranged for the special commission.

There had been an inclination at first on the part of his judges to treat him as a criminal, and to require him to answer standing to the interrogatories propounded to him.   But as the terrible old man advanced into the room, leaning on his staff, and surveying them with the air of haughty command habitual to him, they shrank before his glance, several involuntarily rising, uncovered, to salute him, and making way for him to the fireplace, about which many were standing that wintry morning.[1]

He was thenceforth always accommodated with a seat while he listened to and answered extempore the elaborate series of interrogatories which had been prepared to convict him.

Nearly seven months he had sat with no charges brought against him.   This was in itself a gross violation of the laws of the land, for according to all the ancient charters of Holland it was provided that accusation should follow within six weeks of arrest, or that the prisoner should go free.[2]   But the arrest itself was so gross a violation of law that respect for it was hardly to be expected in the subsequent proceedings. He was a great officer of the states of Holland.   He had been taken under their especial protection.   He was on his way to the High Council.   He was in no sense

[1] Waaragt. Hist.
[2] Charter of Holland of the year 1346.   Grot., Verantw., 139.

a subject of the States-General. He was in the discharge of his official duty. He was doubly and trebly sacred from arrest. The place where he stood was on the territory of Holland and in the very sanctuary of her courts and house of assembly. The States-General were only as guests on her soil, and had no domain or jurisdiction there whatever. He was not apprehended by any warrant or form of law. It was in time of peace, and there was no pretense of martial law. The highest civil functionary of Holland was invited in the name of its first military officer to a conference, and thus entrapped was forcibly imprisoned.

At last a board of twenty-four commissioners was created, twelve from Holland and two from each of the other six provinces.[1] This affectation of concession to Holland was ridiculous. Either the law *de non evocando*, according to which no citizen of Holland could be taken out of the province for trial, was to be respected or it was to be trampled upon. If it was to be trampled upon, it signified little whether more commissioners were to be taken from Holland than from each of the other provinces, or fewer, or none at all. Moreover, it was pretended that a majority of the whole board was to be assigned to that province. But twelve is not a majority of twenty-four. There were three fiscals, or prosecuting officers, Leeuwen of Utrecht, Sylla of Gelderland, and Antony Duyck of Holland. Duyck was notoriously the deadly enemy of Barne-

---

[1] The names of the judges were: Van Essen, De Voogd, Kromhout, Junius, Kouwenburg van Below, Rosa, Van Zwieten, Muis van Holy, Arend Meinardszoon, Beukelszoon van Zanten, Van Broekhoven, Reinier Pauw, Schagen, Bruinink, Manmaker, Schotte, Ploos, Salmius, Van den Sande, Aitsma, Sloot, Van Hemert, Schaffer, Gokkinga. (Wagenaer, x. 340–342.)

veldt, and was destined to succeed to his offices. It would have been as well to select Francis Aertsens himself.

It was necessary to appoint a commission, because there was no tribunal appertaining to the States-General. The general government of the confederacy had no power to deal with an individual. It could only negotiate with the sovereign province to which the individual was responsible, and demand his punishment if proved guilty of an offense. There was no supreme court of appeal. Machinery was provided for settling or attempting to settle disputes among the members of the confederacy, and if there was a culprit in this great process it was Holland itself. Neither the advocate nor any one of his associates had done any act except by authority, express or implied, of that sovereign state. Supposing them unquestionably guilty of blackest crimes against the generality, the dilemma was there which must always exist by the very nature of things in a confederacy. No sovereign can try a fellow-sovereign. The subject can be tried at home by no sovereign but his own.

The accused in this case were amenable to the laws of Holland only.

It was a packed tribunal. Several of the commissioners, like Pauw and Muis for example, were personal enemies of Barneveldt. Many of them were totally ignorant of law. Some of them knew not a word of any language but their mother-tongue, although much of the law which they were to administer was written in Latin.

Before such a court the foremost citizen of the Netherlands, the first living statesman of Europe, was brought day by day during a period of nearly three months, coming down-stairs from the mean and desolate room where he was confined to the comfortable apartment below, which had been fitted up for the commission.

There was no bill of indictment, no arraignment, no counsel. There were no witnesses and no arguments. The court-room contained, as it were, only a prejudiced and partial jury to pronounce both on law and fact, without a judge to direct them, or advocates to sift testimony and contend for or against the prisoner's guilt. The process, for it could not be called a trial, consisted of a vast series of rambling and tangled interrogatories reaching over a space of forty years, without apparent connection or relevancy, skipping fantastically about from one period to another, back and forth, with apparently no other intent than to puzzle the prisoner, throw him off his balance, and lead him into self-contradiction.

The spectacle was not a refreshing one. It was the attempt of a multitude of pygmies to overthrow and bind the giant.

Barneveldt was served with no articles of impeachment. He asked for a list in writing of the charges against him, that he might ponder his answer. The demand was refused. He was forbidden the use of pen and ink or any writing-materials. His papers and books were all taken from him.[1]

[1] He repeatedly demanded pen and ink and paper of his judges, which were steadily refused. (Letter to states of Holland, April or May, 1619, in Leven en Sterven, 237.)

Writing-materials were secretly sent to him from without, however, with the connivance probably of Captain van der Meulen. (Ibid., 227.)

He was allowed to consult neither with an advocate nor even with a single friend. Alone in his chamber of bondage he was to meditate on his defense. Out of his memory and brain, and from these alone, he was to supply himself with the array of historical facts stretching over a longer period than the lifetime of many of his judges, and with the proper legal and historical arguments upon those facts for the justification of his course. That memory and brain were capacious and powerful enough for the task. It was well for the judges that they had bound themselves, at the outset, by an oath never to make known what passed in the court-room, but to bury all the proceedings in profound secrecy forever. Had it been otherwise, had that been known to the contemporary public which has only been revealed more than two centuries later, had a portion only of the calm and austere eloquence been heard in which the advocate set forth his defense, had the frivolous and ignoble nature of the attack been comprehended, it might have moved the very stones in the streets to mutiny. Hateful as the statesman had been made by an organized system of calumny, which was continued with unabated vigor and increased venom since he had been imprisoned, there was enough of justice and of gratitude left in the hearts of Netherlanders to resent the tyranny practised against their greatest man, and the obloquy thus brought against a nation always devoted to their liberties and laws.

That the political system of the country was miserably defective was no fault of Barneveldt. He was bound by oath and duty to administer, not make, the laws. A handful of petty feudal sovereignties such as had once covered the soil of Europe, a multitude of thriving cities which had wrested or purchased a mass of liberties, customs, and laws from their little tyrants, all subjected afterward, without being blended together, to a single foreign family, had at last one by one, or two by two, shaken off that supremacy, and, resuming their ancient and as it were decapitated individualities, had bound themselves by treaty in the midst of a war to stand by each other, as if they were but one province, for purposes of common defense against the common foe.

There had been no pretense of laying down a constitution, of enacting an organic law. The day had not come for even the conception of a popular constitution. The people had not been invented. It was not provinces only, but cities, that had contracted with each other, according to the very first words of the first Article of Union. Some of these cities, like Ghent, Bruges, Antwerp, were Catholic by overwhelming majority, and had subsequently either fallen away from the confederacy or been conquered.

And as if to make assurance doubly sure, the Articles of Union not only reserved to each province all powers not absolutely essential for carrying on the war in common, but by an express article (the thirteenth) declared that Holland and Zealand should regulate the matter of religion according to their own discretion, while the other provinces might conform to the provisions of the Religious Peace—which included mutual protection for Catholics and Protestants—or take such other order as seemed most conducive to the religious and secular rights of the inhabitants. It was stipulated that no province should interfere with another in such matters, and that every individual in them all should remain free in his religion, no man being molested or examined on account of his creed. A further declaration in regard to this famous article was made to the effect that no provinces or cities which held to the Roman Catholic religion were to be excluded from the League of Union if they were ready to conform to its conditions and comport themselves patriotically. Language could not be devised to declare more plainly than was done by this treaty that the central government of the League had neither wish nor right to concern itself with the religious affairs of the separate cities or provinces. If it permitted both papists and Protestants to associate themselves against the common foe, it could hardly have been imagined, when the Articles were drawn, that it would have claimed the exclusive right to define the minutest points in a single Protestant creed.

And if the exclusively secular parts of the polity prevailing in the country were clumsy, irregular, and even monstrous, and if its defects had been flagrantly demonstrated by recent events, a more reasonable method of reforming the laws might have been found than the imprisonment of a man who had faithfully administered them forty years long.

A great commonwealth had grown out of a petty feudal organism, like an oak from an acorn in a crevice, gnarled and distorted, though wide-spreading and vigorous. It seemed perilous to deal radically with such a polity, and an almost timid conservatism on the part of its guardians in such an age of tempests might be pardonable.

Moreover, as before remarked, the apparent imbecility resulting from confederacy and municipalism com-

bined was for a season remedied by the actual prepon-
derance of Holland. Two thirds of the total wealth
and strength of the seven republics being concentrated
in one province, the desired union seemed almost gained
by the practical solution of all in that single republic.
But this was one great cause of the general disaster.

It would be a thankless and tedious task to wander
through the wilderness of interrogatories and answers,
extending over three months of time, which stood in
the place of a trial. The defense of Barneveldt was
his own history, and that I have attempted to give in
the preceding pages. A great part of the accusation
was deduced from his private and official correspondence, and it is for this reason that I have laid such
copious extracts from it before the reader. No man
except the judges and the States-General had access
to those letters, and it was easy, therefore, if needful,
to give them a false coloring. It is only very recently
that they have been seen at all, and they have never
been published from that day to this.

Out of the confused mass of documents appertaining
to the trial, a few generalizations can be made which
show the nature of the attack upon him.[1] He was ac-

---

[1] "Intendit van Oldenbarneveld. Feyten die by de drye fis-
caels by de H. M. H. St. Gᡁ gecommitteert tot t' Instruieren v. d.
Saecken der gevangenen ingestellt zyn tot laste van M. Jan v.
Oldenbarneveld   gevangene," Art. II, Hague   Archives   MS.
This manuscript is in 136 pages, containing 215 sections or
articles, and forms the basis of the sentence afterward delivered
by the judges. From this document, and from the Verhooren,
or interrogatories and answers, published in 1850 by the Historical
Society of Utrecht, from the Verantwoording of Hugo Grotius, and
the Hist. v. d. Rechtspleging, by G. Brandt, the important facts
and arguments in regard to this state trial are deduced.

cused of having permitted Arminius to infuse new opinions into the University of Leyden, and of having subsequently defended the appointment of Vorstius to the same place. He had opposed the national synod. He had made drafts of letters for the King of Great Britain to sign, recommending mutual toleration on the five disputed points regarding predestination. He was the author of the famous Sharp Resolution. He had recommended the enlistment by the provinces and towns of wartgelders, or mercenaries. He had maintained that those mercenaries as well as the regular troops were bound in time of peace to be obedient and faithful not only to the generality and the stadholders, but to the magistrates of the cities and provinces where they were employed, and to the states by whom they were paid. He had sent to Leyden, warning the authorities of the approach of the prince. He had encouraged all the proceedings at Utrecht, writing a letter to the secretary of that province advising a watch to be kept at the city gates as well as in the river, and ordering his letter when read to be burned. He had received presents from foreign potentates. He had attempted to damage the character of his Excellency the Prince by declaring on various occasions that he aspired to the sovereignty of the country. He had held a ciphered correspondence on the subject with foreign ministers of the Republic. He had given great offense to the King of Great Britain by soliciting from him other letters in the sense of those which his Majesty had written in 1613, advising moderation and mutual toleration. He had not brought to condign punishment the author of "The Balance," a pamphlet in which an oration of the English ambassador had been criticized, and aspersions made on the Order of the Garter. He had opposed the formation of the West India Company. He had said many years before to Nicholas van Berk that the provinces had better return to the dominion of Spain. And, in general, all his proceedings had tended to put the provinces into a blood-bath.

There was, however, no accusation that he had received bribes from the enemy or held traitorous communication with him, or that he had committed any act of high treason.

His private letters to Caron and to the ambassadors in Paris, with which the reader has been made familiar, had thus been ransacked to find treasonable matter, but the result was meager in spite of the minute and microscopic analysis instituted to detect traces of poison in them.

But the most subtle and far-reaching research into past transactions was due to the Greffier Cornelis Aertsens, father of the Ambassador Francis, and to a certain Nicholas van Berk, burgomaster of Utrecht.

The process of tale-bearing, hearsay evidence, gossip, and invention went back a dozen years, even to the preliminary and secret conferences in regard to the treaty of truce.

Readers familiar with the history of those memorable negotiations are aware that Cornelis van Aertsens had compromised himself by accepting a valuable diamond and a bill of exchange drawn by Marquis Spinola on a merchant in Amsterdam, Henry Beckman by name, for eighty thousand ducats. These were handed by Father Neyen, the secret agent of the Spanish government, to the greffier as a prospective reward for his services in

furthering the truce. He did not reject them, but he
informed Prince Maurice and the advocate of the transaction.   Both diamond and bill of exchange were subsequently deposited in the hands of the treasurer of the
States-General, Joris de Bie, the assembly being made
officially acquainted with the whole course of the
affair.[1]

It is passing strange that this somewhat tortuous
business, which certainly cast a shade upon the fair
fame of the elder Aertsens, and required him to pub-
lish as good a defense as he could against the consequent scandal, should have furnished a weapon where-
with to strike at the advocate of Holland some dozen
years later.

But so it was.   Cruwel, a relative of Aertsens,
through whom Father Neyen had first obtained access
to the greffier, had stated, so it seemed, that the monk
had, in addition to the bill, handed to him another
draft of Spinola's for one hundred thousand ducats,
to be given to a person of more consideration than
Aertsens.   Cruwel did not know who the person was,
nor whether he took the money.   He expressed his surprise, however, that leading persons in the government,
"even old and authentic beggars," should allow themselves to be so seduced as to accept presents from the
enemy.   He mentioned two such persons, namely, a
burgomaster at Delft and a burgomaster at Haarlem.
Aertsens now deposed that he had informed the advocate of this story, who had said, "Be quiet about it; I
will have it investigated," and some days afterward,

---

[1] Wagenaer, ix. 271, 272.   Van Meteren, xxix. 545, 546.
Grotius, Hist., xvi. 518.   History of the United Netherlands,
vol. vi.

on being questioned, stated that he had made inquiry and found there was something in it.[1]

So the fact that Cornelis Aertsens had taken bribes, and that two burgomasters were strongly suspected by Aertsens of having taken bribes, seems to have been considered as evidence that Barneveldt had taken a bribe. It is true that Aertsens, by advice of Maurice and Barneveldt, had made a clean breast of it to the States-General and had given them over the presents. But the States-General could neither wear the diamond nor cash the bill of exchange, and it would have been better for the greffier not to contaminate his fingers with them, but to leave the gifts in the monk's palm. His revenge against the advocate for helping him out of his dilemma, and for subsequently advancing his son Francis in a brilliant diplomatic career, seems to have been, when the clouds were thickening and every man's hand was against the fallen statesman, to insinuate that he was the anonymous personage who had accepted the apocryphal draft for one hundred thousand ducats.

The case is a pregnant example of the proceedings employed to destroy the advocate.

The testimony of Nicholas van Berk was, at any rate, more direct.

On the 21st December, 1618, the burgomaster testified that the advocate had once declared to him that the differences in regard to divine worship were not so great but that they might be easily composed, asking him at the same time "whether it would not be better that we should submit ourselves again to the King of Spain." Barneveldt had also referred, so said Van

[1] Deposition of Greffier Aertsens, cited by Wagenaer, x. 349.

Berk, to the conduct of the Spanish king toward those who had helped him to the kingdom of Portugal.[1] The burgomaster was unable, however, to specify the date, year, or month in which the advocate had held this language. He remembered only that the conversation occurred when Barneveldt was living on the Spui at The Hague, and that, having been let into the house through the hall on the side of the vestibule, he had been conducted by the advocate down a small staircase into the office.[2]

The only fact proved by the details seems to be that the story had lodged in the tenacious memory of the burgomaster for eight years, as Barneveldt had removed from the Spui to Aremberg House, in the Voorhout, in the year 1611.

No other offers from the King of Spain or the archdukes had ever been made to him, said Van Berk, than those indicated in this deposition against the advocate as coming from that statesman. Nor had Barneveldt ever spoken to him upon such subjects except on that one occasion.

It is not necessary and would be wearisome to follow the unfortunate statesman through the long line of defense which he was obliged to make, in fragmentary and irregular form, against these discursive and confused assaults upon him. A continuous argument might be built up with the isolated parts which should be altogether impregnable. It is superfluous.

Always instructive to his judges as he swept at will through the record of nearly half a century of momentous European history, in which he was himself a conspicuous figure, or expounding the ancient laws and

---

[1] Wagenaer, x. 349 seq.   [2] Ibid., 349, 350.

customs of the country with a wealth and accuracy of illustration which testified to the strength of his memory, he seemed rather like a sage expounding law and history to a class of pupils than a criminal defending himself before a bench of commissioners. Moved occasionally from his austere simplicity, the majestic old man rose to a strain of indignant eloquence which might have shaken the hall of a vast assembly and found echo in the hearts of a thousand hearers as he denounced their petty insults or ignoble insinuations, glaring like a caged lion at his tormenters, who had often shrunk before him when free, and now attempted to drown his voice by contradictions, interruptions, threats, and unmeaning howls.[1]

He protested, from the outset and throughout the proceedings, against the jurisdiction of the tribunal. The Treaty of Union, on which the assembly and States-General were founded, gave that assembly no power over him. They could take no legal cognizance of his person or his acts.[2] He had been deprived of writing-materials, or he would have already drawn up his solemn protest and argument against the existence of the commission. He demanded that they should be pro-

---

[1] " . . . niet gedragen als commissarien maar als formele partye met interrumperen . . . kryten en roepen so dat wy niet vryelick en konden spreeken en meer andere vyandlycke Acten 't welck ooc d' oorsaack is geweest waarom sy haar daarna geschaamt hebben," etc.—H. Grotius, Verantwoording, xiii. 141.

" . . . ende somtijds precipitantelyk dickwyls geturbeert, ende door de vragen moveert, altemets geinterrompeert, oock met refuys van myne allegatien te laten teyckenen."—Letter of Barneveldt to the states of Holland, written in prison (May, 1619) and left unfinished, Leven en Sterven, 238.

[2] Verhooren van Oldenbarneveld, 183–210.

vided for him, together with a clerk to engross his defense. It is needless to say that the demand was refused.

It was notorious to all men, he said, that on the day when violent hands were laid upon him he was not bound to the States-General by oath, allegiance, or commission. He was a well-known inhabitant of The Hague, a householder there, a vassal of the commonwealth of Holland, enfeoffed of many notable estates in that country, serving many honorable offices by commission from his government. By birth, promotion, and conferred dignities he was subject to the supreme authority of Holland, which for forty years had been a free state, possessed of all the attributes of sovereignty, political, religious, judicial, and recognizing no superior save God Almighty alone.

He was amenable to no tribunal save that of their Mightinesses the states of Holland and their ordinary judges. Not only those states, but the Prince of Orange as their governor and vassal, the nobles of Holland, the colleges of justice, the regents of cities, and all other vassals, magistrates, and officers, were by their respective oaths bound to maintain and protect him in these his rights.

After fortifying this position by legal argument and by an array of historical facts within his own experience, and alluding to the repeated instances in which, sorely against his will, he had been solicited and almost compelled to remain in offices of which he was weary, he referred with dignity to the record of his past life. From the youthful days when he had served as a volunteer at his own expense in the perilous sieges of Haarlem and Leyden down to the time of his arrest, through an unbroken course of honorable and most arduous political services, embassies, and great negotiations, he had ever maintained the laws and liberties of the fatherland and his own honor unstained.

That he should now in his seventy-second year be dragged, in violation of every privilege and statute of the country, by extraordinary means, before unknown judges, was a grave matter not for himself alone, but for their Mightinesses the states of Holland and for the other provinces. The precious right *de non evocando* had ever been dear to all the provinces, cities, and inhabitants of the Netherlands. It was the most vital privilege in their possession as well in civil as criminal, in secular as in ecclesiastical affairs.

When the King of Spain, in 1567 and afterward, set up an extraordinary tribunal and a course of extraordinary trials, it was an undeniable fact, he said, that, on the solemn complaint of the states, all princes, nobles, and citizens not only in the Netherlands but in foreign countries, and all foreign kings and sovereigns, held those outrages to be the foremost and fundamental reason for taking up arms against that king and declaring him to have forfeited his right of sovereignty.

Yet that monarch was unquestionably the born and accepted sovereign of each one of the provinces, while the general assembly was but a gathering of confederates and allies, in no sense sovereign. It was an unimaginable thing, he said, that the states of each province should allow their whole authority and right of sovereignty to be transferred to a board of commissioners like this before which he stood. If, for example, a general union of France, England, and the states of the United Netherlands should be formed (and the very words of the Act of Union contemplated such possibility), what greater absurdity could there be than to suppose that a college of administration created for the specific purposes of such union would be competent to perform acts of sovereignty within each of those countries in matters of justice, polity, and religion?

It was known to mankind, he said, that when negotiations were entered into for bestowing the sovereignty of the provinces on France and on England, special and full powers were required from, and furnished by, the states of each individual province.

Had the sovereignty been in the assembly of the States-General, they might have transferred it of their own motion or kept it for themselves.

Even in the ordinary course of affairs the commissioners from each province to the general assembly always required a special power from their constituents before deciding any matter of great importance.

In regard to the defense of the respective provinces and cities, he had never heard it doubted, he said, that the states or the magistrates of cities had full right to provide for it by arming a portion of their own inhabitants or by enlisting paid troops. The sovereign counts of Holland and bishops of Utrecht certainly possessed and exercised that right for many hundred years, and by necessary tradition it passed to the states succeeding to their ancient sovereignty. He then gave from the stores of his memory innumerable instances [1] in which soldiers had been enlisted by provinces and cities all over the Netherlands from the time of the abjuration of Spain down to that moment. Through the whole period of independence in the time of Anjou,

[1] Verhooren, 193–196.

Matthias, Leicester, as well as under the actual government, it had been the invariable custom thus to provide
both by land and sea and on the rivers against robbers,
rebels, pirates, mischief-makers, assailing thieves, domestic or foreign.[1] It had been done by the immortal
William the Silent on many memorable occasions, and
in fact the custom was so notorious that soldiers so
enlisted were known by different and peculiar nick-
names in the different provinces and towns.

That the central government had no right to meddle
with religious matters was almost too self-evident an
axiom to prove. Indeed, the chief difficulty under
which the advocate labored throughout this whole process was the monstrous assumption by his judges of a
political and judicial system which never had any existence even in imagination. The profound secrecy
which inwrapped the proceedings from that day almost
to our own, and an ignorant acquiescence of a considerable portion of the public in accomplished facts, offer
the only explanation of a mystery which must ever
excite our wonder. If there were any impeachment at
all, it was an impeachment of the form of government
itself. If language could mean anything whatever, a
mere perusal of the Articles of Union proved that the
prisoner had never violated that fundamental pact.
How could the general government prescribe an especial formulary for the Reformed Church, and declare
opposition to its decrees treasonable, when it did not
prohibit, but absolutely admitted and invited, provinces and cities exclusively Catholic to enter the Union,
guaranteeing to them entire liberty of religion?[2]

Barneveldt recalled the fact that when the stad-

[1] Verhooren, 207.   [2] Ibid., 43, 196.

holdership of Utrecht, thirty years before, had been conferred on Prince Maurice the states of that province had solemnly reserved for themselves the disposition over religious matters in conformity with the Union, and that Maurice had sworn to support that resolution.

Five years later the prince had himself assured a deputation from Brabant [1] that the states of each province were supreme in religious matters, no interference the one with the other being justifiable or possible. In 1602 the States-General, in letters addressed to the states of the obedient provinces under dominion of the archdukes, had invited them to take up arms to help drive the Spaniards from the provinces and to join the confederacy, assuring them that they should regulate the matter of religion at their good pleasure, and that no one else should be allowed to interfere therewith.

The advocate then went into an historical and critical disquisition, into which we certainly have no need to follow him, rapidly examining the whole subject of predestination and conditional and unconditional damnation from the days of St. Augustine downward, showing a thorough familiarity with a subject of theology which then made up so much of the daily business of life, political and private, and lay at the bottom of the terrible convulsion then existing in the Netherlands. We turn from it with a shudder, reminding the reader only how persistently the statesman then on his trial had advocated conciliation, moderation, and kindness between brethren of the Reformed Church who were not able to think alike on one of the subtlest

[1] Verhooren, 43, 196.

and most mysterious problems that casuistry has ever propounded.

For fifty years, he said, he had been an enemy of all compulsion of the human conscience. He had always opposed rigorous ecclesiastical decrees. He had done his best to further, and did not deny having inspired, the advice given in the famous letters from the King of Great Britain to the states in 1613, that there should be mutual toleration and abstinence from discussion of disputed doctrines, neither of them essential to salvation. He thought that neither Calvin nor Beza would have opposed freedom of opinion on those points. For himself, he believed that the salvation of mankind would be through God's unmerited grace and the redemption of sins through the Savior, and that the man who so held and persevered to the end was predestined to eternal happiness, and that his children dying before the age of reason were destined, not to hell, but to heaven.[1] He had thought fifty years long that the passion and sacrifice of Christ the Savior were more potent to salvation than God's wrath and the sin of Adam and Eve to damnation.[2] He had done his best practically to avert personal bickerings among the clergy. He had been, so far as lay in his power, as friendly to Remonstrants as to Contra-Remonstrants, to Polyander and Festus Hommius as to Uytenbogart and Episcopius. He had almost finished a negotiation with Councilor Kromhout for the peaceable delivery of the Cloister Church on the Thursday preceding the Sunday on which it had been forcibly seized by the Contra-Remonstrants.[3]

When asked by one of his judges how he presumed

---

[1] Verhooren, 36.   [2] Ibid.   [3] Ibid., 68.

to hope for toleration between two parties, each of which abhorred the other's opinions and likened each other to Turks and devil-worshipers, he replied that he had always detested and rebuked those mutual revilings by every means in his power, and would have wished to put down such calumniators of either persuasion by the civil authority, but the iniquity of the times and the exasperation of men's humors had prevented him.

Being perpetually goaded by one judge after another as to his disrespectful conduct toward the King of Great Britain, and asked why his Majesty had not as good right to give the advice of 1617 as the recommendation of tolerance in 1613, he scrupulously abstained, as he had done in all his letters, from saying a desrespectful word as to the glaring inconsistency between the two communications, or to the hostility manifested toward himself personally by the British ambassador. He had always expressed the hope, he said, that the king would adhere to his original position, but did not dispute his right to change his mind, nor the good faith which had inspired his later letters. It had been his object, if possible, to reconcile the two different systems recommended by his Majesty into one harmonious whole.

His whole aim had been to preserve the public peace, as it was the duty of every magistrate, especially in times of such excitement, to do. He could never comprehend why the toleration of the Five Points should be a danger to the Reformed religion. Rather, he thought, it would strengthen the church and attract many Lutherans, Baptists, Catholics, and other good patriots into its pale. He had always opposed the com-

pulsory acceptance by the people of the special opinions
of scribes and doctors. He did not consider, he said,
the difference in doctrine on this disputed point between the Contra-Remonstrants and Remonstrants as
one tenth the value of the civil authority and its right
to make laws and ordinances regulating ecclesiastical
affairs.

He believed the great bulwark of the independence
of the country to be the Reformed Church, and his
efforts had ever been to strengthen that bulwark by pre-
venting the unnecessary schism which might prove its
ruin. Many questions of property, too, were involved in
the question,—the church buildings, lands and pastures
belonging to the counts of Holland and their successors,
—the states having always exercised the right of church
patronage,—*jus patronatus*,—a privilege which, as well
as inherited or purchased advowsons, had been of late
flagrantly interfered with.

He was asked if he had not said that it had never
been the intention of the States-General to carry on the
war for this or that religion.

He replied that he had told certain clergymen, expressing to him their opinion that the war had been
waged solely for the furtherance of their especial shade
of belief, than in his view the war had been undertaken
for the conservation of the liberties and laws of the
land and of its good people. Of that freedom the first
and foremost point was the true Christian religion and
liberty of conscience and opinion. There must be religion in the Republic, he had said, but that the war was
carried on to sustain the opinion of one doctor of divin-
ity or another on differential points was something he
had never heard of and could never believe. The good

citizens of the country had as much right to hold by Melanchthon as by Calvin or Beza. He knew that the first proclamations in regard to the war declared it to be undertaken for freedom of conscience, and so to his own knowledge it had been always carried on.

He was asked if he had not promised during the truce negotiations so to direct matters that the Catholics with time might obtain public exercise of their religion.

He replied that this was a notorious falsehood and calumny, adding that it ill accorded with the proclamation against the Jesuits drawn up by himself some years after the truce. He furthermore stated that it was chiefly by his direction that the discourse of President Jeannin,[1] urging on part of the French king that liberty of worship might be granted to the papists, was kept secret, copies of it not having been furnished even to the commissioners of the provinces.[2]

His indignant denial of this charge, especially taken in connection with his repeated assertions during the trial that among the most patriotic Netherlanders during and since the war were many adherents of the ancient church, seems marvelously in contradiction with his frequent and most earnest pleas for liberty of conscience. But it did not appear contradictory even to his judges nor to any contemporary. His position had always been that the civil authority of each province was supreme in all matters, political or ecclesiastical. The States-General, all the provinces uniting in the vote, had invited the Catholic provinces on more than one occasion to join the Union, promising that there

[1] See History of the United Netherlands, vol. vi. 347–350. Jeannin, Négoc., ii. 589–597.   [2] Verhooren, 67.

should be no interference on the part of any states or individuals with the internal affairs, religious or otherwise, of the provinces accepting the invitation. But it would have been a gross contradiction of his own principle if he had promised so to direct matters that the Catholics should have public right of worship in Holland, where he knew that the civil authority was sure to refuse it, or in any of the other six provinces, in whose internal affairs he had no voice whatever. He was opposed to all tyranny over conscience; he would have done his utmost to prevent inquisition into opinion, violation of domicile, interference with private worship, compulsory attendance in Protestant churches of those professing the Roman creed. This was not attempted. No Catholic was persecuted on account of his religion. Compared with the practice in other countries, this was a great step in advance. Religious tolerance lay on the road to religious equality, a condition which had hardly been imagined then and scarcely exists in Europe even to this day. But among the men in history whose life and death contributed to the advancement of that blessing, it would be vain to deny that Barneveldt occupies a foremost place.

Moreover, it should be remembered that religious equality then would have been a most hazardous experiment. So long as church and state were blended, it was absolutely essential at that epoch for the preservation of Protestantism to assign the predominance to the state. Should the Catholics have obtained religious equality, the probable result would before long have been religious inequality, supremacy of the Catholics in the church, and supremacy of the church over the state. The fruits of the forty years' war would have

become dust and ashes. It would be mere weak senti-
mentalism to doubt, after the bloody history which had
just closed and the awful tragedy then reopening, that
every spark of religious liberty would have soon been
trodden out in the Netherlands. The general onslaught of the League, with Ferdinand, Maximilian of
Bavaria, and Philip of Spain at its head, against the
distracted, irresolute, and wavering line of Protestantism across the whole of Europe was just preparing.
Rather a wilderness to reign over than a single heretic,
was the war-cry of the emperor. The King of Spain,
as we have just been reading in his most secret ciphered
despatches to the archduke at Brussels, was nursing
sanguine hopes and weaving elaborate schemes for recovering his dominion over the United Netherlands,
and proposing to send an army of Jesuits thither to
break the way to the reconquest.[1] To play into his
hands then, by granting public right of worship to the
papists, would have been, in Barneveldt's opinion, like
giving up Jülich and other citadels in the debatable
land to Spain just as the great war between Catholicism and Protestantism was breaking out. There had
been enough of burning and burying alive in the Netherlands during the century which had closed. It was
not desirable to give a chance for their renewal now.

In regard to the synod Barneveldt justified his course
by a simple reference to the thirteenth article of the
Union. Words could not more plainly prohibit the interference by the States-General with the religious
affairs of any one of the provinces than had been done
by that celebrated clause. In 1583 [2] there had been

[1] Vide antea, 21–27.
[2] Grotius, Verantwoording, 19, 20,

an attempt made to amend that article by insertion of
a pledge to maintain the Evangelical, Reformed religion solely, but it was never carried out. He disdained
to argue so self-evident a truth, that a confederacy
which had admitted and constantly invited Catholic
states to membership, under solemn pledge of non-
interference with their religious affairs, had no right
to lay down formulas for the Reformed Church
throughout all the Netherlands. The oath of stadholder and magistrates in Holland to maintain the Reformed religion was framed before this unhappy controversy on predestination had begun, and it was mere
arrogant assumption on the part of the Contra-Remonstrants to claim a monopoly of that religion and to
exclude the Remonstrants from its folds.

He had steadily done his utmost to assuage those
dissensions, while maintaining the laws which he was
sworn to support. He had advocated a provincial
synod to be amicably assisted by divines from neighboring countries. He had opposed a national synod
unless unanimously voted by the seven provinces, because it would have been an open violation of the
fundamental law of the confederacy, of its whole spirit,
and of liberty of conscience. He admitted that he had
himself drawn up a protest on the part of three provinces (Holland, Utrecht, and Overyssel) against the
decree for the national synod as a breach of the Union,
declaring it to be therefore null and void, and binding
upon no man. He had dictated the protest as oldest
member present, while Grotius as the youngest had
acted as scribe. He would have supported the synod
if legally voted, but would have preferred the convocation, under the authority of all the provinces, of a

general, not a national, synod, in which, besides clergy and laymen from the Netherlands, deputations from all Protestant states and churches should take part—a kind of Protestant ecumenical council.

As to the enlistment, by the states of a province, of soldiers to keep the peace and suppress tumults in its cities during times of political and religious excitement, it was the most ordinary of occurrences. In his experience of more than forty years he had never heard the right even questioned. It was pure ignorance of law and history to find it a novelty.

To hire temporarily a sufficient number of professional soldiers he considered a more wholesome means of keeping the peace than to enlist one portion of the citizens of a town against another portion, when party and religious spirit was running high. His experience had taught him that the mutual hatred of the inhabitants, thus inflamed, became more lasting and mischievous than the resentment caused through suppression of disorder by an armed and paid police of strangers.

It was not only the right but the most solemn duty of the civil authority to preserve the tranquillity, property, and lives of citizens committed to their care. "I have said these fifty years," said Barneveldt, "that it is better to be governed by magistrates than mobs. I have always maintained and still maintain that the most disastrous, shameful, and ruinous condition into which this land can fall is that in which the magistrates are overcome by the rabble of the towns and receive laws from them. Nothing but perdition can follow from that."[1]

There had been good reason to believe that the

1 Verhooren, 10.

French garrisons as well as some of the train-bands could not be thoroughly relied upon in emergencies like those constantly breaking out, and there had been advices of invasion by sympathizers from neighboring countries. In many great cities the civil authority had been trampled upon and mob rule had prevailed. Certainly the recent example in the great commercial capital of the country,—where the house of a foremost citizen had been besieged, stormed, and sacked, and a virtuous matron of the higher class hunted like a wild beast through the streets by a rabble grossly ignorant of the very nature of the religious quibble which had driven them mad, pelted with stones, branded with vilest names, and only saved by accident from assassination, while a church-going multitude looked calmly on,—with constantly recurring instances in other important cities, were sufficient reasons for the authorities to be watchful.

He denied that he had initiated the proceedings at Utrecht in conversation with Ledenberg or any one else, but he had not refused, he said, his approval of the perfectly legal measures adopted for keeping the peace there when submitted to him. He was himself a born citizen of that province, and therefore especially interested in its welfare, and there was an old and intimate friendship between Utrecht and Holland. It would have been painful to him to see that splendid city in the control of an ignorant mob, making use of religious problems, which they did not comprehend, to plunder the property and take the lives of peaceful citizens more comfortably housed than themselves.

He had neither suggested nor controlled the proceedings at Utrecht. On the contrary, at an interview with the prince and Count William on the 13th July, and in the presence of nearly thirty members of the general assembly, he had submitted a plan for cashiering the enlisted soldiery and substituting for them other troops, native-born, who should be sworn in the usual form to obey the laws of the Union. The deputation from Holland to Utrecht, according to his personal knowledge, had received no instructions, personal or oral, to authorize active steps by the troops of the Holland quota, but to abstain from them and to request the prince that they should not be used against the will and commands of the states of Utrecht, whom they were bound by oath to obey so long as they were in garrison there.

No man knew better than he whether the military oath which was called newfangled were a novelty or not, for he had himself, he said, drawn it up thirty years before,[1] at command of the States-General, by whom it was then ordained. From that day to this he had never heard a pretense that it justified anything not expressly sanctioned by the Articles of Union, and neither the states of Holland nor those of Utrecht had made any change in the oath.[2] The states of Utrecht were sovereign within their own territory, and in the time of peace neither the Prince of Orange without

[1] Verhooren, 205, 206.

[2] Compare Grotius, Verantwoording, 113, 116.

"That it should seem strange that there are different oaths for soldiers in one province," he says, "comes from ignorance of our form of government and laws. . . . Military officers and soldiers have double obligations of allegiance: first, on account of their office, to the generality; second, on account of the territory (*sic*) where they lie, to the upper and lower authorities of said territory."

their order nor the States-General had the right to
command the troops in their territory. The governor
of a province was sworn to obey the laws of the province and conform to the Articles of the General Union.

He was asked why he wrote the warning letter to
Ledenberg, and why he was so anxious that the letter
should be burned [1]—as if that were a deadly offense.

He said that he could not comprehend why it should
be imputed to him as a crime that he wished in such
turbulent times to warn so important a city as Utrecht,
the capital of his native province, against tumults, dis-
orders, and sudden assaults such as had often happened to her in times past. As for the postscript requesting that the letter might be put in the fire, he
said that, not being a member of the government of
that province, he was simply unwilling to leave a record
that "he had been too curious *in aliena republica*, although that could hardly be considered a grave offense." [2]

In regard to the charge that he had accused Prince
Maurice of aspiring to the sovereignty of the country,
he had much to say. He had never brought such accusation in public or private. He had reason to believe,
however,—he had, indeed, convincing proofs,—that
many people, especially those belonging to the Contra-
Remonstrant party, cherished such schemes. He had
never sought to cast suspicion on the prince himself on
account of those schemes. On the contrary, he had not
even formally opposed them. What he wished had always been that such projects should be discussed formally, legally, and aboveboard. After the lamentable

[1] Vide antea, vol. ii. 303–304. "Being read, *igni*."
[2] Verhooren, 32.

murder of the late prince he had himself recommended to the authorities of some of the cities that the transaction for bestowing the sovereignty of Holland upon William, interrupted by his death, "should be completed in favor of Prince Maurice, in despite of the Spaniard." [1] Recently he had requested Grotius to look up the documents deposited in Rotterdam belonging to this affair, in order that they might be consulted.

He was asked whether, according to Buzanval, the former French ambassador, Prince Maurice had not declared he would rather fling himself from the top of the Hague tower than accept the sovereignty. Barneveldt replied that the prince, according to the same authority, had added, "under the conditions which had been imposed upon his father," [2] a clause which considerably modified the self-denying statement. It was desirable, therefore, to search the acts for the limitations annexed to the sovereignty.

Three years long there had been indications from various sources that a party wished to change the form of government. He had not heard nor ever intimated that the prince suggested such intrigues. In anonymous pamphlets and common street and tavern conversations the Contra-Remonstrants were described by those of their own persuasion as "Prince's Beggars" and the like. [3] He had received from foreign countries information worthy of attention, that it was the design of the Contra-Remonstrants to raise the prince to the sovereignty. He had therefore, in 1616, brought the matter before the nobles and cities in a communication setting forth, to the best of his recollection, that under

[1] Verhooren, 169.   [2] Ibid., 223, 224.   [3] Ibid., 166.

these religious disputes something else was intended. He had desired ripe conclusions on the matter, such as should most conduce to the service of the country. This had been in good faith both to the prince and the provinces, in order that, should a change in the government be thought desirable, proper and peaceful means might be employed to bring it about. He had never had any other intention than to sound the inclinations of those with whom he spoke, and he had many times since that period, by word of mouth and in writing, so lately as the month of April last, assured the prince that he had ever been his sincere and faithful servant and meant to remain so to the end of his life, desiring therefore that he would explain to him his wishes and intentions.

Subsequently he had publicly proposed in full assembly of Holland that the states should ripely deliberate and roundly declare if they were discontented with the form of government, and if so, what change they would desire. He had assured their Mightinesses that they might rely upon him to assist in carrying out their intentions, whatever they might be. He had inferred, however, from the prince's intimations, when he had broached the subject to him in 1617, that he was not inclined toward these supposed projects, and had heard that opinion distinctly expressed from the mouth of Count William.

That the Contra-Remonstrants secretly entertained these schemes, he had been advised from many quarters, at home and abroad. In the year 1618 he had received information to that effect from France. Certain confidential counselors of the prince had been with him recently to confer on the subject. He had told them that, if his Excellency chose to speak to him in regard to it, would listen to his reasoning about it, both as regarded the interests of the country and the prince himself, and then should desire him to propose and advocate it before the assembly, he would do so with earnestness, zeal, and affection. He had desired, however, that, in case the attempt failed, the prince would allow him to be relieved from service and to leave the country. What he wished from the bottom of his heart was that his Excellency would plainly discover to him the exact nature of his sentiments in regard to the business.

He fully admitted receiving a secret letter from Ambassador Langerac, apprising him that a man of quality in France had information of the intention of the Contra-Remonstrants throughout the provinces, should they come into power, to raise Prince Maurice to the sovereignty. He had communicated on the subject with Grotius and other deputies in order that, if this should prove to be the general inclination, the affair might be handled according to law, without confusion or disorder. This, he said, would be serving both the country and the prince most judiciously.

He was asked why he had not communicated directly with Maurice. He replied that he had already seen how unwillingly the prince heard him allude to the subject, and that, moreover, there was another clause in the letter of different meaning, and in his view worthy of grave consideration by the states.

No question was asked him as to this clause, but we have seen that it referred to the communication by Du Agean to Langerac of a scheme for bestowing the sovereignty of the provinces on the King of France. The reader will also recollect that Barneveldt had advised the ambassador to communicate the whole intelligence to the prince himself.[1]

Barneveldt proceeded to inform the judges that he had never said a word to cast suspicion upon the prince, but had been actuated solely by the desire to find out the inclination of the states. The communications which he had made on the subject were neither for discrediting the prince nor for counteracting the schemes for his advancement. On the contrary, he had conferred with deputies from great cities like Dordrecht, Enkhuizen, and Amsterdam, most devoted to the Contra-Remonstrant party, and had told them that, if they chose to propose the subject themselves, he would conduct himself to the best of his abilities in accordance with the wishes of the prince.

It would seem almost impossible for a statesman placed in Barneveldt's position to bear himself with more perfect loyalty both to the country and to the stadholder. His duty was to maintain the constitution and laws so long as they remained unchanged. Should it appear that the states, which legally represented the country, found the constitution defective, he was ready to aid in its amendment by fair public and legal methods.

If Maurice wished to propose himself openly as a candidate for the sovereignty which had a generation before been conferred upon his father, Barneveldt would not only acquiesce in the scheme, but propose it.

Should it fail, he claimed the right to lay down all his offices and go into exile.

He had never said that the prince was intriguing

---

[1] Vide antea, 34–39.

for, or even desired, the sovereignty. That the project existed among the party most opposed to himself, he had sufficient proof. To the leaders of that party, therefore, he suggested that the subject should be publicly discussed, guaranteeing freedom of debate and his loyal support so far as lay within his power.

This was his answer to the accusation that he had meanly, secretly, and falsely circulated statements that the prince was aspiring to the sovereignty.[1]

[1] Verhooren, 102, 103.

Great pains were taken, in the course of the interrogatories, to elicit proof that the advocate had concealed important diplomatic information from the prince. He was asked why, in his secret instructions to Ambassador Langerac, he ordered him by an express article to be very cautious about making communications to the prince. Searching questions were put in regard to these secret instructions, which I have read in the archives, and a copy of which now lies before me. They are in the form of questions, some of them almost puerile ones, addressed to Barneveldt by the ambassador, then just departing on his mission to France in 1614, with the answers written in the margin by the advocate. The following is all that has reference to the prince:

"Of what matters may I ordinarily write to his Excellency?"

Answer: "Of all great and important matters."

It was difficult to find much that was treasonable in that.

Another question was: "Would it not be advisable for me privately to pick up secrets through my secretary from the secretaries of princes and other gentlemen about the court, but to reveal nothing, and write to no one about them except to M. de Barneveldt?" The answer of the advocate was: "You must act in such matters with discretion, caution, and foresight. I shall take the orders of my lords the states whether you are to write of such things in public or private letters, and advise you accordingly." And there is nothing more vital in the whole list of questions than these.

The paper is called "Vraechstucken ende poincten by my ingestellt ende by den adv. Oldenbarneveld geappostilleert tot

Among the heterogeneous articles of accusation he was asked why he had given no attention to those who had so frequently proposed the formation of the West India Company.

He replied [1] that it had from old time been the opinion of the states of Holland, and always his own, that special and private licenses for traffic, navigation, and foreign commerce were prejudicial to the welfare of the land. He had always been most earnestly opposed to them, detesting monopolies which interfered with that free trade and navigation which should be common to all mankind. He had taken great pains, however, in the years 1596 and 1597, to study the nature of the navigation and trade to the East Indies, in regard to the nations to be dealt with in those regions, the nature of the wares bought and sold there, the opposition to be encountered from the Spaniards and Portuguese against the commerce of the Netherlanders, and the necessity of equipping vessels both for traffic and defense, and had come to the conclusion that these matters could best be directed by a general company. He explained in detail the manner in which he had procured the blending of all the isolated chambers into one great East India corporation, the enormous pains which it had cost him to bring it about, and the great commercial and national success which had been the result. The admiral of Aragon, when a prisoner after the bat-

myner onderrichtinge ende instructie voor myn vertreck naer Vranckryk 1614," G. van Boetzelaer van Asperen, Hague Archives MS.

It was sent to Prince Maurice on January 29, 1619, together with the answers to the points alluded to by Langerac in the letter already cited.

[1] Verhooren, 72.

tle of Nieuport, had told him, he said, that the union
of these petty corporations into one great whole had
been as disastrous a blow to the kingdoms of Spain
and Portugal as the Union of the provinces at Utrecht
had been. In regard to the West India Company, its
sole object, so far as he could comprehend it, had been
to equip armed vessels, not for trade, but to capture
and plunder Spanish merchantmen and silver-fleets in
the West Indies and South America. This was an ad-
vantageous war measure, which he had favored while
the war lasted. It was in no sense a commercial scheme,
however, and when the truce had been made, the company not having come into existence, he failed to comprehend how its formation could be profitable for the
Netherlanders. On the contrary, it would expressly
invite or irritate the Spaniards into a resumption of
the war, an object which, in his humble opinion, was
not at all desirable.[1]

Certainly these ideas were not especially reprehen-
sible, but had they been as shallow and despicable as
they seem to us enlightened, it is passing strange that
they should have furnished matter for a criminal
prosecution.

It was doubtless a disappointment for the promoters
of the company, the chief of whom was a bankrupt, to
fail in obtaining their charter, but it was scarcely high
treason to oppose it. There is no doubt, however, that
the disapprobation with which Barneveldt regarded
the West India Company, the seat of which was at
Amsterdam, was a leading cause of the deadly hostility entertained for him by the great commercial
metropolis.

[1] Verhooren, 75.

It was bad enough for the advocate to oppose unconditional predestination and the damnation of infants,
but to frustrate a magnificent system of privateering
on the Spaniards in time of truce was an unpardonable crime.

The patience with which the venerable statesman
submitted to the taunts, ignorant and insolent cross-
questionings, and noisy interruptions of his judges,
was not less remarkable than the tenacity of memory
which enabled him thus day after day, alone, unaided
by books, manuscripts, or friendly counsel, to recon-
struct the record of forty years, and to expound the
laws of the land, by an array of authorities, instances,
and illustrations, in a manner that would be deemed
masterly by one who had all the resources of libraries,
documents, witnesses, and secretaries at command.

Only when insidious questions were put tending to
impute to him corruption, venality, and treacherous
correspondence with the enemy—for they never once
dared formally to accuse him of treason—did that almost superhuman patience desert him.

He was questioned as to certain payments made by
him to a certain Van der Veecken in Spanish coin. He
replied briefly, at first, that his money transactions with
that man of business extended over a period of twenty
or thirty years, and amounted to many hundred thousands of florins, growing out of purchases and sales of
lands, agricultural enterprises on his estates, moneys
derived from his professional or official business, and
the like. It was impossible for him to remember the
details of every especial money payment that might
have occurred between them.

Then suddenly breaking forth into a storm of indignation, he could mark from these questions, he said, that his enemies, not satisfied with having wounded his heart with their falsehoods, vile forgeries, and honor-robbing libels, were determined to break it. This he prayed that God Almighty might avert and righteously judge between him and them.

It was plain that among other things they were alluding to the stale and senseless story of the sledge [1] —filled with baskets of coin sent by the Spanish envoys on their departure from The Hague, on conclusion of the truce, to defray expenses incurred by them for board and lodging of servants, forage of horses, and the like—which had accidentally stopped at Barneveldt's door and was forthwith sent on to John Spronsen, superintendent of such affairs. Passing over this wanton bit of calumny with disgust, he solemnly asserted that he had never at any period of his life received one penny nor the value of one penny from the King of Spain, the archdukes, Spinola, or any other person connected with the enemy, saving only the presents publicly and mutually conferred, according to invariable custom, by the high contracting parties upon the respective negotiators at conclusion of the treaty of truce. Even these gifts Barneveldt had moved his colleagues not to accept, but proposed that they should all be paid into the public treasury. He had been overruled, he said, but that any dispassionate man of tolerable intelligence could imagine him, whose whole life had been a perpetual offense to Spain, to be in suspicious relations with that power seemed to him impossible. The most intense party spirit, yes, envy itself, must confess that he had been among the fore-

[1] See History of the United Netherlands, vi. 314.

most to take up arms for his country's liberties, and
had through life never faltered in their defense. And
once more in that mean chamber, and before a row of
personal enemies calling themselves judges, he burst
into an eloquent and most justifiable sketch of the
career of one whom there was none else to justify and
so many to assail.

From his youth, he said, he had made himself by his
honorable and patriotic deeds hopelessly irreconcilable
with the Spaniards. He was one of the advocates practising in the Supreme Court of Holland who, in the
very teeth of the Duke of Alva, had proclaimed him a
tyrant and had sworn obedience to the Prince of
Orange as the lawful governor of the land. He was
one of those who in the same year had promoted and
attended private gatherings for the advancement of
the Reformed religion. He had helped to levy, and
had contributed to, funds for the national defense in
the early days of the revolt. These were things which
led directly to the Council of Blood and the gibbet.
He had borne arms himself on various bloody fields
and had been perpetually a deputy to the rebel camps.
He had been the original mover of the Treaty of Union
which was concluded between the provinces at Utrecht.
He had been the first to propose and to draw up the
declaration of Netherland independence and the abjuration of the King of Spain. He had been one of those
who had drawn and passed the act establishing the
late Prince of Orange as stadholder. Of the sixty
signers of these memorable declarations none were now
living save himself and two others. When the prince
had been assassinated, he had done his best to secure
for his son Maurice the sovereign position of which

murder had so suddenly deprived the father. He had been member of the memorable embassies to France and England by which invaluable support for the struggling provinces had been obtained.

And thus he rapidly sketched the history of the great war of independence, in which he had ever been conspicuously employed on the patriotic side. When the late King of France, at the close of the century, had made peace with Spain, he had been sent as special ambassador to that monarch, and had prevailed on him, notwithstanding his treaty with the enemy, to continue his secret alliance with the states and to promise them a large subsidy, pledges which had been sacredly fulfilled. It was on that occasion that Henry, who was his debtor for past services, professional, official, and perfectly legitimate, had agreed, when his finances should be in better condition, to discharge his obligations, over and above the customary diplomatic present which he received publicly in common with his colleague Admiral Nassau. This promise, fulfilled a dozen years later, had been one of the senseless charges of corruption brought against him. He had been one of the negotiators of the truce, in which Spain had been compelled to treat with her revolted provinces as with free states and her equals. He had promoted the Union of the Protestant princes and their alliance with France and the United States in opposition to the designs of Spain and the League. He had organized and directed the policy by which the forces of England, France, and Protestant Germany had possessed themselves of the debatable land. He had resisted every scheme by which it was hoped to force the states from their hold of those important citadels. He had been one of the foremost promoters of the East India Company, an organization which the Spaniards confessed had been as damaging to them as the Union of the provinces itself had been.

The idiotic and circumstantial statements that he had conducted Burgomaster van Berk through a secret staircase of his house into his private study for the purpose of informing him that the only way for the states to get out of the war was to submit themselves once more to their old masters, so often forced upon him by the judges, he contradicted with disdain and disgust. He had ever abhorred and dreaded, he said, the house of Spain, Austria, and Burgundy. His life had passed in open hostility to that house, as was known to all mankind. His mere personal interests, apart from higher considerations, would make an approach to the former sovereign impossible, for besides the deeds he had already alluded to, he had committed at least twelve distinct and separate acts each one of which would be held high treason by the house of Austria, and he had learned from childhood that these are things which monarchs never forget. The tales of Van Berk were those of a personal enemy, falsehoods scarcely worth contradicting.

He was grossly and enormously aggrieved by the illegal constitution of the commission. He had protested and continued to protest against it. If that protest were unheeded, he claimed at least that those men should be excluded from the board and the right to sit in judgment upon his person and his deeds who had proved themselves by words and works to be his capital enemies, of which fact he could produce irrefragable evidence. He claimed that the Supreme

Court of Holland, or the High Council, or both together, should decide upon that point. He held as his
personal enemies, he said, all those who had declared
that he, before or since the truce down to the day of
his arrest, had held correspondence with the Spaniards,
the archdukes, the Marquis Spinola, or any one on that
side, had received money, money value, or promises of
money from them, and in consequence had done or
omitted to do anything whatever. He denounced such
tales as notorious, shameful, and villainous falsehoods,
the utterers and circulators of them as wilful liars, and
this he was ready to maintain in every appropriate
way for the vindication of the truth and his own honor.
He declared solemnly before God Almighty to the
States-General and to the states of Holland that his
course in the religious matter had been solely directed
to the strengthening of the Reformed religion and to
the political security of the provinces and cities. He
had simply desired that, in the awful and mysterious
matter of predestination, the consciences of many
preachers and many thousands of good citizens might
be placed in tranquillity, with moderate and Christian
limitations against all excesses.

From all these reasons, he said, the commissioners,
the States-General, the prince, and every man in the
land could clearly see, and were bound to see, that he
was the same man now that he was at the beginning
of the war, had ever been, and with God's help should
ever remain.

The proceedings were kept secret from the public,
and, as a matter of course, there had been conflicting
rumors from day to day as to the probable result of
these great state trials. In general, however, it was

thought that the prisoner would be acquitted of the graver charges, or that at most he would be permanently displaced from all office and declared incapable thenceforth to serve the state. The triumph of the Contra-Remonstrants since the stadholder had placed himself at the head of them, and the complete metamorphosis of the city governments even in the strongholds of the Arminian party, seemed to render the permanent political disgrace of the advocate almost a matter of certainty.

The first step that gave rise to a belief that he might be perhaps more severely dealt with than had been anticipated was the proclamation by the States-General of a public fast and humiliation for the 17th April.

In this document it was announced that "church and state, during several years past having been brought into great danger of utter destruction through certain persons in furtherance of their ambitious designs, had been saved by the convocation of a national synod; that a lawful sentence was soon to be expected upon those who had been disturbing the commonwealth; that through this sentence general tranquillity would probably be restored; and that men were now to thank God for this result, and pray to him that he would bring the wicked counsels and stratagems of the enemy against these provinces to naught."

All the prisoners were asked if they, too, would like in their chambers of bondage to participate in the solemnity, although the motive for the fasting and prayer was not mentioned to them. Each of them in his separate prison-room, of course without communication together, selected the Seventh Psalm [1] and sang it with his servant and doorkeeper.

From the date of this fast-day Barneveldt looked upon the result of his trial as likely to be serious.

Many clergymen refused or objected to comply with the terms of this declaration. Others conformed with it greedily, and preached lengthy thanksgiving sermons, giving praise to God that he had confounded the devices of the ambitious and saved the country from the blood-bath which they had been preparing for it.

The friends of Barneveldt became alarmed at the sinister language of this proclamation, in which for the first time allusions had been made to a forthcoming sentence against the accused.

Especially the stanch and indefatigable Du Maurier at once addressed himself again to the States-General. De Boississe had returned to France, having found that the government of a country torn, weakened, and rendered almost impotent by its own internecine factions was not likely to exert any very potent influence on the fate of the illustrious prisoner.

The states had given him to understand that they

[1] Carleton, 358.   Van Rees and Brill, iii. 192.

How nobly pathetic are some of the verses as sung by Barneveldt in his prison! "O Lord my God, in thee do I put my trust. . . . O Lord my God, if I have done this; if there be iniquity in my hands; if I have rewarded evil unto him that was at peace with me; . . . let the enemy persecute my soul, and take it; yea, let him tread down my life upon the earth, and lay mine honor in the dust. Arise, O Lord, in thine anger, lift up thyself because of the rage of mine enemies: and awake for me to the judgment that thou hast commanded. . . . My defense is of God, which saveth the upright in heart. . . . God is angry with the wicked. . . . He travaileth with iniquity, and hath conceived mischief, and brought forth falsehood. . . . His mischief shall return upon his own head."

were wearied with his perpetual appeals, intercessions, and sermons in behalf of mercy. They made him feel, in short, that Louis XIII. and Henry IV. were two entirely different personages.[1]

Du Maurier, however, obtained a hearing before the assembly on the 1st May, where he made a powerful and manly speech in presence of the prince, urging that the prisoners ought to be discharged unless they could be convicted of treason, and that the states ought to show as much deference to his sovereign as they had always done to Elizabeth of England. He made a personal appeal to Prince Maurice, urging upon him how much it would redound to his glory if he should now in generous and princely fashion step forward in behalf of those by whom he deemed himself to have been personally offended.[2]

His speech fell upon ears hardened against such eloquence and produced no effect.

Meantime the family of Barneveldt, not yet reduced to despair, chose to take a less gloomy view of the proclamation. Relying on the innocence of the great statesman, whose aims, in their firm belief, had ever been for the welfare and glory of his fatherland, and in whose heart there had never been kindled one spark of treason, they bravely expected his triumphant release from his long and, as they deemed it, his iniquitous imprisonment.

On this very 1st May, in accordance with ancient custom, a May-pole was erected on the Voorhout before the mansion of the captive statesman,[3] and wreaths of

---

[1] Wagenaer, x. 356, 357.   [2] Ibid., 358.

[3] Groen van Prinsterer, Archives de la Maison d'Orange, 2de série, ii. 567, 568.

spring flowers and garlands of evergreen decorated the walls within which were such bruised and bleeding hearts. These demonstrations of a noble hypocrisy, if such it were, excited the wrath, not the compassion, of the stadholder, who thought that the aged matron and her sons and daughters who dwelt in that house of mourning should rather have sat in sackcloth, with ashes on their heads, than indulge in these insolent marks of hope and joyful expectation.

It is certain, however, that Count Louis William, who, although most stanch on the Contra-Remonstrant side, had a veneration for the advocate and desired warmly to save him, made a last strenuous effort for that purpose.

It was believed then, and it seems almost certain, that, if the friends of the advocate had been willing to implore pardon for him, the sentence would have been remitted or commuted. Their application would have been successful, for through it his guilt would seem to be acknowledged.

Count William sent for the Fiscal Duyck.[1] He asked him if there were no means of saving the life of a man who was so old and had done the country so much service. After long deliberation, it was decided that Prince Maurice should be approached on the subject. Duyck wished that the count himself would speak with his cousin, but was convinced by his reasoning that it would be better that the fiscal should do it. Duyck had a long interview, accordingly, with Maurice, which was followed by a very secret one between them both and Count William. The three were locked up together three hours long in the prince's private

[1] Brandt, Rechtspl., 166, 167.

cabinet. It was then decided that Count William
should go, as if of his own accord, to the Princess
Dowager Louise, and induce her to send for some one
of Barneveldt's children and urge that the family
should ask pardon for him. She asked if this was
done with the knowledge of the Prince of Orange, or
whether he would not take it amiss. The count eluded
the question, but implored her to follow his advice.

The result was an interview between the princess
and Madame de Groeneveld, wife of the eldest son.
That lady was besought to apply, with the rest of the
advocate's children, for pardon to the lords states, but
to act as if it were done of her own impulse, and to
keep their interview profoundly secret.

Madame de Groeneveld took time to consult the
other members of the family and some friends. Soon
afterward she came again to the princess, and informed
her that she had spoken with the other children, and
that they could not agree to the suggestion. "They
would not move one step in it—no, not if it should cost
him his head."

The princess reported the result of this interview to
Count William, at which both were so distressed that
they determined to leave The Hague.[1]

There is something almost superhuman in the stern-
ness of this stoicism. Yet it lay in the proud and
highly tempered character of the Netherlanders. There
can be no doubt that the advocate would have expressly
dictated this proceeding if he had been consulted. It
was precisely the course adopted by himself. Death
rather than life with a false acknowledgment of guilt
and therefore with disgrace. The loss of his honor

[1] Brandt, Rechtspl., 166, 167.

would have been an infinitely greater triumph to his enemies than the loss of his head.

There was no delay in drawing up the sentence. Previously to this interview with the widow of William the Silent, the family of the advocate had presented to the judges three separate documents, rather in the way of arguments than petitions, undertaking to prove by elaborate reasoning and citations of precedents and texts of the civil law that the proceedings against him were wholly illegal, and that he was innocent of every crime.[1]

No notice had been taken of those appeals.

Upon the questions and answers as already set forth the sentence soon followed, and it may be as well that the reader should be aware, at this point in the narrative, of the substance of that sentence so soon to be pronounced. There had been no indictment, no specification of crime. There had been no testimony or evidence. There had been no argument for the prosecution or the defense. There had been no trial whatever. The prisoner was convicted on a set of questions to which he had put in satisfactory replies. He was sentenced on a preamble. The sentence was a string of vague generalities, intolerably long, and as tangled as the interrogatories. His proceedings during a long career had, on the whole, tended to something called a "blood-bath"—but the blood-bath had never occurred.

With an effrontery which did not lack ingenuity, Barneveldt's defense was called by the commissioners his confession, and was formally registered as such in the process and the sentence; while the facts that he

[1] Wagenaer, ubi sup. They are printed at length in the Waaragtige Historie van Oldenbarneveld, 310 seq.

had not been stretched upon the rack during his trial, nor kept in chains for the eight months of his imprisonment, were complacently mentioned as proofs of exceptional indulgence.

"Whereas the prisoner John of Barneveldt," said the sentence, "without being put to the torture and without fetters of iron, has confessed . . . to having perturbed religion, greatly afflicted the church of God, and carried into practice exorbitant and pernicious maxims of state, . . . inculcating by himself and accomplices that each province had the right to regulate religious affairs within its own territory, and that other provinces were not to concern themselves therewith,"[1] therefore and for many other reasons he merited punishment.

He had instigated a protest by vote of three provinces against the national synod. He had despised the salutary advice of many princes and notable personages. He had obtained from the King of Great Britain certain letters furthering his own opinions, the drafts of which he had himself suggested, and corrected and sent over to the states' ambassador in London, and when written out, signed, and addressed by the king to the States-General, had delivered them without stating how they had been procured.

Afterward he had attempted to get other letters of a similar nature from the king, and not succeeding, had defamed his Majesty as being a cause of the troubles in the provinces. He had permitted unsound theologians to be appointed to church offices, and had employed

---

[1] "Sententie uitghesprooken ende ghepronuncieert over Johan v. Oldenbarneveld," etc., appended to the Verhooren, 317–331 (Utrecht, 1850).

such functionaries in political affairs as were most likely to be the instruments of his own purposes. He had not prevented vigorous decrees from being enforced in several places against those of the true religion. He had made them odious by calling them Puritans, foreigners, and "Flanderizers," although the United Provinces had solemnly pledged to each other their lives, fortunes, and blood by various conventions, to some of which the prisoner was himself a party, to maintain the Reformed, Evangelical religion only, and to suffer no change in it to be made forevermore.

In order to carry out his design and perturb the political state of the provinces he had drawn up and caused to be enacted the Sharp Resolution of 4th August, 1617. He had thus nullified the ordinary course of justice. He had stimulated the magistrates to disobedience, and advised them to strengthen themselves with freshly enlisted military companies. He had suggested newfangled oaths for the soldiers, authorizing them to refuse obedience to the States-General and his Excellency. He had especially stimulated the proceedings at Utrecht. When it was understood that the prince was to pass through Utrecht, the states of that province, not without the prisoner's knowledge, had addressed a letter to his Excellency requesting him not to pass through their city. He had written a letter to Ledenberg suggesting that good watch should be held at the town gates and up and down the river Lek. He had desired that Ledenberg, having read that letter, should burn it. He had interfered with the cashiering of the mercenaries at Utrecht. He had said that such cashiering without the consent of the states of that province was an act of force which would justify resistance by force.

Although those states had sent commissioners to concert measures with the prince for that purpose, he had advised them to conceal their instructions until his own plan for the disbandment could be carried out. At a secret meeting in the house of Tressel, clerk of the States-General, between Grotius, Hoogerbeets, and other accomplices, it was decided that this advice should be taken. Report accordingly was made to the prisoner. He had advised them to continue in their opposition to the national synod.

He had sought to calumniate and blacken his Excellency by saying that he aspired to the sovereignty of the provinces. He had received intelligence on that subject from abroad in ciphered letters.

He had of his own accord rejected a certain proposed, notable alliance of the utmost importance to this Republic.[1]

[1] This refers, I think, without doubt, to the conversation between King James and Caron at the end of the year 1615.

The MS. memorandum of April 15, 1619, sent by the ambassador for the use of the judges, gives briefly the substance of his letter to Barneveldt recounting that conversation, and a couple of lines indicating the cautious nature of the advocate's reply. (Vide antea.)

In the learned and accurate Continuation of Arend's Allg. Geschiedenis des Vaderlands, by Professor O. van Rees and Dr. W. G. Brill (deel iii. stuk iii. 228, note 1), the paragraph is thought to refer to a proposed alliance with the French princes against the government of the queen regent. I venture, however, to believe that the very distinct expressions used by Caron in describing the language of the British king— " . . . die my seyde dat het nu goet waere dat H. M. H. de Gen. Staeten alhier souden willen senden eenighe commissarissen omme met haer een nieuw

He had received from foreign potentates various large sums of money and other presents.

All "these proceedings tended to put the city of Utrecht into a blood-bath, and likewise to bring the whole country and the person of his Excellency into the uttermost danger."

This is the substance of the sentence, amplified by repetitions and exasperating tautology into thirty or forty pages.

It will have been perceived by our analysis of Barneveldt's answers to the commissioners that all the graver charges which he was now said to have confessed had been indignantly denied by him or triumphantly justified.

It will also be observed that he was condemned for no categorical crime—lese-majesty, treason, or rebellion. The commissioners never ventured to assert that the States-General were sovereign, or that the central government had a right to prescribe a religious formulary for all the United Provinces. They never dared to say that the prisoner had been in communication with the enemy or had received bribes from him.

tractaet te maaken ende te handelen van alle voirvallende saaken die daar dagelicx in questie vielen tusschen haere ondersaten ende onse landen; . . . omme alsoe een vaster unie ende accord te maeken ende elcanderen beter te verstaen waertoe sy verclaerde wel geneghen te wesen; want, seyde sy, indien wy ons tsaemen wel unieren ende met elckanderen connen verstaen wy en hebben nyemant naest God te vresen hoe machtig die oick souden connen wesen" (Arch. of the Realm MS.)—point to this conversation as the foundation of the charge, absurd and unreasonable as it was. The king's overtures were mere loose expressions of friendly inclinations which he happened to entertain for the moment. That they contained an offer of an alliance, offensive and defensive, is a preposterous idea.

Of insinuation and implication there was much, of assertion very little, of demonstration nothing whatever.

But supposing that all the charges had been admitted or proved, what course would naturally be taken in consequence? How was a statesman who adhered to the political, constitutional, and religious opinions on which he had acted, with the general acquiescence, during a career of more than forty years, but which were said to be no longer in accordance with public opinion, to be dealt with? Would the commissioners request him to retire honorably from the high functions which he had over and over again offered to resign? Would they consider that, having fairly impeached and found him guilty of disturbing the public peace by continuing to act on his well-known legal theories, they might deprive him summarily of power and declare him incapable of holding office again?

The conclusion of the commissioners was somewhat more severe than either of these measures. Their long, rambling preamble ended with these decisive words:

"Therefore the judges, in name of the Lords States-General, condemn the prisoner to be taken to the Binnenhof, there to be executed with the sword that death may follow, and they declare all his property confiscated."

The execution was to take place so soon as the sentence had been read to the prisoner.

After the 1st May Barneveldt had not appeared before his judges. He had been examined in all about sixty times.

In the beginning of May his servant became impatient. "You must not be impatient," said his master.

"The time seems much longer because we get no news now from the outside. But the end will soon come. This delay cannot last forever."

Intimation reached him on Saturday the 11th May that the sentence was ready and would soon be pronounced.

"It is a bitter folk," said Barneveldt as he went to bed. "I have nothing good to expect of them." Next day was occupied in sewing up and concealing his papers, including a long account of his examination, with the questions and answers, in his Spanish arm-chair. Next day Van der Meulen said to the servant, "I will bet you a hundred florins you 'll not be here next Thursday."

The faithful John was delighted, not dreaming of the impending result.[1]

It was Sunday afternoon, 12th May, and about half-past five o'clock. Barneveldt sat in his prison-chamber, occupied as usual in writing, reviewing the history of the past, and doing his best to reduce into something like order the rambling and miscellaneous interrogatories out of which his trial had been concocted, while the points dwelt in his memory, and to draw up a concluding argument in his own defense. Work which according to any equitable, reasonable, or even decent procedure should have been intrusted to the first lawyers of the country—preparing the case upon the law and the facts with the documents before them, with the power of cross-questioning witnesses and sifting evidence, and enlightened by constant conferences with the illustrious prisoner himself—came entirely upon his own shoulders, enfeebled as he was by age, physical

[1] Leven en Sterven, 22.

illness, and by the exhaustion of a long imprisonment. Without books, notes of evidence, or even copies of the charges of which he stood accused, he was obliged to draw up his counter-arguments against the impeachment, and then by aid of a faithful valet to conceal his manuscripts behind the tapestry of the chamber, or cause them to be sewed up in the lining of his easy-chair, lest they should be taken from him by order of the judges who sat in the chamber below.

While he was thus occupied in preparations for his next encounter with the tribunal, the door opened, and three gentlemen entered. Two were the prosecuting officers of the government, Fiscal Sylla and Fiscal van Leeuwen. The other was the provost-marshal, Carel de Nijs. The servant was directed to leave the room.[1]

Barneveldt had stepped into his dressing-room on hearing footsteps, but came out again with his long furred gown about him as the three entered. He greeted them courteously and remained standing, with his hands placed on the back of his chair and with one knee resting carelessly against the arm of it. Van Leeuwen asked him if he would not rather be seated, as they brought a communication from the judges. He answered in the negative. Van Leeuwen then informed him that he was summoned to appear before the judges the next morning to hear his sentence of death.

"The sentence of death!" he exclaimed, without in the least changing his position; "the sentence of death! the sentence of death!" saying the words over thrice, with an air of astonishment rather than of horror. "I never expected that. I thought they were going to

---

[1] Waaragt. Hist., 399 seq.

hear my defense again. I had intended to make some change in my previous statements, having set some things down when beside myself with choler.''

He then made reference to his long services. Van Leeuwen expressed himself as well acquainted with them. ''He was sorry,'' he said, ''that his Lordship took this message ill of him.''

''I do not take it ill of you,'' said Barneveldt, ''but let them''—meaning the judges—''see how they will answer it before God. Are they thus to deal with a true patriot? Let me have pen, ink, and paper, that for the last time I may write farewell to my wife.''

''I will go ask permission of the judges,'' said Van Leeuwen, ''and I cannot think that my lord's request will be refused.''

While Van Leeuwen was absent, the advocate exclaimed, looking at the other legal officer:

''Oh, Sylla, Sylla, if your father could only have seen to what uses they would put you!''[1]

Sylla was silent.

Permission to write the letter was soon received from De Voogd, president of the commission. Pen, ink, and paper were brought, and the prisoner calmly sat down to write, without the slightest trace of discomposure upon his countenance or in any of his movements.

While he was writing, Sylla said with some authority: ''Beware, my lord, what you write, lest you put down something which may furnish cause for not delivering the letter.''

Barneveldt paused in his writing, took the glasses from his eyes, and looked Sylla in the face.

''Well, Sylla,'' he said very calmly, ''will you in

[1] Waaragt. Hist., 401.

these my last moments lay down the law to me as to what I shall write to my wife?"

He then added, with a half-smile: "Well, what is expected of me?"

"We have no commission whatever to lay down the law," said Van Leeuwen. "Your worship will write whatever you like."

While he was writing, Anthony Walaeus came in, a preacher and professor of Middelburg, a deputy to the Synod of Dordrecht, a learned and amiable man, sent by the States-General to minister to the prisoner on this supreme occasion, and not unworthy to be thus selected.[1]

The advocate, not knowing him, asked him why he came.

"I am not here without commission," said the clergyman. "I come to console my lord in his tribulation."

"I am a man," said Barneveldt, "have come to my present age, and I know how to console myself. I must write, and have now other things to do."

The preacher said that he would withdraw and return when his worship was at leisure.

"Do as you like," said the advocate, calmly going on with his writing.

When the letter was finished, it was sent to the judges for their inspection, by whom it was at once forwarded to the family mansion in the Voorhout, hardly a stone's throw from the prison-chamber.

Thus it ran:

"VERY DEARLY BELOVED WIFE, CHILDREN, SONS-IN-LAW, AND GRANDCHILDREN: I greet you all together

[1] Wagenaer, x.

most affectionately. I receive at this moment the very heavy and sorrowful tidings that I, an old man, for all my services done well and faithfully to the fatherland for so many years (after having performed all respectful and friendly offices to his Excellency the Prince with upright affection so far as my official duty and vocation would permit, shown friendship to many people of all sorts, and wittingly injured no man), must prepare myself to die to-morrow.

"I console myself in God the Lord, who knows all hearts, and who will judge all men. I beg you all together to do the same. I have steadily and faithfully served my lords the states of Holland and their nobles and cities. To the states of Utrecht, as sovereigns of my own fatherland, I have imparted at their request upright and faithful counsel, in order to save them from tumults of the populace, and from the bloodshed with which they have so long been threatened. I had the same views for the cities of Holland, in order that every one might be protected and no one injured.

"Live together in love and peace. Pray for me to Almighty God, who will graciously hold us all in his holy keeping.

"From my chamber of sorrow, the 12th May, 1619.

"Your very dear husband, father, father-in-law, and grandfather,

"JOHN OF BARNEVELDT." [1]

It was thought strange that the judges should permit so simple and clear a statement, an argument in itself, to be forwarded. The theory of his condemnation was to rest before the public on his confessions of

[1] Waaragt. Hist., 404.

guilt, and here in the instant of learning the nature of
the sentence in a few hours to be pronounced upon him
he had in a few telling periods declared his entire innocence.   Nevertheless, the letter had been sent at once to
its address.

So soon as this sad business had been disposed of,
Anthony Walaeus returned.   The advocate apologized
to the preacher for his somewhat abrupt greeting on
his first appearance.   He was much occupied and did
not know him, he said, although he had often heard of
him.   He begged him, as well as the provost-marshal,
to join him at supper, which was soon brought.

Barneveldt ate with his usual appetite, conversed
cheerfully on various topics, and pledged the health of
each of his guests in a glass of beer.   Contrary to his
wont, he drank at that repast no wine.   After supper
he went out into the little antechamber and called his
servant, asking him how he had been faring.   Now,
John Franken had just heard with grief unspeakable
the melancholy news of his master's condemnation
from two soldiers of the guard, who had been sent by
the judges to keep additional watch over the prisoner.
He was, however, as great a stoic as his master, and,
with no outward and superfluous manifestations of woe,
had simply implored the captain-at-arms, Van der
Meulen, to intercede with the judges that he might be
allowed to stay with his lord to the last.   Meantime he
had been expressly informed that he was to say nothing
to the advocate in secret, and that his master was
not to speak to him in a low tone nor whisper in
his ear.[1]

When the advocate came out into the antechamber

---

[1] Waaragt. Hist., 405.

and, looking over his shoulder, saw the two soldiers, he at once lowered his voice.

"Hush! Speak low," he whispered; "this is too cruel." John then informed him of Van der Meulen's orders, and that the soldiers had also been instructed to look to it sharply that no word was exchanged between master and man except in a loud voice.

"Is it possible," said the advocate, "that so close an inspection is held over me in these last hours? Can I not speak a word or two in freedom? This is a needless mark of disrespect."

The soldiers begged him not to take their conduct amiss, as they were obliged strictly to obey orders.[1]

He returned to his chamber, sat down in his chair, and begged Walaeus to go on his behalf to Prince Maurice.

"Tell his Excellency," said he, "that I have always served him with upright affection so far as my office, duties, and principles permitted. If I, in the discharge of my oath and official functions, have ever done anything contrary to his views, I hope that he will forgive it, and that he will hold my children in his gracious favor."

It was then ten o'clock. The preacher went downstairs and crossed the courtyard to the stadholder's apartments, where he at once gained admittance.

Maurice heard the message with tears in his eyes, assuring Walaeus that he felt deeply for the advocate's misfortunes. He had always had much affection for him, he said, and had often warned him against his mistaken courses. Two things, however, had always excited his indignation. One was that Barneveldt had

[1] Waaragt. Hist., 405.

accused him of aspiring to sovereignty; the other, that he had placed him in such danger at Utrecht. Yet he forgave him all. As regarded his sons, so long as they behaved themselves well they might rely on his favor.

As Walaeus was about to leave the apartment, the prince called him back.

"Did he say anything of a pardon?" he asked, with some eagerness.

"My lord," answered the clergyman, "I cannot with truth say that I understood him to make any allusion to it." [1]

Walaeus returned immediately to the prison-chamber and made his report of the interview. He was unwilling, however, to state the particulars of the offense which Maurice declared himself to have taken at the acts of the advocate.

But as the prisoner insisted upon knowing, the clergyman repeated the whole conversation.

"His Excellency has been deceived in regard to the Utrecht business," said Barneveldt, "especially as to one point. But it is true that I had fear and apprehension that he aspired to the sovereignty or to more authority in the country. Ever since the year 1600 I have felt this fear and have tried that these apprehensions might be rightly understood."

While Walaeus had been absent, the Rev. Jean la Motte (or Lamotius) and another clergyman of The Hague had come to the prisoner's apartment. La Motte could not look upon the advocate's face without weeping,[2] but the others were more collected. Conversation now ensued among the four, the preachers wish-

---

[1] Waaragt. Hist., 406.   [2] Ibid.

ing to turn the doomed statesman's thought to the consolations of religion.

But it was characteristic of the old lawyer's frame of mind that even now he looked at the tragical position in which he found himself from a constitutional and controversial point of view. He was perfectly calm and undaunted at the awful fate so suddenly and unexpectedly opened before his eyes, but he was indignant at what he esteemed the ignorance, injustice, and stupidity of the sentence to be pronounced against him.

"I am ready enough to die," he said to the three clergymen, "but I cannot comprehend why I am to die. I have done nothing except in obedience to the laws and privileges of the land and according to my oath, honor, and conscience.

"These judges," he continued, "come in a time when other maxims prevail in the state than those of my day. They have no right, therefore, to sit in judgment upon me." [1]

The clergymen replied that the twenty-four judges who had tried the case were no children and were conscientious men; that it was no small thing to condemn a man, and that they would have to answer it before the Supreme Judge of all.

"I console myself," he answered, "in the Lord my God, who knows all hearts and shall judge all men. God is just.

"They have not dealt with me," he continued, "as

[1] Baudartius, xi. 55.

This observation having been subsequently reported to the stadholder in presence of Count Louis William, Maurice observed that Barneveldt did not find those maxims of his prevailing in the state, but tried to introduce them there, and that their adoption would have caused the ruin of the church and the country. (Ibid.)

according to law and justice they were bound to deal.
They have taken away from me my own sovereign lords
and masters and deposed them. To them alone I was
responsible. In their place they have put many of my
enemies who were never before in the government, and
almost all of whom are young men who have not seen
much or read much. I have seen and read much, and
know that from such examples no good can follow.
After my death they will learn for the first time what
governing means.[1]

"The twenty-four judges are nearly all of them my
enemies. What they have reproached me with, I have
been obliged to hear. I have appealed against these
judges, but it has been of no avail. They have examined me in piecemeal, not in statesmanlike fashion.
The proceedings against me have been much too hard.
I have frequently requested to see the notes of my examination as it proceeded, and to confer upon it with aid
and counsel of friends, as would be the case in all lands
governed by law. The request was refused. During
this long and wearisome affliction and misery I have
not once been allowed to speak to my wife and children.
These are indecent proceedings against a man seventy-
two years of age, who has served his country faithfully
for three-and-forty years. I bore arms with the volun-
teers at my own charges at the siege of Haarlem and
barely escaped with life."[2]

It was not unnatural that the aged statesman's
thoughts should revert in this supreme moment to the
heroic scenes in which he had been an actor almost a
half-century before. He could not but think with bitterness of those long-past but never-forgotten days

[1] Waaragt. Hist., 408, 409.   [2] Ibid.

when he, with other patriotic youths, had faced the
terrible legions of Alva in defense of the fatherland,
at a time when the men who were now dooming him to
a traitor's death were unborn, and who, but for his
labors, courage, wisdom, and sacrifices, might have
never had a fatherland to serve, or a judgment-seat on
which to pronounce his condemnation.

Not in a spirit of fretfulness, but with disdainful
calm, he criticized and censured the proceedings against
himself as a violation of the laws of the land and of the
first principles of justice, discussing them as lucidly
and steadily as if they had been against a third
person.

The preachers listened, but had nothing to say.
They knew not of such matters, they said, and had no
instructions to speak of them. They had been sent to
call him to repentance for his open and hidden sins
and to offer the consolations of religion.

"I know that very well," he said, "but I, too, have
something to say notwithstanding." The conversation
then turned upon religious topics, and the preachers
spoke of predestination.

"I have never been able to believe in the matter of
high predestination," said the advocate. "I have left
it in the hands of God the Lord. I hold that a good
Christian man must believe that he through God's
grace and by the expiation of his sin through our Redeemer Jesus Christ is predestined to be saved, and
that this belief in his salvation, founded alone on God's
grace and the merits of our Redeemer Jesus Christ,
comes to him through the same grace of God. And if
he falls into great sins, his firm hope and confidence
must be that the Lord God will not allow him to con-

tinue in them, but that, through prayer for grace and repentance, he will be converted from evil and remain in the faith to the end of his life."[1]

These feelings, he said, he had expressed fifty-two years before to three eminent professors of theology in whom he confided, and they had assured him that he might tranquilly continue in such belief without examining further. "And this has always been my creed," he said.

The preachers replied that faith is a gift of God and not given to all men, that it must be given out of heaven to a man before he could be saved. Hereupon they began to dispute, and the advocate spoke so earnestly and well that the clergymen were astonished and sat for a time listening to him in silence.[2]

He asked afterward about the synod, and was informed that its decrees had not yet been promulgated, but that the Remonstrants had been condemned.

"It is a pity," said he. "One is trying to act on the old papal system, but it will never do. Things have gone too far. As to the synod, if my lords the states of Holland had been heeded there would have been first a provincial synod and then a national one. But," he added, looking the preachers in the face, "had you been more gentle with each other, matters would not have taken so high a turn. But you have been too fierce one against the other, too full of bitter party spirit."[3]

They replied that it was impossible for them to act against their conscience and the supreme authority. And then they asked him if there was nothing that troubled him in his conscience in the matters for which

---

[1] Waaragt. Hist., 409, 410.   [2] Ibid.   [3] Ibid.

he must die; nothing for which he repented and sorrowed, and for which he would call upon God for mercy.

"This I know well," he said, "that I have never willingly done wrong to any man. People have been ransacking my letters to Caron—confidential ones written several years ago to an old friend when I was troubled and seeking for counsel and consolation. It is hard that matter of impeachment against me to-day should be sought for thus."

And then he fell into political discourse again on the subject of the wartgelders and the state rights, and the villainous pasquils and libels that had circulated so long through the country.

"I have sometimes spoken hastily, I confess," he said; "but that was when I was stung by the daily swarm of infamous and loathsome pamphlets, especially those directed against my sovereign masters the states of Holland. That I could not bear. Old men cannot well brush such things aside. All that was directly aimed at me in particular I endeavored to overcome with such patience as I could muster. The disunion and mutual enmity in the country have wounded me to the heart. I have made use of all means in my power to accommodate matters, to effect with all gentleness a mutual reconciliation. I have always felt a fear lest the enemy should make use of our internal dissensions to strike a blow against us. I can say with perfect truth that ever since the year '77 I have been as resolutely and unchangeably opposed to the Spaniards and their adherents, and their pretensions over these provinces, as any man in the world, no one excepted, and as ready to sacrifice property and shed my

blood in defense of the fatherland. I have been so
devoted to the service of the country that I have not
been able to take the necessary care of my own private
affairs.'' [1]

So spoke the great statesman in the seclusion of his
prison, in the presence of those clergymen whom he
respected, at a supreme moment, when, if ever, a man
might be expected to tell the truth. And his whole life,
which belonged to history and had been passed on the
world's stage before the eyes of two generations of spectators, was a demonstration of the truth of his words.

But Burgomaster van Berk knew better. Had he
not informed the twenty-four commissioners that,
twelve years before, the advocate wished to subject the
country to Spain, and that Spinola had drawn a bill
of exchange for one hundred thousand ducats as a
compensation for his efforts?

It was eleven o'clock. Barneveldt requested one of
the brethren to say an evening prayer. This was done
by La Motte, and they were then requested to return by
three or four o'clock next morning. They had been directed, they said, to remain with him all night. ''That
is unnecessary,'' said the advocate, and they retired.

His servant then helped his master to undress, and he
went to bed as usual. Taking off his signet-ring, he
gave it to John Franken.

''For my eldest son,'' he said.

The valet sat down at the head of his bed in order
that his master might speak to him before he slept.
But the soldiers ordered him away and compelled him
to sit in a distant part of the room.

An hour after midnight, the advocate having been

[1] Waaragt. Hist., 410–413.

unable to lose himself, his servant observed that Isaac, one of the soldiers, was fast asleep. He begged the other, Tilman Schenk by name, to permit him some private words with his master. He had probably last messages, he thought, to send to his wife and children, and the eldest son, M. de Groeneveld, would no doubt reward him well for it. But the soldier was obstinate in obedience to the orders of the judges.

Barneveldt, finding it impossible to sleep, asked his servant to read to him from the Prayer-book. The soldier called in a clergyman, however, another one named Hugo Bayerus, who had been sent to the prison, and who now read to him the Consolations of the Sick. As he read, he made exhortations and expositions, which led to animated discussion, in which the advocate expressed himself with so much fervor and eloquence that all present were astonished, and the preacher sat mute a half-hour long at the bedside.

"Had there been ten clergymen," said the simple-hearted sentry to the valet, "your master would have enough to say to all of them." [1]

Barneveldt asked where the place had been prepared in which he was to die.

"In front of the great hall, as I understand," said Bayerus; "but I don't know the localities well, having lived here but little."

"Have you heard whether my Grotius is to die, and Hoogerbeets also?" he asked. [2]

"I have heard nothing to that effect," replied the clergyman.

"I should most deeply grieve for those two gentlemen," said Barneveldt, "were that the case. They

[1] Waaragt. Hist., 414, 415.   [2] Ibid. Wagenaer, x. 362.

may yet live to do the land great service. That great rising light, De Groot, is still young, but a very wise and learned gentleman, devoted to his fatherland with all zeal, heart, and soul, and ready to stand up for her privileges, laws, and rights. As for me, I am an old and worn-out man. I can do no more. I have already done more than I was really able to do. I have worked so zealously in public matters that I have neglected my private business. I had expressly ordered my house at Loosduinen [a villa by the seaside] to be got ready, that I might establish myself there and put my affairs in order. I have repeatedly asked the states of Holland for my discharge, but could never obtain it. It seems that the Almighty had otherwise disposed of me.''

He then said he would try once more if he could sleep. The clergyman and the servant withdrew for an hour, but his attempt was unsuccessful. After an hour he called for his French Psalm-book and read in it for some time. Sometime after two o'clock the clergymen came in again and conversed with him. They asked him if he had slept, if he hoped to meet Christ, and if there was anything that troubled his conscience.

''I have not slept, but am perfectly tranquil,'' he replied. ''I am ready to die, but cannot comprehend why I must die. I wish from my heart that, through my death and my blood, all disunion and discord in this land may cease.''

He bade them carry his last greetings to his fellow-prisoners. ''Say farewell for me to my good Grotius,'' said he, ''and tell him that I must die.'' [1]

[1] K. Brandt, Leven van de Groot, 196, from MS. annotations of William de Groot on the Waaragt. Historie van Oldenbarneveld.

The clergymen then left him, intending to return between five and six o'clock.

He remained quiet for a little while and then ordered his valet to cut open the front of his shirt. When this was done, he said, "John, are you to stay by me to the last?"

"Yes," he replied, "if the judges permit it."

"Remind me to send one of the clergymen to the judges with the request," said his master.

The faithful John, than whom no servant or friend could be more devoted, seized the occasion, with the thrift and stoicism of a true Hollander, to suggest that his lord might at the same time make some testamentary disposition in his favor.

"Tell my wife and children," said the advocate, "that they must console each other in mutual love and union. Say that through God's grace I am perfectly at ease, and hope that they will be equally tranquil. Tell my children that I trust they will be loving and friendly to their mother during the short time she has yet to live. Say that I wish to recommend you to them, that they may help you to a good situation either with themselves or with others. Tell them that this was my last request."

He bade him further to communicate to the family the messages sent that night through Walaeus by the stadholder.

The valet begged his master to repeat these instructions in presence of the clergymen, or to request one of them to convey them himself to the family. He promised to do so.

"As long as I live," said the grateful servant, "I shall remember your Lordship in my prayers."

"No, John," said the advocate; "that is popish. When I am dead, it is all over with prayers. Pray for me while I still live. Now is the time to pray. When one is dead, one should no longer be prayed for." [1]

La Motte came in. Barneveldt repeated his last wishes exactly as he desired them to be communicated to his wife and children. The preacher made no response. "Will you take the message?" asked the prisoner. La Motte nodded, but did not speak, nor did he subsequently fulfil the request.

Before five o'clock the servant heard the bell ring in the apartment of the judges, directly below the prison-chamber, and told his master he had understood that they were to assemble at five o'clock.

"I may as well get up, then," said the advocate; "they mean to begin early, I suppose. Give me my doublet and but one pair of stockings."

He was accustomed to wear two or three pairs at a time.

He took off his under-waistcoat, saying that the silver box which was in one of the pockets was to be taken to his wife, and that the servant should keep the loose money there for himself. Then he found an opportunity to whisper to him, "Take good care of the papers which are in the apartment." He meant the elaborate writings which he had prepared during his imprisonment and concealed in the tapestry and within the linings of the chair.

As his valet handed him the combs and brushes, he said, with a smile, "John, this is for the last time."

When he was dressed, he tried, in rehearsal of the

[1] Waaragt. Hist., 417.

approaching scene, to pull over his eyes the silk skull-cap which he usually wore under his hat. Finding it too tight, he told the valet to put the nightcap in his pocket and give it him when he should call for it. He then swallowed a half-glass of wine with a strengthening cordial in it, which he was wont to take.

The clergymen then reëntered, and asked if he had been able to sleep. He answered no, but that he had been much consoled by many noble things which he had been reading in the French Psalm-book. The clergymen said that they had been thinking much of the beautiful confession of faith which he had made to them that evening. They rejoiced at it, they said, on his account, and had never thought it of him. He said that such had always been his creed.[1]

At his request Walaeus now offered a morning prayer. Barneveldt fell on his knees and prayed inwardly, without uttering a sound. La Motte asked when he had concluded, "Did my lord say Amen?" "Yes, Lamotius," he replied. "Amen." "Has either of the brethren," he added, "prepared a prayer to be offered outside there?"

La Motte informed him that this duty had been confided to him. Some passages from Isaiah were now read aloud, and soon afterward Walaeus was sent for to speak with the judges. He came back and said to the prisoner, "Has my lord any desire to speak with his wife or children, or any of his friends?" It was then six o'clock, and Barneveldt replied: "No; the time is drawing near. It would excite a new emotion." Walaeus went back to the judges with this answer, who thereupon made this official report:

[1] Waaragt. Hist., 418.

"The husband and father of the petitioners, being asked if he desired that any of the petitioners should come to him, declared that he did not approve of it, saying that it would cause too great an emotion for himself as well as for them. This is to serve as an answer to the petitioners." [1]

Now, the advocate knew nothing of the petition. Up to the last moment his family had been sanguine as to his ultimate acquittal and release. They relied on a promise which they had received, or imagined that they had received, from the stadholder that no harm should come to the prisoner in consequence of the arrest made of his person in the prince's apartments on the 8th August. They had opened this tragical month of May with flagstaffs and flower-garlands, and were making daily preparations to receive back the revered statesman in triumph.

The letter written by him from his "chamber of sorrow," late in the evening of 12th May, had at last dispelled every illusion. It would be idle to attempt to paint the grief and consternation into which the household in the Voorhout was plunged, from the venerable dame at its head, surrounded by her sons and daughters and children's children, down to the humblest servant in their employment. For all revered and loved the austere statesman, but simple and benignant father and master.

No heed had been taken of the three elaborate and argumentative petitions which, prepared by learned counsel in name of the relatives, had been addressed to the judges. They had not been answered because they were difficult to answer, and because it was not in-

---

[1] Waaragt. Hist., 421.

tended that the accused should have the benefit of counsel.

An urgent and last appeal was now written late at night, and signed by each member of the family, to his Excellency the Prince and the judge commissioners, to this effect:

"The afflicted wife and children of M. van Barneveldt humbly show that, having heard the sorrowful tidings of his coming execution, they humbly beg that it may be granted them to see and speak to him for the last time."[1]

The two sons delivered this petition at four o'clock in the morning into the hands of De Voogd, one of the judges. It was duly laid before the commission, but the prisoner was never informed, when declining a last interview with his family, how urgently they had themselves solicited the boon.

Louise de Coligny, on hearing late at night the awful news, had been struck with grief and horror. She endeavored, late as it was, to do something to avert the doom of one she so much revered, the man on whom her illustrious husband had leaned his life long as on a staff of iron. She besought an interview of the stadholder, but it was refused.[2] The wife of William the Silent had no influence at that dire moment with her stepson. She was informed at first that Maurice was asleep, and at four in the morning that all intervention was useless.

The faithful and energetic Du Maurier, who had already exhausted himself in efforts to save the life of the great prisoner, now made a last appeal. He, too, heard at four o'clock in the morning of the 13th that

---

[1] Waaragt. Hist., 419, 420.   [2] Wagenaer, x. 362, 363.

LOUIZE DE COLIGNY,
Prinsesse Weduwe van Oranje.

LOUISE DE COLIGNY.
After a contemporaneous engraving, reëngraved by Houbracken.

sentence of death was to be pronounced. Before five o'clock he made urgent application to be heard before the assembly of the States-General as ambassador of a friendly sovereign who took the deepest interest in the welfare of the Republic and the fate of its illustrious statesman. The appeal was refused. As a last resource he drew up an earnest and eloquent letter to the States-General, urging clemency in the name of his king. It was of no avail. The letter may still be seen in the Royal Archives at The Hague, drawn up entirely in Du Maurier's clear and beautiful handwriting. Although possibly a first draft, written as it was under such a mortal pressure for time, its pages have not one erasure or correction.[1]

It was seven o'clock. Barneveldt, having observed by the preacher La Motte's manner that he was not likely to convey the last messages which he had mentioned to his wife and children, sent a request to the judges to be allowed to write one more letter. Captain van der Meulen came back with the permission, saying he would wait and take it to the judges for their revision.

"Must they see this too? Why, it is only a line in favor of John," said the prisoner, sitting quietly down to write this letter:

"VERY DEAR WIFE AND CHILDREN: It is going to an end with me. I am, through the grace of God, very tranquil. I hope that you are equally so, and that you may by mutual love, union, and peace help each other to overcome all things, which I pray to the Omnipo-

---

[1] The letter has been often published; in the Waaragt. Hist., for instance, 423–426.

tent as my last request. John Franken has served me faithfully for many years and throughout all these my afflictions, and is to remain with me to the end. He deserves to be recommended to you and to be furthered to good employments with you or with others. I request you herewith to see to this.

"I have requested his Princely Excellency to hold my sons and children in his favor, to which he has answered that so long as you conduct yourselves well this shall be the case. I recommend this to you in the best form and give you all into God's holy keeping. Kiss each other and all my grandchildren for the last time in my name, and fare you well. Out of the chamber of sorrow, 13th May, 1619. Your dear husband and father,   JOHN OF BARNEVELDT.

"P. S. You will make John Franken a present in memory of me."[1]

Certainly it would be difficult to find a more truly calm, courageous, or religious spirit than that manifested by this aged statesman at an hour when, if ever, a human soul is tried and is apt to reveal its innermost depths or shallows. Whatever Gomarus, or Bogerman, or the whole council of Dordrecht may have thought of his theology, it had at least taught him forgiveness of his enemies, kindness to his friends, and submission to the will of the Omnipotent. Every moment of his last days on earth had been watched and jealously scrutinized, and his bitterest enemies had failed to discover one trace of frailty, one manifestation of any vacillating, ignoble, or malignant sentiment.

[1] Waaragt. Hist., 428, 429,

The drums had been sounding through the quiet but anxiously expectant town since four o'clock that morning, and the tramp of soldiers marching to the Inner Court had long been audible in the prison-chamber.

Walaeus now came back with a message from the judges. "The high commissioners," he said, "think it is beginning. Will my lord please to prepare himself?"

"Very well, very well," said the prisoner. "Shall we go at once?"

But Walaeus suggested a prayer. Upon its conclusion, Barneveldt gave his hand to the provost-marshal and to the two soldiers, bidding them adieu, and walked down-stairs, attended by them, to the chamber of the judges. As soon as he appeared at the door, he was informed that there had been a misunderstanding, and he was requested to wait a little. He accordingly went up-stairs again with perfect calmness, sat down in his chamber again, and read in his French Psalm-book.[1] Half an hour later he was once more summoned, the provost-marshal and Captain van der Meulen reappearing to escort him. "Mr. Provost," said the prisoner, as they went down the narrow staircase, "I have always been a good friend to you." "It is true," replied that officer, "and most deeply do I grieve to see you in this affliction."

He was about to enter the judges' chamber as usual, but was informed that the sentence would be read in the great hall of judicature. They descended accordingly to the basement story, and passed down the narrow flight of steps which then, as now, connected the more modern structure, where the advocate had been

[1] Waaragt. Hist., 431.

imprisoned and tried, with what remained of the ancient palace of the counts of Holland. In the center of the vast hall—once the banqueting-chamber of those petty sovereigns, with its high, vaulted roof of cedar, which had so often in ancient days rung with the sounds of mirth and revelry—was a great table at which the twenty-four judges and the three prosecuting officers were seated, in their black caps and gowns of office. The room was lined with soldiers and crowded with a dark, surging mass of spectators, who had been waiting there all night.

A chair was placed for the prisoner. He sat down, and the clerk of the commission, Pots by name, proceeded at once to read the sentence.[1] A summary of this long, rambling, and tiresome paper has been already laid before the reader. If ever a man could have found it tedious to listen to his own death-sentence, the great statesman might have been in that condition as he listened to Secretary Pots.

During the reading of the sentence the advocate moved uneasily on his seat, and seemed about to interrupt the clerk at several passages which seemed to him especially preposterous. But he controlled himself by a strong effort, and the clerk went steadily on to the conclusion.

Then Barneveldt said:

"The judges have put down many things which they have no right to draw from my confession. Let this protest be added.

"I thought, too," he continued, "that my lords the States-General would have had enough in my life and blood, and that my wife and children might keep what

---

[1] Waaragt. Hist., 421 and 442–466.

belongs to them. Is this my recompense for forty-three years' service to these provinces?''

President de Voogd rose.

''Your sentence has been pronounced,'' he said. ''Away, away!'' So saying, he pointed to the door into which one of the great windows at the southeastern front of the hall had been converted.[1]

Without another word the old man rose from his chair and strode, leaning on his staff, across the hall, accompanied by his faithful valet and the provost, and escorted by a file of soldiers. The mob of spectators flowed out after him at every door into the inner court-yard in front of the ancient palace.

[1] Waaragt. Hist., 432.   Wagenaer, x. 366.

CHAPTER XXI

Barneveldt's execution—The advocate's conduct on the scaffold—
The sentence printed and sent to the provinces—The proceedings
irregular and inequitable.

In the beautiful village capital of the "Count's Park,"
commonly called The Hague, the most striking and pic-
turesque spot then, as now, was that where the transformed remains of the old moated castle of those feudal
sovereigns were still to be seen. A three-storied range
of simple, substantial buildings in brown brickwork,
picked out with white stone in a style since made familiar both in England and America, and associated with
a somewhat later epoch in the history of the house of
Orange, surrounded three sides of a spacious inner
paved quadrangle called the Inner Court, the fourth or
eastern side being overshadowed by a beechen grove.
A square tower flanked each angle, and on both sides
of the southwestern turret extended the commodious
apartments of the stadholder. The great gateway on
the southwest opened into a wide open space called the
Outer Courtyard. Along the northwest side a broad
and beautiful sheet of water, in which the walls, turrets, and chapel spires of the inclosed castle mirrored
themselves, was spread between the mass of buildings
and an umbrageous promenade called the Vyverberg,
consisting of a sextuple alley of lime-trees and embow-

ering here and there a stately villa. A small island,
fringed with weeping-willows and tufted all over with
lilacs, laburnums, and other shrubs then in full flower,
lay in the center of the miniature lake, and the tall,
solid tower of the Great Church, surmounted by a light
openwork spire, looked down from a little distance over
the scene.

It was a bright morning in May. The white swans
were sailing tranquilly to and fro over the silver basin,
and the mavis, blackbird, and nightingale, which
haunted the groves surrounding the castle and the
town, were singing as if the daybreak were ushering in
a summer festival.

But it was not to a merrymaking that the soldiers
were marching and the citizens thronging so eagerly
from every street and alley toward the castle. By four
o'clock the Outer and Inner courts had been lined with
detachments of the prince's guard and companies of
other regiments to the number of twelve hundred men.
Occupying the northeastern side of the court rose the
grim, time-worn front of the ancient hall, consisting
of one tall, pyramidal gable of ancient gray brickwork flanked with two tall, slender towers, the whole
with the lancet-shaped windows and severe style of the
twelfth century, excepting a rose-window in the center with the decorated mullions of a somewhat later
period.

In front of the lower window, with its Gothic archway hastily converted into a door, a shapeless platform
of rough, unhewn planks had that night been rudely
patched together. This was the scaffold. A slight
railing around it served to protect it from the crowd,
and a heap of coarse sand had been thrown upon it.

A squalid, unclean box of unplaned boards, originally prepared as a coffin for a Frenchman who some time before had been condemned to death for murdering the son of Goswyn Menskens, a Hague tavern-keeper, but pardoned by the stadholder, lay on the scaffold. It was recognized from having been left for a long time, half forgotten, at the public execution-place of The Hague.[1]

Upon this coffin now sat two common soldiers of ruffianly aspect, playing at dice, betting whether the Lord or the devil would get the soul of Barneveldt.[2] Many a foul and ribald jest at the expense of the prisoner was exchanged between these gamblers, some of their comrades, and a few townsmen who were grouped about at that early hour. The horrible libels, caricatures, and calumnies which had been circulated, exhibited, and sung in all the streets for so many months had at last thoroughly poisoned the minds of the vulgar against the fallen statesman.

The great mass of the spectators had forced their way by daybreak into the hall itself to hear the sentence, so that the Inner Courtyard had remained comparatively empty.

At last, at half-past nine o'clock, a shout arose, "There he comes! There he comes!"[3] and the populace flowed out from the hall of judgment into the courtyard like a tidal wave.

In an instant the Binnenhof was filled with more than three thousand spectators.

---

[1] Letter written May 13, 1619, by an eye-witness, Pr. Hanneman to his cousin, Abraham van der Bruggen, student at Leyden; printed in Waaragt. Hist., 433–437.

[2] Ibid.   [3] Ibid., 432.

The old statesman, leaning on his staff, walked out upon the scaffold and calmly surveyed the scene. Lifting his eyes to heaven, he was heard to murmur, "O God, what does man come to!" Then he said bitterly once more: "This, then, is the reward of forty years' service to the state!"

La Motte, who attended him, said fervently: "It is no longer time to think of this. Let us prepare your coming before God."

"Is there no cushion or stool to kneel upon?" said Barneveldt, looking around him.[1]

The provost said he would send for one, but the old man knelt at once on the bare planks. His servant, who waited upon him as calmly and composedly as if he had been serving him at dinner, held him by the arm. It was remarked that neither master nor man, true stoics and Hollanders both, shed a single tear upon the scaffold.[2]

La Motte prayed for a quarter of an hour, the advocate remaining on his knees.

He then rose and said to John Franken, "See that he does not come near me," pointing to the executioner, who stood in the background grasping his long double-handed sword. Barneveldt then rapidly unbuttoned his doublet with his own hands, and the valet helped him off with it. "Make haste! Make haste!" said his master.

The statesman then came forward and said in a loud, firm voice to the people:

"Men, do not believe that I am a traitor to the coun-

[1] Remark of an eye-witness in a broadsheet account of the execution published on the following day.

[2] Waaragt. Hist., 432, 433.

try.   I have ever acted uprightly and loyally as a good patriot, and as such I shall die.''

The crowd was perfectly silent.

He then took his cap from John Franken, drew it over his eyes, and went forward toward the sand, saying:

''Christ shall be my guide.   O Lord, my heavenly Father, receive my spirit.''

As he was about to kneel with his face to the south, the provost said:

''My lord will be pleased to move to the other side, not where the sun is in his face.''

He knelt accordingly with his face toward his own house.   The servant took farewell of him, and Barneveldt said to the executioner:

''Be quick about it.   Be quick.''

The executioner then struck his head off at a single blow.

Many persons from the crowd now sprang, in spite of all opposition, upon the scaffold and dipped their handkerchiefs in his blood, cut wet splinters from the boards, or grubbed up the sand that was steeped in it; driving many bargains afterward for these relics, to be treasured with various feelings of sorrow, joy, glutted or expiated vengeance.

It has been recorded, and has been constantly repeated to this day, that the stadholder, whose windows exactly faced the scaffold, looked out upon the execution with a spy-glass, saying as he did so:

''See the old scoundrel, how he trembles!   He is afraid of the stroke.'' [1]

[1] Wagenaer, x. 367;   Cl. Sarravii Epist., 196 ; Brandt, Rechtspl., 213 ; and many engravings and broadsheets of the period.   See also Vondel's tragedy of Palamedes.

But this is calumny. Colonel Hauterive declared that he was with Maurice in his cabinet during the whole period of the execution, that by order of the prince all the windows and shutters were kept closed, that no person wearing his livery was allowed to be abroad, that he anxiously received messages as to the proceedings, and heard of the final catastrophe with sorrowful emotion.[1]

It must be admitted, however, that the letter which Maurice wrote on the same morning to his cousin Louis William does not show much pathos.

"After the judges," he said, "have been busy here with the sentence against the Advocate Barneveldt for several days, at last it has been pronounced, and this morning, between nine o'clock and half-past, carried into execution with the sword, in the Binnenhof before the great hall.

"The reasons they had for this you will see from the sentence, which will doubtless be printed, and which I will send you.

"The wife of the aforesaid Barneveldt and also some of his sons and sons-in-law or other friends have never presented any supplication for his pardon, but till now have vehemently demanded that law and justice should be done to him, and have daily let the report run through the people that he would soon come out. They also planted a May-pole before their house adorned with garlands and ribbons, and practised other jollities and impertinences, while they ought to have conducted themselves in a humble and lowly fashion. This is no proper manner of behaving, and, moreover, not a

---

[1] Van der Kemp, iv. 129. Da Costa, Karakt. van Prins Maurits, 80.

practical one to move the judges to any favor, even
if they had been thereto inclined."[1]

The sentence was printed and sent to the separate
provinces. It was accompanied by a declaration of the
States-General that they had received information
from the judges of various points, not mentioned in
the sentence, which had been laid to the charge of the
late advocate, and which gave much reason to doubt
whether he had not perhaps turned his eyes toward the
enemy. They could not, however, legally give judgment to that effect without a sharper investigation,
which on account of his great age and for other reasons it was thought best to spare him.[2]

A meaner or more malignant postscript to a state
paper recounting the issue of a great trial it would be
difficult to imagine. The first statesman of the country had just been condemned and executed on a narrative, without indictment of any specified crime. And
now, by a kind of apologetic afterthought, six or eight
individuals calling themselves the States-General in-
sinuated that he had been looking toward the enemy,
and that, had they not mercifully spared him the rack,
which is all that could be meant by their "sharper
investigation," he would probably have confessed the
charge.

And thus the dead man's fame was blackened by
those who had not hesitated to kill him, but had shrunk
from inquiring into his alleged crime.

Not entirely without semblance of truth did Grotius
subsequently say that the men who had taken his life
would hardly have abstained from torturing him if

[1] Groen van Prinsterer, Archives de la Maison d'Orange.
[2] Wagenaer, x. 368, 369.

they had really hoped by so doing to extract from him
a confession of treason.[1]

The sentence was sent likewise to France, accompanied with a statement that Barneveldt had been
guilty of unpardonable crimes which had not been set
down in the act of condemnation.[2] Complaints were
also made of the conduct of Du Maurier in thrusting
himself into the internal affairs of the states and taking sides so ostentatiously against the government.
The king and his ministers were indignant with these
rebukes, and sustained the ambassador. Jeannin and
De Boississe expressed the opinion that he had died
innocent of any crime, and only by reason of his strong
political opposition to the prince.[3]

The judges had been unanimous in finding him guilty
of the acts recorded in their narrative, but three of
them had held out for some time in favor of a sentence
of perpetual imprisonment rather than decapitation.

They withdrew at last their opposition to the death-
penalty for the wonderful reason that reports had been
circulated of attempts likely to be made to assassinate
Prince Maurice. The stadholder himself treated these
rumors and the consequent admonition of the States-
General that he would take more than usual precautions for his safety with perfect indifference, but they
were conclusive with the judges of Barneveldt.[4]

"Respublica poscit exemplum," said Commissioner
Junius, one of the three, as he sided with the death-
warrant party.[5]

[1] Wagenaer, x. 368, 369. Grotius, Verantw., cap. xx. 289.

[2] Wagenaer, ubi sup.   [3] Ibid. Uytenbog. Leven, xv. 309 seq.

[4] Van der Kemp, iv. 123. Resol. St.-Gen., April 23 and May 9,
1619, in Van der Kemp, iv. 305, 306.

[5] Van der Kemp, ubi sup.

The same Dr. Junius a year afterward happened to dine, in company of one of his fellow-commissioners, with Attorney-General Sylla at Utrecht, and took occasion to ask them why it was supposed that Barneveldt had been hanging his head toward Spain, as not one word of that stood in the sentence.

The question was ingenuous on the part of one learned judge to his colleagues in one of the most famous state trials of history, propounded as a bit of after-dinner casuistry, when the victim had been more than a year in his grave.

But perhaps the answer was still more artless. His brother lawyers replied that the charge was easily to be deduced from the sentence, because a man who breaks up the foundation of the state makes the country indefensible, and therefore invites the enemy to invade it. And this Barneveldt had done, who had turned the Union, religion, alliances, and finances upside down by his proceedings.[1]

Certainly if every constitutional minister accused by the opposition party of turning things upside down by his proceedings were assumed to be guilty of deliberately inviting a hostile invasion of his country, there would have been few from that day to this to escape hanging.

Constructive treason could scarcely go further than it was made to do in these attempts to prove, after his death, that the advocate had, as it was euphuistically expressed, been looking toward the enemy.

And no better demonstrations than these have ever been discovered.

[1] Van der Kemp, iv. 305, citing a letter of William de Groot in Vollenhoven Broed Gevankenis, 109,

He died at the age of seventy-one years seven months and eighteen days.[1]

His body and head were huddled into the box upon which the soldiers had been shaking the dice, and this was placed that night in the vault of the chapel in the Inner Court.

It was subsequently granted as a boon to the widow and children that it might be taken thence and decently buried in the family vault at Amersfoort.

On the day of the execution a formal entry was made in the register of the states of Holland:

"Monday, 13th May, 1619. To-day was executed with the sword here in The Hague, on a scaffold thereto erected in the Binnenhof before the steps of the great hall, Mr. John of Barneveldt, in his life Knight, Lord of Berkel, Rodenrys, etc., Advocate of Holland and West Friesland, for reasons expressed in the sentence and otherwise, with confiscation of his property, after he had served the state thirty-three years two months and five days since 8th March, 1586; a man of great activity, business, memory, and wisdom—yes, extraordinary in every respect. He that stands let him see that he does not fall, and may God be merciful to his soul. Amen."[2]

A year later, on application made by the widow and children of the deceased to compound for the confiscation of his property by payment of a certain sum, eighty florins or a similar trifle, according to an ancient privilege of the order of nobility, the question was raised whether he had been guilty of high treason, as he had not been sentenced for such a crime, and as it was

---

[1] Wagenaer, x. 367. Brandt, Rechtspl., 179–184.
[2] Resol. Holl., May 13, 1619, 102.

only in case of sentence for lese-majesty that this composition was disallowed. It was deemed proper, therefore, to ask the court for what crime the prisoner had been condemned. Certainly a more sarcastic question could not have been asked. But the court had ceased to exist. The commission had done its work and was dissolved. Some of its members were dead. Letters, however, were addressed by the States-General to the individual commissioners requesting them to assemble at The Hague for the purpose of stating whether it was because the prisoner had committed lese-majesty that his property had been confiscated. They never assembled. Some of them were perhaps ignorant of the exact nature of that crime. Several of them did not understand the words. Twelve of them, among whom were a few jurists, sent written answers to the question proposed. The question was, "Did you confiscate the property because the crime was lese-majesty?" The reply was, "The crime was lese-majesty, although not so stated in the sentence, because we confiscated the property." In one of these remarkable documents this was stated to be "the unanimous opinion of almost all the judges."[1]

The point was referred to the commissioners, some of whom attended the court of The Hague in person, while others sent written opinions. All agreed that the criminal had committed high treason, because otherwise his property would not have been confiscated.[2]

[1] " . . . het einhellig gevoelen van meest alle den Heeren Rechteren."—MS. pieces belonging to the process of Barneveldt, Hague Archives.

[2] These written opinions of the ex-commissioners are among the MSS. belonging to the process of Barneveldt in the Hague Archives.

A more wonderful example of the argument in a circle was never heard of. Moreover, it is difficult to understand by what right the high commission, which had been dissolved a year before, after having completed its work, could be deemed competent to emit afterward a judicial decision. But the fact is curious as giving one more proof of the irregular, unphilosophical, and inequitable nature of these famous proceedings.

Two days after the execution of the advocate, judgment was pronounced upon Gillis van Ledenberg. It
would have been difficult to try him, or to extort a
confession of high treason from him by the rack or
otherwise, as the unfortunate gentleman had been dead
for more than seven months.

Not often has a court of justice pronounced a man
without trial to be guilty of a capital offense. Not
often has a dead man been condemned and executed.
But this was the lot of Secretary Ledenberg. He was
sentenced to be hanged, his property declared confiscated.

His unburied corpse, reduced to the condition of a
mummy, was brought out of its lurking-place, thrust
into a coffin, dragged on a hurdle to the Golgotha outside The Hague, on the road to Ryswyk, and there
hung on the gibbet in company of the bodies of other
malefactors swinging there in chains.[1]

His prudent scheme to save his property for his

[1] Wagenaer, x. 370. Baudartius, et mult. al.

children by committing suicide in prison was thus thwarted.

The reading of the sentence of Ledenberg, as had been previously the case with that of Barneveldt, had been heard by Grotius through the open window of his prison, as he lay on his bed.[1] The scaffold on which the advocate had suffered was left standing, three executioners were still in the town, and there was every reason for both Grotius and Hoogerbeets to expect a similar doom. Great efforts were made to induce the friends of the distinguished prisoners to sue for their pardon. But, even as in the case of the Barneveldt family, these attempts were fruitless. The austere stoicism both on the part of the sufferers and their relatives excites something like wonder.

Three of the judges went in person to the prison-chamber of Hoogerbeets, urging him to ask forgiveness himself or to allow his friends to demand it for him.

"If my wife and children do ask," he said, "I will protest against it. I need no pardon. Let justice take its course. Think not, gentlemen, that I mean by asking for pardon to justify your proceedings."

He stoutly refused to do either. The judges, astonished, took their departure, saying:

"Then you will fare as Barneveldt. The scaffold is still standing."

He expected consequently nothing but death, and said many years afterward that he knew from personal experience how a man feels who goes out of prison to be beheaded.[2]

The wife of Grotius sternly replied to urgent intima-

[1] K. Brandt, Leven van H. de Groot, 195.
[2] Wagenaer, x. 369, 370. Brandt, Rechtspl., 264.

tions from a high source that she should ask pardon
for her husband, "I shall not do it. If he has deserved it, let them strike off his head." [1]

Yet no woman could be more devoted to her husband
than was Maria van Reigersbergen to Hugo de Groot,
as time was to prove. The prince subsequently told
her at a personal interview that "one of two roads must
be taken, that of the law or that of pardon." [2]

Soon after the arrest it was rumored that Grotius
was ready to make important revelations if he could
first be assured of the prince's protection.

His friends were indignant at the statement. His
wife stoutly denied its truth, but, to make sure, wrote
to her husband on the subject.

"One thing amazes me," she said: "some people here
pretend to say that you have stated to one gentleman
in private that you have something to disclose greatly
important to the country, but that you desired beforehand to be taken under the protection of his Excellency. I have not chosen to believe this, nor do I, for I
hold that to be certain which you have already told me
—that you know no secrets. I see no reason, therefore, why you should require the protection of any
man. And there is no one to believe this, but I thought
best to write to you of it. Let me, in order that I may
contradict the story with more authority, have by the
bearer of this a simple yes or no. Study quietly, take
care of your health, have some days' patience, for the
advocate has not yet been heard."

The answer has not been preserved, but there is an
allusion to the subject in an unpublished memorandum
of Grotius written while he was in prison.

[1] K. Brandt, Leven, 196.   [2] Wagenaer, x. 370.

It must be confessed that the heart of the great theo-
logian and jurist seems to have somewhat failed him
after his arrest, and although he was incapable of
treachery—even if he had been possessed of any secrets,
which certainly was not the case—he did not show the
same Spartan firmness as his wife, and was very far
from possessing the heroic calm of Barneveldt. He
was much disposed to extricate himself from his unhappy plight by making humble, if not abject, submission to Maurice. He differed from his wife in thinking that he had no need of the prince's protection.
"I begged the chamberlain, Matthew de Cors," he said,
a few days after his arrest, "that I might be allowed to
speak with his Excellency of certain things which I
would not willingly trust to the pen. My meaning
was to leave all public employment and to offer my
service to his Excellency in his domestic affairs. Thus
I hoped that the motives for my imprisonment would
cease. This was afterward misinterpreted as if I had
had wonderful things to reveal." [1]

But Grotius toward the end of his trial showed still
greater weakness. After repeated refusals, he had at
last obtained permission of the judges to draw up in
writing the heads of his defense. To do this he was
allowed a single sheet of paper and four hours of time,
the trial having lasted several months. And in the
document thus prepared he showed faltering in his
faith as to his great friend's innocence, and admitted,
without any reason whatever, the possibility of there
being truth in some of the vile and anonymous calumnies against him.[2]

"The friendship of the advocate of Holland I had

[1] Brandt, Rechtspl. (second edition), 11.   [2] Ibid., 102.

always highly prized," he said, "hoping from the conversation of so wise and experienced a person to learn much that was good. . . . I firmly believed that his Excellency, notwithstanding occasional differences as to the conduct of public affairs, considered him a true and upright servant of the land. . . . I have been, therefore, surprised to understand, during my imprisonment, that the gentlemen had proofs in hand not alone of his correspondence with the enemy, but also of his having received money from them.

"He being thus accused, I have vindicated by word of mouth and afterward resumed in writing all matters which I thought—the above-mentioned proofs being made good—might be thereto indirectly referred, in order to show that for me no friendships were so dear as the preservation of the freedom of the land. I wish that he may give explanation of all to the contentment of the judges, and that therefore his actions—which, supposing the said correspondence to be true, are subject to a bad interpretation—may be taken in another sense."

Alas! could the advocate, among whose first words after hearing of his own condemnation to death were, "And must my Grotius die too?" adding, with a sigh of relief when assured of the contrary, "I should deeply grieve for that; he is so young and may live to do the state much service"—could he have read those faltering and ungenerous words from one he so held in his heart, he would have felt them like the stab of Brutus.

Grotius lived to know that there were no such proofs, that the judges did not dare even allude to the charge in their sentence, and long years afterward he drew a picture of the martyred patriot such as one might have expected from his pen.[1]

But these written words of doubt must have haunted him to his grave.

On the 18th May, 1619,—on the fifty-first anniversary, as Grotius remarked, of the condemnation of Egmont and Horn by the Blood-Tribunal of Alva,— the two remaining victims were summoned to receive their doom. The Fiscal Sylla, entering De Groot's chamber early in the morning to conduct him before the judges, informed him that he was not instructed to communicate the nature of the sentence. "But," he said maliciously, "you are aware of what has befallen the advocate."

"I have heard with my own ears," answered Grotius, "the judgment pronounced upon Barneveldt and upon Ledenberg. Whatever may be my fate, I have patience to bear it."[2]

The sentence, read in the same place and in the same manner as had been that upon the advocate, condemned both Hoogerbeets and Grotius to perpetual imprisonment.

The course of the trial and the enumeration of the offenses were nearly identical with the leading process which has been elaborately described.

Grotius made no remark whatever in the court-room. On returning to his chamber he observed that his admissions of facts had been tortured into confessions of guilt, that he had been tried and sentenced against all principles and forms of law, and that he had been deprived of what the humblest criminal could claim, the right of defense and the examination of testimony. In

[1] Brandt, Rechtspl., 185.   [2] K. Brandt, Leven, etc., 197.

regard to the penalty against him, he said, there was no such thing as perpetual imprisonment except in hell. Alluding to the leading cause of all these troubles, he observed that it was with the stadholder and the advocate as Cato had said of Cæsar and Pompey: the great misery had come, not from their being enemies, but from their having once been friends.[1]

On the night of 5th June the prisoners were taken from their prison in The Hague and conveyed to the castle of Loevenstein.

This fortress, destined thenceforth to be famous in history and, from its frequent use in after times as a state prison for men of similar constitutional views to those of Grotius and the advocate, to give its name to a political party, was a place of extraordinary strength. Nature and art had made it, according to military ideas of that age, almost impregnable. As a prison it seemed the very castle of despair. "Abandon all hope, ye who enter," seemed engraven over its portal.

Situate in the very narrow, acute angle where the broad, deep, and turbid Waal—the chief of the three branches into which the Rhine divides itself on entering the Netherlands—mingles its current with the silver Meuse, whose name it adopts as the united rivers roll to the sea, it was guarded on many sides by these deep and dangerous streams. On the land side it was surrounded by high walls and a double foss, which protected it against any hostile invasion from Brabant. As the Twelve Years' Truce was running to its close, it was certain that pains would be taken to strengthen the walls and deepen the ditches, that the place might be proof against all marauders and land-robbers likely

[1] K. Brandt, Leven, 211. See Verantw., 163.

to swarm over from the territory of the archdukes.
The town of Gorcum was exactly opposite on the northern side of the Waal, while Worcum was about a
league's distance from the castle on the southern side,
but separated from it by the Meuse.

The prisoners, after crossing the drawbridge, were
led through thirteen separate doors, each one secured
by iron bolts and heavy locks, until they reached their
separate apartments.

They were never to see or have any communication
with each other. It had been accorded by the States-
General, however, that the wives of the two gentlemen
were to have access to their prison, were to cook for
them in the castle kitchen, and, if they chose to inhabit
the fortress, might cross to the neighboring town of
Gorcum from time to time to make purchases, and even
make visits to The Hague. Twenty-four stivers, or
two shillings, a day were allowed by the States-General
for the support of each prisoner and his family.[1] As
the family property of Grotius was at once sequestered,
with a view to its ultimate confiscation, it was clear
that abject indigence as well as imprisonment was to
be the lifelong lot of this illustrious person, who had
hitherto lived in modest affluence, occupying the most
considerable of social positions.

The commandant of the fortress was inspired from
the outset with a desire to render the prisoner's situation as hateful as it was in his power to make it. And
much was in his power. He resolved that the family
should really live upon their daily pittance. Yet
Madame de Groot, before the final confiscation of her
own and her husband's estates, had been able to effect

[1] K. Brandt, Leven, 211.

considerable loans, both to carry on process against
government for what the prisoners contended was an
unjust confiscation, and for providing for the household on a decent scale and somewhat in accordance
with the requirements of the prisoner's health. Thus
there was a wearisome and ignoble altercation, revived
from day to day, between the commandant and Madame
de Groot. It might have been thought enough of torture for this virtuous and accomplished lady, but twenty-nine years of age and belonging to one of the eminent families of the country, to see her husband, for
his genius and accomplishments the wonder of Europe,
thus cut off in the flower of his age and doomed to a
living grave. She was nevertheless to be subjected to
the perpetual inquisition of the market-basket, which
she was not ashamed with her maid to take to and from
Gorcum, and to petty wrangles about the kitchen fire,
where she was proud to superintend the cooking of the
scanty fare for her husband and her five children.[1]

There was a reason for the spite of the military
jailer. Lieutenant Proninck, called Deventer, commandant of Loevenstein, was son of the notorious Ge-
rard Proninck, formerly burgomaster of Utrecht, one
of the ringleaders of the Leicester faction in the days
when the earl made his famous attempts upon the four
cities.[2] He had sworn revenge upon all those concerned in his father's downfall, and it was a delight,
therefore, to wreak a personal vengeance on one who
had since become so illustrious a member of that party
by which the former burgomaster had been deposed,

[1] K. Brandt, Leven, 211.

[2] See History of the United Netherlands, vol. ii. 301, 302, 303,
367.

although Grotius at the time of Leicester's government had scarcely left his cradle.

Thus these ladies were to work in the kitchen and go to market from time to time, performing this menial drudgery under the personal inspection of the warrior who governed the garrison and fortress, but who in vain attempted to make Maria van Reigersbergen tremble at his frown.

Hugo de Groot, when thus for life immured, after having already undergone a preliminary imprisonment of nine months, was just thirty-six years of age. Although comparatively so young, he had been long regarded as one of the great luminaries of Europe for learning and genius. Of an ancient and knightly race, his immediate ancestors had been as famous for literature, science, and municipal abilities as their more distant progenitors for deeds of arms in the feudal struggles of Holland in the middle ages.

His father and grandfather had alike been eminent for Hebrew, Greek, and Latin scholarship, and both had occupied high positions in the University of Leyden from its beginning. Hugo, born and nurtured under such quickening influences, had been a scholar and poet almost from his cradle. He wrote respectable Latin verses at the age of seven,[1] he was matriculated at Leyden at the age of eleven. That school, founded

---

[1] Here are verses written by him in the year 1591, in his eighth year, on the capture of Nimwegen by Prince Maurice:

"Plaudite Mauritio Victori quotquot adestis;
   Namque is Cæsaream Neomagum venit in urbem,
   Vel potius Domino Victori plaudite Christo,
   Namque is Mauritio Neomagum tradidit urbem."

(K. Brandt, Leven, 6.)

amid the storms and darkness of terrible war, was not lightly to be entered. It was already illustrated by a galaxy of shining lights in science and letters, which radiated over Christendom. His professors were Joseph Scaliger, Francis Junius, Paulus Merula, and a host of others. His fellow-students were men like Scriverius, Vossius, Baudius, Daniel Heinsius. The famous soldier and poet Dousa, who had commanded the forces of Leyden during the immortal siege, addressed him on his admission to the university as ''Magne puer magni dignissime cura parentis,'' in a copy of eloquent verses.

When fourteen years old he took his bachelor's degree, after a rigorous examination not only in the classics but astronomy, mathematics, jurisprudence, and theology, at an age when most youths would have been accounted brilliant if able to enter that high school with credit.

On leaving the university he was attached to the embassy of Barneveldt and Justinus van Nassau to the court of Henry IV. Here he attracted the attention of that monarch, who pointed him out to his courtiers as the ''miracle of Holland,'' presented him with a gold chain with his miniature attached to it, and proposed to confer on him the dignity of knighthood, which the boy from motives of family pride appears to have refused. While in France he received from the University of Orléans, before the age of fifteen, the honorary degree of doctor of laws in a very eulogistic diploma. On his return to Holland he published an edition of the poet Johannes Capella with valuable annotations, besides giving to the public other learned and classical works and several tragedies of more or less merit. At the age of seventeen he was already an advocate in full practice before the supreme tribunals of The Hague, and when twenty-three years old he was selected by Prince Maurice from a list of three candidates for the important post of fiscal or attorney-general of Holland. Other civic dignities, embassies, and offices of various kinds had been thrust upon him one after another, in all of which he had acquitted himself with dignity and brilliancy. He was but twenty-six when he published his argument for the liberty of the sea, the famous "Mare Liberum," and a little later appeared his work on the "Antiquity of the Batavian Republic," which procured for him in Spain the title of "Hugo Grotius, auctor damnatus." At the age of twenty-nine he had completed his Latin history of the Netherlands from the period immediately preceding the war of independence down to the conclusion of the truce, 1550–1609—a work which has been a classic ever since its appearance, although not published until after his death. A chief magistrate of Rotterdam, member of the states of Holland and the States-General, jurist, advocate, attorney-general, poet, scholar, historian, editor of the Greek and Latin classics, writer of tragedies, of law treatises, of theological disquisitions, he stood foremost among a crowd of famous contemporaries. His genius, eloquence, and learning were esteemed among the treasures not only of his own country but of Europe. He had been part and parcel of his country's history from his earliest manhood, and although a child in years compared to Barneveldt, it was upon him that the great statesman had mainly relied ever since the youth's first appearance in public affairs. Impressible, emotional, and susceptive, he had been accused from time to time, perhaps not entirely, without reason, of infirmity of purpose, or at least of vacillation in opinion; but his worst enemies had never assailed the purity of his heart or integrity of his character. He had not yet written the great work on the "Rights of War and Peace," which was to make an epoch in the history of civilization and to be the foundation of a new science, but the materials lay already in the ample storehouse of his memory and his brain.

Possessed of singular personal beauty, which the masterly portraits of Mierevelt attest to the present day, tall, brown-haired, straight-featured, with a delicate aquiline nose and piercing dark-blue eyes, he was also athletic of frame and a proficient in manly exercises. This was the statesman and the scholar, of whom it is difficult to speak but in terms of affectionate but not exaggerated eulogy, and for whom the Republic of the Netherlands could now find no better use than to shut him up in the grim fortress of Loevenstein for the remainder of his days. A commonwealth must have deemed itself rich in men which, after cutting off the head of Barneveldt, could afford to bury alive Hugo Grotius.

His deportment in prison was a magnificent moral lesson. Shut up in a kind of cage consisting of a bedroom and a study, he was debarred from physical exercise, so necessary for his mental and bodily health. Not choosing for the gratification of Lieutenant Deventer to indulge in weak complaints, he procured a huge top,[1] which he employed himself in whipping several hours a day; while for intellectual employment he plunged once more into those classical, juridical,

---

[1] K. Brandt, Leven, 235, 236.

HUGO GROTIUS

and theological studies which had always employed his leisure hours from childhood upward.

It had been forbidden by the States-General to sell his likeness in the shops. The copperplates on which they had been engraved had as far as possible been destroyed.

The wish of the government, especially of his judges, was that his name and memory should die at once and forever. They were not destined to be successful, for it would be equally difficult to-day to find an educated man in Christendom ignorant of the name of Hugo Grotius, or acquainted with that of a single one of his judges.

And his friends had not forgotten him as he lay there living in his tomb. Especially the learned Scriverius, Vossius, and other professors were permitted to correspond with him at intervals on literary subjects, the letters being subjected to preliminary inspection. Scriverius sent him many books from his well-stocked library, De Groot's own books and papers having been confiscated by the government. At a somewhat later period the celebrated Orientalist Erpenius sent him from time to time a large chest of books, the precious freight being occasionally renewed and the chest passing to and from Loevenstein by way of Gorcum. At this town lived a sister of Erpenius, married to one Daatselaer, a considerable dealer in thread and ribbons, which he exported to England. The house of Daatselaer became a place of constant resort for Madame de Groot as well as the wife of Hoogerbeets, both dames going every few days from the castle across the Waal to Gorcum, to make their various purchases for the use of their forlorn little household in the prison. Madame Daatselaer therefore received and forwarded into Loevenstein or into Holland many parcels and boxes, besides attending to the periodical transmission of the mighty chest of books.[1]

Professor Vossius was then publishing a new edition of the tragedies of Seneca, and at his request Grotius enriched that work, from his prison, with valuable notes. He employed himself also in translating the moral sentences extracted by Stobæus from the Greek tragedies, drawing consolation from the ethics and philosophy of the ancient dramatists, whom he had always admired, especially the tragedies of Euripides. He formed a complete moral anthology from that poet and from the works of Sophocles, Menander, and others, which he translated into fluent Dutch verse. Becoming more and more interested in the subject, he executed a masterly rhymed translation of the "Theban Brothers" of Euripides, thus seeking distraction from his own tragic doom in the portraiture of antique, distant, and heroic sorrow.

Turning again to legal science, he completed an "Introduction to the Jurisprudence of Holland," a work which as soon as published became thenceforward a text-book and an oracle in the law courts and the high schools of the country. Not forgetting theology, he composed for the use of the humbler classes, especially for sailors, in whose lot, so exposed to danger and temptation, he ever took deep interest, a work on the proofs of Christianity in easy and familiar rhyme—a book of gold, as it was called once, which became rapidly popular with those for whom it was designed.

At a somewhat later period Professor Erpenius, publishing a new edition of the New Testament in Greek,

1 K. Brandt, Leven, 235, 236.

with translations in Arabic, Syriac, and Ethopian, solicited his friend's help both in translations and in the
Latin commentaries and expositions with which he proposed to accompany the work. The prisoner began
with a modest disclaimer, saying that after the labors
of Erasmus and Beza, Maldonatus and Jasenius, there
was little for him to glean. Becoming more enthusiastic as he went on, he completed a masterly commen-
tary on the Four Evangelists, a work for which the
learned and religious world has ever recognized a kind
of debt of gratitude to the castle of Loevenstein, and
hailed in him the founder of a school of manly biblical
criticism.

And thus nearly two years wore away. Spinning
his great top for exercise; soothing his active and pro-
lific brain with Greek tragedy, with Flemish verse, with
jurisprudence, history, theology; creating, expounding,
adorning, by the warmth of his vivid intellect; moving
the world and doing good to his race from the depths
of his stony sepulcher, Hugo Grotius rose superior to
his doom and took captivity captive. The man is not
to be envied who is not moved by so noble an example
of great calamity manfully endured.

The wife of Hoogerbeets, already advanced in years,
sickened during the imprisonment, and died at Loevenstein after a lingering illness, leaving six children to
the care of her unfortunate husband. Madame de
Groot had not been permitted by the prison authorities
to minister to her in sickness, nor to her children after
her death.[1]

Early in the year 1621 Francis Aertsens, Lord of
Sommelsdyk, the arch-enemy of Barneveldt and Gro-

[1] K. Brandt, Leven, 236 seq.

tius, was appointed special ambassador to Paris. The intelligence, although hardly unexpected, for the stratagems of Aertsens had been completely successful, moved the prisoner deeply. He felt that this mortal enemy, not glutted with vengeance by the beheading of the advocate and the perpetual imprisonment of his friend, would do his best at the French court to defame and to blacken him. He did what he could to obviate this danger by urgent letters to friends on whom he could rely.

At about the same time Muis van Holy, one of the twenty-four commissioners, not yet satisfied with the misery he had helped to inflict, informed the States-General that Madame de Groot had been buying ropes at Gorcum. On his motion a committee was sent to investigate the matter at Castle Loevenstein, where it was believed that the ropes had been concealed for the purpose of enabling Grotius to make his escape from prison.

Lieutenant Deventer had heard nothing of the story. He was in high spirits at the rumor, however, and conducted the committee very eagerly over the castle, causing minute search to be made in the apartment of Grotius for the ropes which, as they were assured by him and his wife, had never existed save in the imagination of Judge Muis. They succeeded at least in inflicting much superfluous annoyance on their victims, and in satisfying themselves that it would be as easy for the prisoner to fly out of the fortress on wings as to make his escape with ropes, even if he had them.

Grotius soon afterward addressed a letter to the States-General denouncing the statement of Muis as a fable, and these persistent attempts to injure him as cowardly and wicked.

A few months later Madame de Groot happened to be in the house of Daatselaer on one of her periodical visits to Gorcum. Conversation turning on these rumors of attempts at escape, she asked Madame Daatselaer if she would not be much embarrassed should Grotius suddenly make his appearance there.

"Oh, no," said the good woman, with a laugh; "only let him come. We will take excellent care of him."

At another visit one Saturday, 20th March, Madame de Groot asked her friend why all the bells of Gorcum were ringing.

"Because to-morrow begins our yearly fair," replied Dame Daatselaer.

"Well, I suppose that all exiles and outlaws may come to Gorcum on this occasion," said Madame de Groot.

"Such is the law, they say," answered her friend.

"And my husband might come too?"

"No doubt," said Madame Daatselaer, with a merry laugh, rejoiced at finding the wife of Grotius able to speak so cheerfully of her husband in his perpetual and hopeless captivity. "Send him hither. He shall have a warm welcome."

"What a good woman you are!" said Madame de Groot, with a sigh, as she rose to take leave. "But you know very well that if he were a bird he could never get out of the castle, so closely he is caged there."

Next morning a wild equinoctial storm was howling around the battlements of the castle. Of a sudden Cornelia, daughter of the De Groots, nine years of age, said to her mother, without any reason whatever:

"To-morrow papa must be off to Gorcum, whatever the weather may be."

De Groot, as well as his wife, was aghast at the child's remark, and took it as a direct indication from Heaven.[1]

For while Madame Daatselaer had considered the recent observations of her visitor from Loevenstein as idle jests, and perhaps wondered that Madame de Groot could be frivolous and apparently light-hearted on so dismal a topic, there had been really a hidden meaning in her words.

For several weeks past the prisoner had been brooding over a means of escape. His wife, whose every thought was devoted to him, had often cast her eyes on the great chest or trunk in which the books of Erpenius had been conveyed between Loevenstein and Gorcum for the use of the prisoner. At first the trunk had been carefully opened and its contents examined every time it entered or left the castle. As nothing had ever been found in it save Hebrew, Greek, and Latin folios, uninviting enough to the commandant, that warrior had gradually ceased to inspect the chest very closely, and had at last discontinued the practice altogether.

It had been kept for some weeks past in the prisoner's study. His wife thought, although it was two finger-breadths less than four feet in length, and not very broad or deep in proportion, that it might be possible for him to get into it. He was considerably above middle height, but found that by curling himself up very closely he could just manage to lie in it with the cover closed. Very secretly they had many times rehearsed the scheme which had now taken possession of their minds, but had not breathed a word of it to any one. He had lain in the chest with the lid fas-

[1] K. Brandt, Leven, vi. 242–286.

tened, and with his wife sitting upon the top of it, two hours at a time by the hour-glass. They had decided at last that the plan, though fraught with danger, was not absolutely impossible, and they were only waiting now for a favorable opportunity. The chance remark of the child Cornelia settled the time for hazarding the adventure. By a strange coincidence, too, the commandant of the fortress, Lieutenant Deventer, had just been promoted to a captaincy, and was to go to Heusden to receive his company. He left the castle for a brief absence that very Sunday evening. As a precautionary measure, the trunk filled with books had been sent to Gorcum and returned after the usual interval only a few days before.

The maid-servant of the De Groots, a young girl of twenty, Elsje van Houwening by name, quick, intelligent, devoted, and courageous, was now taken into their confidence. The scheme was explained to her, and she was asked if she were willing to take the chest under her charge with her master in it, instead of the usual freight of books, and accompany it to Gorcum.

She naturally asked what punishment could be inflicted upon her in case the plot were discovered.

"None legally," answered her master; "but I, too, am innocent of any crime, and you see to what sufferings I have been condemned."

"Whatever come of it," said Elsje, stoutly, "I will take the risk and accompany my master." [1]

Every detail was then secretly arranged, and it was provided beforehand, as well as possible, what should be said or done in the many contingencies that might arise.

[1] K. Brandt, Leven, vi. 242–286.

On Sunday evening Madame de Groot then went to the wife of the commandant, with whom she had always been on more friendly terms than with her malicious husband. She had also recently propitiated her affections by means of venison and other dainties brought from Gorcum. She expressed the hope that, notwithstanding the absence of Captain Deventer, she might be permitted to send the trunk full of books next day from the castle.

"My husband is wearing himself out," she said, "with his perpetual studies. I shall be glad for a little time to be rid of some of these folios."

The commandant's wife made no objection to this slight request.

On Monday morning the gale continued to beat with unabated violence on the turrets. The turbid Waal, swollen by the tempest, rolled darkly and dangerously along the castle walls.

But the die was cast. Grotius rose betimes, fell on his knees, and prayed fervently an hour long. Dressed only in linen underclothes, with a pair of silk stockings, he got into the chest with the help of his wife. The big Testament of Erpenius, with some bunches of thread placed upon it, served him as a pillow. A few books and papers were placed in the interstices left by the curves of his body, and as much pains as possible taken to prevent his being seriously injured or incommoded during the hazardous journey he was contemplating. His wife then took solemn farewell of him, fastened the lock, which she kissed, and gave the key to Elsje.

The usual garments worn by the prisoner were thrown on a chair by the bedside, and his slippers placed before it. Madame de Groot then returned to her bed, drew the curtains close, and rang the bell.

It was answered by the servant who usually waited on the prisoner, and who was now informed by the lady that it had been her intention to go herself to Gorcum, taking charge of the books, which were valuable. As the weather was so tempestuous, however, and as she was somewhat indisposed, it had been decided that Elsje should accompany the trunk.

She requested that some soldiers might be sent as usual to take it down to the vessel. Two or three of the garrison came accordingly, and seeing the clothes and slippers of Grotius lying about, and the bed-curtains closed, felt no suspicion.

On lifting the chest, however, one of them said, half in jest:

"The Arminian must be in it himself, it seems so heavy."

"Not the Arminian," replied Madame de Groot, in a careless voice, from the bed; "only heavy Arminian books." [1]

Partly lifting, partly dragging the ponderous box, the soldiers managed to get it down the stairs and through the thirteen barred and bolted doors. Four several times one or other of the soldiers expressed the opinion that Grotius himself must be locked within it, but they never spoke quite seriously, and Elsje was ever ready to turn aside the remark with a jest. A soldier's wife, just as the box was approaching the wharf, told a story of a malefactor who had once been carried out of the castle in a chest.

"And if a malefactor, why not a lawyer?" she

[1] K. Brandt, Leven, vi. 242–286.

added. A soldier said he would get a gimlet and bore a hole into the Arminian. "Then you must get a gimlet that will reach to the top of the castle, where the Arminian lies abed and asleep," said Elsje.[1]

Not much heed was given to this careless talk, the soldiers, before leaving the chamber of Grotius, having satisfied themselves that there were no apertures in the chest save the keyhole, and that it would be impossible by that means alone for sufficient air to penetrate to keep a man inclosed in it from smothering.

Madame Deventer was asked if she chose to inspect the contents of the trunk, and she inquired whether the commandant had been wont so to do. When told that such search had been for a long time discontinued, as nothing had ever been found there but books, she observed that there was no reason why she should be more strict than her husband, and ordered the soldiers to take their heavy load to the vessel.

Elsje insisted that the boatmen should place a doubly thick plank for sliding the box on board, as it seemed probable, she said, that the usual one would break in two, and then the valuable books borrowed of Professor Erpenius would be damaged or destroyed. The request caused much further grumbling, but was complied with at last and the chest deposited on the deck. The wind still continued to blow with great fury, and as soon as the sails were set the vessel heeled over so much that Elsje implored the skipper to cause the box to be securely lashed, as it seemed in imminent danger, at the first lurch of the vessel, of sliding into the sea.

This done, Elsje sat herself down and threw her

[1] K. Brandt, Leven, vi. 245.

white handkerchief over her head, letting it flutter in the wind. One of the crew asked her why she did so, and she replied that the servant in the castle had been tormenting her, saying that she would never dare to sail to Gorcum in such tempestuous weather, and she was now signaling him that she had been as good as her word. Whereupon she continued to wave the handkerchief.

In reality the signal was for her mistress, who was now straining her eyes from the barred window which looked out upon the Waal, and with whom the maid had agreed that if all went prosperously she would give this token of success. Otherwise she would sit with her head in her hands.

During the voyage an officer of the garrison, who happened to be on board, threw himself upon the chest as a convenient seat, and began drumming and pounding with his heels upon it. The ever-watchful Elsje, feeling the dreadful inconvenience to the prisoner of these proceedings, who perhaps was already smothering and would struggle for air if not relieved, politely addressed the gentleman and induced him to remove to another seat by telling him that, besides the books, there was some valuable porcelain in the chest which might easily be broken.

No further incident occurred. The wind, although violent, was favorable, and Gorcum in due time was reached. Elsje insisted upon having her own precious freight carried first into the town, although the skipper for some time was obstinately bent on leaving it to the very last, while all the other merchandise in the vessel should be previously unshipped.

At last, on promise of payment of ten stivers, which

was considered an exorbitant sum, the skipper and son agreed to transport the chest between them on a handbarrow. While they were trudging with it to the town, the son remarked to his father that there was some living thing in the box. For the prisoner, in the anguish of his confinement, had not been able to restrain a slight movement.

"Do you hear what my son says?" cried the skipper to Elsje. "He says you have got something alive in your trunk."

"Yes, yes," replied the cheerful maid-servant; "Arminian books are always alive, always full of motion and spirit." [1]

They arrived at Daatselaer's house, moving with difficulty through the crowd which, notwithstanding the boisterous weather, had been collected by the annual fair. Many people were assembled in front of the building, which was a warehouse of great resort, while next door was a bookseller's shop, thronged with professors, clergymen, and other literary persons. The carriers accordingly entered by the back way, and Elsje, deliberately paying them their ten stivers and seeing them depart, left the box lying in a room at the rear and hastened to the shop in front.

Here she found the thread- and ribbon-dealer and his wife, busy with their customers, unpacking and exhibiting their wares. She instantly whispered in Madame Daatselaer's ear, "I have got my master here in your back parlor."

The dame turned white as a sheet, and was near fainting on the spot. It was the first imprudence Elsje had committed. The good woman recovered some-

[1] K. Brandt, Leven, vi. 246.

what of her composure by a strong effort, however, and instantly went with Elsje to the rear of the house.

"Master, master!" cried Elsje, rapping on the chest. There was no answer.

"My God, my God!" shrieked the poor maid-servant. "My poor master is dead."

"Ah!" said Madame Daatselaer, "your mistress has made a bad business of it. Yesterday she had a living husband. Now she has a dead one."

But soon there was a vigorous rap on the inside of the lid, and a cry from the prisoner:

"Open the chest! I am not dead, but did not at first recognize your voice."

The lock was instantly unfastened, the lid thrown open, and Grotius arose in his linen clothing, like a dead man from his coffin.[1]

The dame instantly accompanied the two through a trap-door into an upper room.

Grotius asked her if she was always so deadly pale.

"No," she replied, " but I am frightened to see you here. My lord is no common person. The whole world is talking of you. I fear this will cause the loss of all my property and perhaps bring my husband into prison in your place."

Grotius rejoined: "I made my prayers to God before as much as this had been gained, and I have just been uttering fervent thanks to him for my deliverance so far as it has been effected. But if the consequences are to be as you fear, I am ready at once to get into the chest again and be carried back to prison."

But she answered: "No; whatever comes of it, we

[1] K. Brandt, Leven, vi. 248,

have you here and will do all that we can to help
you on."

Grotius being faint from his sufferings, the lady
brought him a glass of Spanish wine, but was too much
flustered to find even a cloak or shawl to throw over
him.   Leaving him sitting there in his very thin attire,
just as he had got out of the chest, she went to the
front warehouse to call her husband.   But he pru-
dently declined to go to his unexpected guest.   It
would be better in the examination sure to follow, he
said, for him to say with truth that he had not seen
him and knew nothing of the escape from first to last.

Grotius entirely approved of the answer when told
to him.   Meantime Madame Daatselaer had gone to her
brother-in-law Van der Veen, a clothier by trade, whom
she found in his shop talking with an officer of the
Loevenstein garrison.   She whispered in the clothier's
ear, and he, making an excuse to the officer, followed
her home at once.   They found Grotius sitting where
he had been left.   Van der Veen gave him his hand,
saying:

"Sir, you are the man of whom the whole country is
talking."

"Yes, here I am," was the reply, "and I put myself
in your hands."

"There is n't a moment to lose," replied the clothier.
"We must help you away at once."

He went immediately in search of one John Lambertsen, a man in whom he knew he could confide, a Lu-
theran in religion, a master mason by occupation.   He
found him on a scaffold against the gable-end of a
house, working at his trade.

He told him that there was a good deed to be done

which he could do better than any man, that his conscience would never reproach him for it, and that he
would at the same time earn no trifling reward.

He begged the mason to procure a complete dress as
for a journeyman, and to follow him to the house of his
brother-in-law Daatselaer.

Lambertsen soon made his appearance with the doublet, trunk-hose, and shoes of a bricklayer, together with
trowel and measuring-rod. He was informed who his
new journeyman was to be, and Grotius at once put
on the disguise.

The doublet did not reach to the waistband of the
trunk-hose, while those nether garments stopped short
of his knees, the whole attire belonging to a smaller
man than the unfortunate statesman.   His delicate
white hands, much exposed by the shortness of the
sleeves, looked very unlike those of a day-laborer, and
altogether the new mason presented a somewhat incongruous and woebegone aspect.   Grotius was fearful,
too, lest some of the preachers and professors frequent-
ing the book-shop next door would recognize him
through his disguise.   Madame Daatselaer smeared his
face and hands with chalk and plaster, however, and
whispered encouragement, and so, with a felt hat
slouched over his forehead and a yardstick in his hand,
he walked calmly forth into the thronged market-place
and through the town to the ferry, accompanied by the
friendly Lambertsen.   It had been agreed that Van der
Veen should leave the house in another direction and
meet them at the landing-place.[1]

When they got to the ferry, they found the weather
as boisterous as ever.   The boatmen absolutely refused

[1] K. Brandt, Leven, vi. 248, 249 seq.

to make the dangerous crossing to the Merwede, over which their course lay to the land of Altona, and so into the Spanish Netherlands, for two such insignificant personages as this mason and his scarecrow journeyman.

Lambertsen assured them that it was of the utmost importance that he should cross the water at once. He had a large contract for purchasing stone at Altona for a public building on which he was engaged. Van der Veen, coming up, added his entreaties, protesting that he, too, was interested in this great stone purchase, and so, by means of offering a larger price than they at first dared to propose, they were able to effect their passage.

After landing, Lambertsen and Grotius walked to Waalwyk, Van der Veen returning the same evening to Gorcum. It was four o'clock in the afternoon when they reached Waalwyk, where a carriage was hired to convey the fugitive to Antwerp. The friendly mason here took leave of his illustrious journeyman, having first told the driver that his companion was a disguised bankrupt fleeing from Holland into foreign territory to avoid pursuit by his creditors. This would explain his slightly concealing his face in passing through a crowd in any village.

Grotius proved so ignorant of the value of different coins in making small payments on the road that the honest wagoner, on being occasionally asked who the odd-looking stranger was, answered that he was a bankrupt, and no wonder, for he did not know one piece of money from another. For his part, he thought him little better than a fool.

Such was the depreciatory opinion formed by the

Waalwyk coachman as to the "rising light of the world" and the "miracle of Holland." They traveled all night, and arriving on the morning of the 21st within a few leagues of Antwerp, met a patrol of soldiers, who asked Grotius for his passport. He inquired in whose service they were, and was told in that of "Red Rod," as the chief bailiff of Antwerp was called. That functionary happened to be near, and the traveler, approaching him, said that his passport was on his feet, and forthwith told him his name and story.

Red Rod treated him at once with perfect courtesy, offered him a horse for himself with a mounted escort, and so furthered his immediate entrance to Antwerp. Grotius rode straight to the house of a banished friend of his, the preacher Grevinkhoven. He was told by the daughter of that clergyman that her father was upstairs ministering at the bedside of his sick wife. But so soon as the traveler had sent up his name, both the preacher and the invalid came rushing down-stairs to fall upon the neck of one who seemed as if risen from the dead.

The news spread, and Episcopius and other exiled friends soon thronged to the house of Grevinkhoven, where they all dined together in great glee, Grotius, still in his journeyman's clothes, narrating the particulars of his wonderful escape.

He had no intention of tarrying in his resting-place at Antwerp longer than was absolutely necessary. Intimations were covertly made to him that a brilliant destiny might be in store for him should he consent to enter the service of the archdukes; nor were there wanting rumors, circulated as a matter of course by his host of enemies, that he was about to become a renegade to country and religion. There was as much truth in the slanders as in the rest of the calumnies of which he had been the victim during his career. He placed on record a proof of his loyal devotion to his country in the letters which he wrote from Antwerp within a week of his arrival there.[1] With his subsequent history, his appearance and long residence at the French court as ambassadcr of Sweden, his memorable labors in history, diplomacy, poetry, theology, the present narrative is not concerned. Driven from the service of his fatherland, of which his name to all time is one of the proudest garlands, he continued to be a benefactor not only to her but to all mankind. If refutation is sought of the charge that republics are ungrateful, it will certainly not be found in the history of Hugo Grotius or John of Barneveldt.

Nor is there need to portray the wrath of Captain Deventer when he returned to Castle Loevenstein.

"Here is the cage, but your bird is flown," said corpulent Maria Grotius, with a placid smile. The commandant solaced himself by uttering imprecations on her, on her husband, and on Elsje van Houwening. But these curses could not bring back the fugitive. He flew to Gorcum to browbeat the Daatselaers and to search the famous trunk. He found in it the big New Testament and some skeins of thread, together with an octavo or two of theology and of Greek tragedies; but the Arminian was not in it, and was gone from the custody of the valiant Deventer forever.

After a brief period Madame de Groot was released and rejoined her husband. Elsje van Houwening, true

[1] The letters were dated March 26 and 30, 1621, and are printed in K. Brandt's Leven, etc., 256–258.

heroine of the adventure, was subsequently married to the faithful servant of Grotius, who during the two years' imprisonment had been taught Latin and the rudiments of law by his master, so that he subsequently rose to be a thriving and respectable advocate at the tribunals of Holland.

The stadholder, when informed of the escape of the prisoner, observed, "I always thought the black pig was deceiving me," making not very complimentary allusion to the complexion and size of the lady who had thus aided the escape of her husband.

He is also reported as saying that it "is no wonder they could not keep Grotius in prison, as he has more wit than all his judges put together." [1]

[1] K. Brandt, Leven, 258.   Van der Kemp, 138.   The following epigram was written in the album of David Kempenaer at Antwerp by Grotius on the eighth day after his escape:

> "Quos matris alvus Carcer edit in lucem,
> Queis corpus animum more Carceris vincit,
> Quos morte functos terra Carcer exspectat,
> Nunquam nimis timere Carcerem debent."
>
> (K. Brandt, Leven, etc., 259.)

CHAPTER XXIII

Barneveldt's sons plot against Maurice—The conspiracy betrayed to Maurice—Escape of Stoutenburg—Groeneveld is arrested—Mary of Barneveldt appeals to the stadholder—Groeneveld condemned to death—Execution of Groeneveld.

THE widow of Barneveldt had remained, since the last scene of the fatal tragedy on the Binnenhof, in hopeless desolation. The wife of the man who during a whole generation of mankind had stood foremost among the foremost of the world, and had been one of those chief actors and directors in human affairs to whom men's eyes turned instinctively from near and from afar, had led a life of unbroken prosperity. An heiress in her own right, Maria van Utrecht had laid the foundation of her husband's wealth by her union with the rising young lawyer and statesman. Her two sons and two daughters had grown up around her, all four being married into the leading families of the land, and with apparently long lives of prosperity and usefulness before them. And now the headsman's sword had shivered all this grandeur and happiness at a blow. The name of the dead statesman had become a word of scoffing and reproach; vagabond mountebanks enacted ribald scenes to his dishonor in the public squares and streets; balladmongers yelled blasphemous libels upon him in the very ears of his widow and children. For

266

party hatred was not yet glutted with the blood it had drunk.

It would be idle to paint the misery of this broken-hearted woman.

The great painters of the epoch have preserved her face to posterity—the grief-stricken face of a hard-featured but commanding and not uncomely woman, the fountains of whose tears seem exhausted; a face of austere and noble despair. A decorous veil should be thrown over the form of that aged matron, for whose long life of prosperity Fate took such merciless vengeance at last.

For the woes of Maria of Barneveldt had scarcely begun. Desolation had become her portion, but dishonor had not yet crossed her threshold. There were sterner strokes in store for her than that which smote her husband on the scaffold.

She had two sons, both in the prime of life. The eldest, Reinier, Lord of Groeneveld, who had married a widow of rank and wealth, Madame de Brandwyk, was living since the death of his father in comparative ease, but entire obscurity. An easy-tempered, genial, kindly gentleman, he had been always much beloved by his friends and, until the great family catastrophe, was popular with the public, but of an infirm and vacillating character, easily impressed by others, and apt to be led by stronger natures than his own. He had held the lucrative office of head forester of Delfland, of which he had now been deprived.

The younger son, William, called, from an estate conferred on him by his father, Lord of Stoutenburg, was of a far different mold. We have seen him at an earlier period of this narrative attached to the embassy of

Francis Aertsens in Paris, bearing then from another estate the unmusical title of Craimgepolder, and giving his subtle and dangerous chief great cause of complaint by his irregular, expensive habits. He had been, however, rather a favorite with Henry IV., who had so profound a respect for the father as to consult him, and him only of all foreign statesmen, in the gravest affairs of his reign, and he had even held an office of honor and emolument at his court. Subsequently he had embraced the military career, and was esteemed a soldier of courage and promise. As captain of cavalry and governor of the fortress of Bergen-op-Zoom, he occupied a distinguished and lucrative position, and was likely, so soon as the truce ran to its close, to make a name for himself in that gigantic political and religious war which had already opened in Bohemia, and in which it was evident the Republic would soon be desperately involved. His wife, Walburg de Marnix, was daughter to one of the noblest characters in the history of the Netherlands, or of any history, the illustrious Sainte-Aldegonde. Two thousand florins a year from his father's estate had been settled on him at his marriage, which, in addition to his official and military income, placed him in a position of affluence.[1]

After the death of his father the family estates were confiscated, and he was likewise deprived of his captaincy and his governorship. He was reduced at a blow from luxury and high station to beggary and obscurity. At the renewal of the war he found himself, through no fault of his own, excluded from the service of his country. Yet the advocate almost in his last breath had recommended his sons to the stadholder,

[1] Brandt, Hist. Ref., vol. iv. bk. lix. 901 seq.

and Maurice had sent a message in response that so long as the sons conducted themselves well they might rely upon his support.

Hitherto they had not conducted themselves otherwise than well. Stoutenburg, who now dwelt in his house with his mother, was of a dark, revengeful, turbulent disposition. In the career of arms he had a right to look forward to success, but thus condemned to brood in idleness on the cruel wrongs to himself and his house it was not improbable that he might become dangerous.

Years long he fed on projects of vengeance as his daily bread. He was convinced that his personal grievances were closely entwined with the welfare of the commonwealth, and he had sworn to avenge the death of his father, the misery of his mother, and the wrongs which he was himself suffering, upon the stadholder, whom he considered the author of all their woe. To effect a revolution in the government, and to bring back to power all the municipal regents whom Maurice had displaced so summarily, in order, as the son believed, to effect the downfall of the hated advocate, this was the determination of Stoutenburg.

He did not pause to reflect whether the arm which had been strong enough to smite to nothingness the venerable statesman in the plenitude of his power would be too weak to repel the attack of an obscure and disarmed partizan. He saw only a hated tyrant, murderer, and oppressor, as he considered him, and he meant to have his life.

He had around him a set of daring and desperate men to whom he had from time to time half confided his designs. A certain unfrocked preacher of the Re-

monstrant persuasion, who, according to the fashion of
the learned of that day, had translated his name out
of Hendrik Slaet into Henricus Slatius, was one of
his most unscrupulous instruments. Slatius, a big,
swarthy, shag-eared, beetle-browed Hollander, possessed
learning of no ordinary degree, a tempestuous kind of
eloquence, and a habit of dealing with men, especially
those of the humbler classes. He was passionate,
greedy, overbearing, violent, and loose of life. He had
sworn vengeance upon the Remonstrants in consequence of a private quarrel, but this did not prevent
him from breathing fire and fury against the Contra-
Remonstrants also, and especially against the stadholder, whom he affected to consider the arch-enemy of
the whole commonwealth.

Another twelvemonth went by. The advocate had
been nearly four years in his grave. The terrible German war was in full blaze. The Twelve Years' Truce
had expired, the Republic was once more at war, and
Stoutenburg, forbidden at the head of his troop to
campaign with the stadholder against the archdukes,
nourished more fiercely than ever his plans against the
stadholder's life.

Besides the ferocious Slatius he had other associates.
There was his cousin by marriage, Van der Dussen, a
Catholic gentleman, who had married a daughter of
Elias Barneveldt, and who shared all Stoutenburg's
feelings of resentment toward Maurice. There was
Korenwinder, another Catholic, formerly occupying
an official position of responsibility as secretary of the
town of Berkel, a man of immense corpulence, but none
the less an active and dangerous conspirator.[1]

[1] Brandt, Hist. Ref., vol. iv. lix. 901 seq.

There was Van Dyk, ex-secretary of Bleiswyk,
equally active and dangerous, and as lean and hungry
as Korenwinder was fat.[1]   Stoutenburg, besides other
rewards, had promised him a cornetcy of cavalry,
should their plans be successful.   And there was the
brother-in-law of Slatius, one Cornelis Gerritsen, a
joiner by trade, living at Rotterdam, who made himself
very useful in all the details of the conspiracy.

For the plot was now arranged, the men just mentioned being its active agents and in constant communication with Stoutenburg.

Korenwinder and Van Dyk, in the last days of December, 1622, drew up a scheme on paper, which was
submitted to their chief and met with his approval.
The document began with a violent invective against
the crimes and tyranny of the stadholder, demonstrated
the necessity of a general change in the government,
and of getting rid of Maurice as an indispensable preliminary, and laid down the means and method of
doing this deed.

The prince was in the daily habit of driving, unat-
tended by his body-guard, to Ryswyk, about two miles
from The Hague.   It would not be difficult for a determined band of men divided into two parties to set
upon him between the stables and his coach, either
when alighting from or about to enter it—the one
party to kill him while the other protected the retreat
of the assassins and beat down such defense as the few
lackeys of the stadholder could offer.

The scheme thus mapped out was submitted to Stoutenburg, who gave it his approval after suggesting a
few amendments.   The document was then burned.   It

[1] Brandt, ubi sup.

was estimated that twenty men would be needed for the job, and that to pay them handsomely would require about six thousand guilders.

The expenses and other details of the infamous plot were discussed as calmly as if it had been an industrial or commercial speculation. But six thousand guilders was an immense sum to raise, and the Seigneur de Stoutenburg was a beggar. His associates were as forlorn as himself, but his brother-in-law, the ex-Ambassador van der Myle, was living at Beverwyk under the supervision of the police, his property not having been confiscated. Stoutenburg paid him a visit, accompanied by the Reverend Slatius, in hopes of getting funds from him; but at the first obscure hint of the infamous design Van der Myle faced them with such looks, gestures, and words of disgust and indignation that the murderous couple recoiled, the son of Barneveldt saying to the ex-preacher: "Let us be off, Slaet. 'T is a mere cur. Nothing is to be made of him." [1]

The other son of Barneveldt, the Seigneur de Groeneveld, had means and credit. His brother had darkly hinted to him the necessity of getting rid of Maurice, and tried to draw him into the plot. Groeneveld, more unstable than water, neither repelled nor encouraged these advances. He joined in many conversations with Stoutenburg, Van Dyk, and Korenwinder, but always weakly affected not to know what they were driving at. "When we talk of business," said Van Dyk to him one day, "you are always turning off from us and from the subject. You had better remain." Many anonymous letters were sent to him, calling on him to strike for vengeance on the murderer of his father, and for the

[1] Brandt, Hist. Ref., vol. iv. lix. 901 seq.

redemption of his native land and the Remonstrant religion from foul oppression.

At last yielding to the persuasions and threats of his fierce younger brother, who assured him that the plot would succeed, the government be revolutionized, and that then all property would be at the mercy of the victors, he agreed to indorse certain bills which Korenwinder undertook to negotiate.[1] Nothing could be meaner, more cowardly, and more murderous than the proceedings of the Seigneur de Groeneveld. He seems to have felt no intense desire of vengeance upon Maurice, which certainly would not have been unnatural, but he was willing to supply money for his assassination. At the same time he was careful to insist that this pecuniary advance was by no means a free gift, but only a loan to be repaid by his more bloodthirsty brother upon demand with interest. With a business-like caution, in ghastly contrast with the foulness of the contract, he exacted a note of hand from Stoutenburg covering the whole amount of his disbursements. There might come a time, he thought, when his brother's paper would be more negotiable than it was at that moment.

Korenwinder found no difficulty in discounting Groeneveld's bills, and the necessary capital was thus raised for the vile enterprise. Van Dyk, the lean and hungry conspirator, now occupied himself vigorously in engaging the assassins, while his corpulent colleague remained as treasurer of the company. Two brothers Blansaert, woolen-manufacturers at Leyden, one of whom had been a student of theology in the Remonstrant Church and had occasionally preached, and a

---

[1] Brandt, Hist. Ref., iv. 936 seq.

certain William Party, a Walloon by birth, but likewise a woolen-worker at Leyden, agreed to the secretary's propositions. He had at first told them that
their services would be merely required for the for-
cible liberation of two Remonstrant clergymen, Niel-
lius and Poppius, from the prison at Haarlem. Entertaining his new companions at dinner, however, toward
the end of January, Van Dyk, getting very drunk, informed them that the object of the enterprise was to
kill the stadholder; that arrangements had been made
for effecting an immediate change in the magistracies
in all the chief cities of Holland so soon as the deed
was done; that all the recently deposed regents would
enter The Hague at once, supported by a train of
armed peasants from the country; and that better times
for the oppressed religion, for the fatherland, and especially for every one engaged in the great undertaking, would begin with the death of the tyrant. Each
man taking direct part in the assassination would receive at least three hundred guilders, besides being
advanced to offices of honor and profit according to his
capacity.[1]

The Blansaerts assured their superior that entire
reliance might be placed on their fidelity, and that they
knew of three or four other men in Leyden "as firm as
trees and fierce as lions," whom they would engage—
a fustian-worker, a tailor, a chimney-sweeper, and one
or two other mechanics. The looseness and utter reck-
lessness with which this hideous conspiracy was arranged excites amazement. Van Dyk gave the two
brothers one hundred pistoles in gold—a coin about
equal to a guinea—for their immediate reward as well

[1] Brandt, Hist. Ref., iv. 936 seq.

as for that of the comrades to be engaged. Yet it seems almost certain from subsequent revelations that they were intending all the time to deceive him, to take as much money as they could get from him, "to milk the cow as long as she would give milk," as William Party expressed it, and then to turn round upon and betray him. It was a dangerous game, however, which might not prove entirely successful.

Van Dyk duly communicated with Stoutenburg, who grew more and more feverish with hatred and impatience as the time for gratifying those passions drew nigh, and frequently said that he would like to tear the stadholder to pieces with his own hands. He preferred, however, to act as controlling director over the band of murderers now enrolled.

For in addition to the Leyden party, the Reverend Slatius, supplied with funds by Van Dyk, had engaged at Rotterdam his brother-in-law Gerritsen, a joiner, living in that city, together with three sailors named respectively Dirk, John, and Hermann.

The ex-clergyman's house was also the arsenal of the conspiracy, and here were stored away a stock of pistols, snaphances, and sledge-hammers, together with that other death-dealing machinery, the whole edition of the "Clear-shining Torch," an inflammatory pamphlet by Slatius, all to be used on the fatal day fast approaching.

On the 1st February Van Dyk visited Slatius at Rotterdam.[1] He found Gerritsen hard at work.

There in a dark back kitchen, by the lurid light of the fire in a dim wintry afternoon, stood the burly Slatius, with his swarthy face and heavy eyebrows, accom-

[1] Brandt. Hist. Ref., iv. 59, 936 seq.

panied by his brother-in-law the joiner, both in work-
man's dress, melting lead, running bullets, drying pow-
der, and burnishing and arranging the firearms and
other tools to be used in the great crime now so rapidly
maturing.   The lean, busy, restless Van Dyk, with his
adust and sinister visage, came peering in upon the
couple thus engaged, and observed their preparations
with warm approval.

He recommended that, in addition to Dirk, John, and
Hermann, a few more hardy seafaring men should be
engaged, and Slatius accordingly secured next day the
services of one Jerome Ewouts and three other sailors.
They were not informed of the exact nature of the enterprise, but were told that it was a dangerous although
not a desperate one, and sure to be of great service to
the fatherland.   They received, as all the rest had
done, between two and three hundred guilders in gold,
with a promise of further reward and an intimation
that they would all be promoted to be captains and
first mates.

It was agreed that all the conspirators should assemble four days later at The Hague, on Sunday, the 5th
February, at the inn of the "Golden Helmet."   The
next day, Monday, the 6th, had been fixed by Stoutenburg for doing the deed.   Van Dyk, who had great
confidence in the eloquence of William Party, the Walloon wool-manufacturer, had arranged that he should
make a discourse to them all in a solitary place in the
downs between that city and the sea-shore, taking for
his theme or brief the "Clear-shining Torch" of
Slatius.

On Saturday that eminent divine entertained his
sister and her husband Gerritsen, Jerome Ewouts, who

was at dinner but half informed as to the scope of the
great enterprise, and several other friends who were
entirely ignorant of it. Slatius was in high spirits,
although his sister, who had at last become acquainted
with the vile plot, had done nothing but weep all day
long. They had better be worms, she said, and eat dirt
for their food, than crawl in so base a business. Her
brother comforted her with assurances that the project
was sure to result in a triumph for religion and fatherland, and drank many healths at his table to the success of all engaged in it. That evening he sent off a
great chest filled with arms and ammunition to the
Golden Helmet at The Hague, under the charge of
Jerome Ewouts and his three mates. Van Dyk had already written a letter to the landlord of that hostelry
engaging a room there, and saying that the chest contained valuable books and documents to be used in a
lawsuit, in which he was soon to be engaged, before the
supreme tribunal.

On the Sunday this bustling conspirator had John
Blansaert and William Party to dine with him at the
Golden Helmet in The Hague, and produced seven
packages neatly folded, each containing gold pieces to
the amount of twenty pounds sterling. These were
for themselves and the others whom they had reported
as engaged by them in Leyden. Getting drunk as
usual, he began to bluster of the great political revolution impending, and after dinner examined the carbines of his guests. He asked if those weapons were
to be relied upon. "We can blow a hair to pieces with
them at twenty paces," they replied. "Ah, would
that I too could be of the party!" said Van Dyk, seizing one of the carbines. "No, no," said John Blan-

saert; "we can do the deed better without you than with you. You must look out for the defense."

Van Dyk then informed them that they, with one of the Rotterdam sailors, were to attack Maurice as he got out of his coach at Ryswyk, pin him between the stables and the coach, and then and there do him to death. "You are not to leave him," he cried, "till his soul has left his body." [1]

The two expressed their hearty concurrence with this arrangement, and took leave of their host for the night, going, they said, to distribute the seven packages of blood-money. They found Adam Blansaert waiting for them in the downs, and immediately divided the whole amount between themselves and him—the chimney-sweeper, tailor, and fustian-worker, "firm as trees and fierce as lions," having never had any existence save in their fertile imaginations.

On Monday, 6th February, Van Dyk had a closing interview with Stoutenburg and his brother at the house of Groeneveld, and informed them that the execution of the plot had been deferred to the following day. Stoutenburg expressed disgust and impatience at the delay. "I should like to tear the stadholder to pieces with my own hands!" he cried. He was pacified on hearing that the arrangements had been securely made for the morrow, and turning to his brother, observed: "Remember that you can never retract. You are in our power, and all your estates at our mercy." He then explained the manner in which the magistracies of Leyden, Gouda, Rotterdam, and other cities were to be instantly remodeled after the death of Maurice, the ex-regents of The Hague, at the head of a band of

[1] Brandt, Hist. Ref., iv. 913 seq.

armed peasants, being ready at a moment's warning to take possession of the political capital.

Prince Frederick Henry, moreover, he hinted darkly and falsely, but in a manner not to be mistaken, was favorable to the movement, and would after the murder of Maurice take the government into his hands.[1]

Stoutenburg then went quietly home to pass the day and sleep at his mother's house, awaiting the eventful morning of Tuesday.

Van Dyk went back to his room at the Golden Helmet and began inspecting the contents of the arms- and ammunition-chest which Jerome Ewouts and his three mates had brought the night before from Rotterdam. He had been somewhat unquiet at having seen nothing of those mariners during the day, when, looking out of window, he saw one of them in conference with some soldiers. A minute afterward he heard a bustle in the rooms below, and found that the house was occupied by a guard, and that Gerritsen, with the three first-engaged sailors, Dirk, John, and Hermann, had been arrested at the Zotje. He tried in vain to throw the arms back into the chest and conceal it under the bed, but it was too late. Seizing his hat and wrapping himself in his cloak, with his sword by his side, he walked calmly down the stairs, looking carelessly at the group of soldiers and prisoners who filled the passages. A waiter informed the provost-marshal in command that the gentleman was a respectable boarder at the tavern, well known to him for many years. The conspirator passed unchallenged and went straight to inform Stoutenburg.

The four mariners last engaged by Slatius at Rotter-

[1] Brandt, Hist. Ref., iv. 920 seq.

dam had signally exemplified the danger of half-confidences. Surprised that they should have been so mysteriously intrusted with the execution of an enterprise the particulars of which were concealed from them, and suspecting that crime alone could command such very high prices as had been paid and promised by the ex-clergyman, they had gone straight to the residence of the stadholder after depositing the chest at the Golden Helmet.

Finding that he had driven as usual to Ryswyk, they followed him thither, and by dint of much importunity obtained an audience. If the enterprise was a patriotic one, they reasoned, he would probably know of it and approve it. If it were criminal, it would be useful for them to reveal and dangerous to conceal it.

They told the story so far as they knew it to the prince, and showed him the money, three hundred guilders apiece, which they had already received from Slatius. Maurice hesitated not an instant. It was evident that a dark conspiracy was afoot. He ordered the sailors to return to The Hague by another and circuitous road through Voorburg, while he lost not a moment himself in hurrying back as fast as his horses would carry him. Summoning the president and several councilors of the chief tribunal, he took instant measures to take possession of the two taverns and arrest all the strangers found in them.

Meantime Van Dyk came into the house of the Widow Barneveldt and found Stoutenburg in the stable-yard. He told him the plot was discovered, the chest of arms at the Golden Helmet found. "Are there any private letters or papers in the box?" asked

Stoutenburg. "None relating to the affair," was the answer.

"Take yourself off as fast as possible," said Stoutenburg. Van Dyk needed no urging. He escaped through the stables and across the fields in the direction of Leyden. After skulking about for a week, however, and making very little progress, he was arrested at Hazerswoude, having broken through the ice while attempting to skate across the inundated and frozen pastures in that region.[1]

Proclamations were at once made denouncing the foul conspiracy in which the sons of the late Advocate Barneveldt, the Remonstrant clergyman Slatius, and others were the ringleaders, and offering four thousand florins each for their apprehension. A public thanksgiving for the deliverance was made in all the churches on the 8th February.

On the 12th February the States-General sent letters to all their ambassadors and foreign agents informing them of this execrable plot to overthrow the commonwealth and take the life of the stadholder, set on foot by certain Arminian preachers and others of that faction, and this too in winter, when the ice and snow made hostile invasion practicable, and when the enemy was encamped in so many places in the neighborhood. "The Arminians," said the despatch, "are so filled with bitterness that they would rather the Republic should be lost than that their pretended grievances should go unredressed."[2]   Almost every pulpit shook with Contra-Remonstrant thunder against the whole society of Remonstrants, who were held up to the world as rebels and prince-murderers, the criminal conspiracy

[1] Brandt, Hist. Ref., iv. lix.   [2] Ibid.

being charged upon them as a body. Hardly a man of that persuasion dared venture into the streets and public places, for fear of being put to death by the rabble. The Chevalier William of Nassau, natural son of the stadholder, was very loud and violent in all the taverns and tap-rooms, drinking mighty draughts to the damnation of the Arminians.

Many of the timid in consequence shrank away from the society and joined the Contra-Remonstrant Church, while the more courageous members, together with the leaders of that now abhorred communion, published long and stirring appeals to the universal sense of justice, which was outraged by the spectacle of a whole sect being punished for a crime committed by a few individuals who had once been unworthy members of it.

Meantime hue and cry was made after the fugitive conspirators. The Blansaerts and William Party having set off from Leyden toward The Hague on Monday night, in order, as they said, to betray their employers, whose money they had taken, and whose criminal orders they had agreed to execute, attempted to escape, but were arrested within ten days. They were exhibited at their prison at Amsterdam to an immense concourse at a skilling a peep, the sums thus collected being distributed to the poor. Slatius made his way disguised as a boor into Friesland, and after various adventures attempted to cross the Bourtange Moor to Lingen. Stopping to refresh himself at a tavern near Coevorden, he found himself in the tap-room in presence of Quartermaster Blau and a company of soldiers from the garrison. The dark, scowling boor, travel-stained and weary, with felt hat slouched over his forbidding visage, fierce and timorous at once like a hunted wild beast, excited their suspicion. Seeing himself watched, he got up, paid his scot, and departed, leaving his can of beer untasted. This decided the quartermaster, who accordingly followed the peasant out of the house, and arrested him as a Spanish spy on the watch for the train of specie which the soldiers were then conveying into Coevorden Castle.

Slatius protested his innocence of any such design, and vehemently besought the officer to release him, telling him, as a reason for his urgency and an explanation of his unprepossessing aspect, that he was an oculist from Amsterdam, John Hermansen by name, that he had just committed a homicide in that place, and was fleeing from justice.[1]

The honest quartermaster saw no reason why a suspected spy should go free because he proclaimed himself a murderer, nor why an oculist should escape the penalties of homicide. "The more reason," he said, "why thou shouldst be my prisoner." The ex-preacher was arrested and shut up in the state prison at The Hague.

The famous engraver Visser executed a likeness on copperplate of the grim malefactor as he appeared in his boor's disguise. The portrait, accompanied by a fiercely written broadsheet attacking the Remonstrant Church, had a great circulation, and deepened the animosity against the sect upon which the unfrocked preacher had sworn vengeance. His evil face and fame thus became familiar to the public, while the term "Hendrik Slaet" became a proverb at pot-houses, being held equivalent among tipplers to shirking the bottle.[2]

---

[1] Brandt, Hist. Ref., iv. lix.
[2] Ibid. Wagenaer, x. 470–472.

Korenwinder, the treasurer of the association, coming to visit Stoutenburg soon after Van Dyk had left him, was informed of the discovery of the plot and did his best to escape, but was arrested within a fortnight's time.

Stoutenburg himself acted with his usual promptness and coolness. Having gone straightway to his brother to notify him of the discovery and to urge him to instant flight, he contrived to disappear. A few days later a chest of merchandise was brought to the house of a certain citizen of Rotterdam, who had once been a fiddler, but was now a man of considerable property. The chest, when opened, was found to contain the Seigneur de Stoutenburg, who in past times had laid the fiddler under obligations, and in whose house he now lay concealed for many days, and until the strictness with which all roads and ferries in the neighborhood were watched at first had somewhat given way. Meantime his cousin Van der Dussen had also effected his escape, and had joined him in Rotterdam. The faithful fiddler then, for a thousand florins, chartered a trading-vessel commanded by one Jacob Beltje to take a cargo of Dutch cheese to Wesel on the Rhine. By this means, after a few adventures, they effected their escape, and arriving not long afterward at Brussels, were formally taken under the protection of the Archduchess Isabella.[1]

Stoutenburg afterward traveled in France and Italy, and returned to Brussels. His wife, loathing his crime and spurning all further communication with him, abandoned him to his fate.[2] The daughter of Marnix of

[1] Brandt, Hist. Ref., iv. lix.   Wagenaer, x. 465, 466.

[2] Brandt, ubi sup.

Sainte-Aldegonde had endured poverty, obscurity, and unmerited obloquy, which had become the lot of the great statesman's family after his tragic end, but she came of a race that would not brook dishonor. The conspirator and suborner of murder and treason, the hirer and companion of assassins, was no mate for her.

Stoutenburg hesitated for years as to his future career, strangely enough keeping up a hope of being allowed to return to his country.

Subsequently he embraced the cause of his country's enemies, converted himself to the Roman Church, and obtained a captaincy of horse in the Spanish service. He was seen one day, to the disgust of many spectators, to enter Antwerp in black foreign uniform, at the head of his troopers, waving a standard with a death's-head embroidered upon it, and wearing, like his soldiers, a sable scarf and plume. History disdains to follow further the career of the renegade, traitor, and assassin.

When the Seigneur de Groeneveld learned from his younger brother, on the eventful 6th February, that the plot had been discovered, he gave himself up for lost. Remorse and despair, fastening upon his naturally feeble character, seemed to render him powerless. His wife, of more hopeful disposition than himself and of less heroic mold than Walburg de Marnix, encouraged him to fly. He fled accordingly, through the desolate sandy downs which roll between The Hague and the sea, to Scheveningen, then an obscure fishing-village on the coast, at a league's distance from the capital. Here a fisherman, devoted to him and his family, received him in his hut, disguised him in boatman's attire, and went with him to the strand, proposing to launch his pinky, put out at once to sea, and to land him on the English coast, the French coast, in Hamburg—where he would.

The sight of that long, sandy beach stretching for more than seventy miles in an unbroken, melancholy line, without cove, curve, or indentation to break its cruel monotony, and with the wild waves of the German Ocean, lashed by a wintry storm, breaking into white foam as far as the eye could reach, appalled the fugitive criminal. With the certainty of an ignominious death behind him, he shrank abjectly from the terrors of the sea, and, despite the honest fisherman's entreaties, refused to enter the boat and face the storm. He wandered feebly along the coast, still accompanied by his humble friend, to another little village, where the fisherman procured a wagon, which took them as far as Sandvoort. Thence he made his way through Egmond and Petten and across the Marsdiep to Texel, where, not deeming himself safe, he had himself ferried over to the neighboring island of Vlieland. Here among the quicksands, whirlpools, and shallows which mark the last verge of habitable Holland, the unhappy fugitive stood at bay.

Meantime information had come to the authorities that a suspicious stranger had been seen at Scheveningen. The fisherman's wife was arrested. Threatened with torture, she at last confessed with whom her husband had fled and whither. Information was sent to the bailiff of Vlieland, who with a party of followers made a strict search through his narrow precincts. A group of seamen seated on the sands was soon discovered, among whom, dressed in shaggy pea-jacket [1] with long fisherman's boots, was the Seigneur de Groeneveld,

[1] "Py.'

who, easily recognized through his disguise, submitted
to his captors without a struggle.   The Scheveningen
fisherman who had been so faithful to him, making a
sudden spring, eluded his pursuers and disappeared,
thus escaping the gibbet which would probably have
been his doom instead of the reward of four thousand
golden guilders which he might have had for betraying
him.   Thus a sum more than double the amount originally furnished by Groeneveld, as the capital of the
assassination company, had been rejected by the Rotterdam boatman who saved Stoutenburg, and by the
Scheveningen fisherman who was ready to save Groeneveld.   On the 19th February, within less than a fortnight from the explosion of the conspiracy, the eldest
son of Barneveldt was lodged in the Gevangen Poort,
or state prison of The Hague.[1]

The awful news of the 6th February had struck the
widow of Barneveldt as with a thunderbolt.   Both her
sons were proclaimed as murderers and suborners of
assassins, and a price put upon their heads.   She remained for days neither speaking nor weeping, scarcely
eating, drinking, or sleeping.   She seemed frozen to
stone.   Her daughters and friends could not tell
whether she were dying or had lost her reason.   At
length the escape of Stoutenburg and the capture of
Groeneveld seemed to rouse her from her trance.   She
then stooped to do what she had sternly refused to do
when her husband was in the hands of the authorities.
Accompanied by the wife and infant son of Groeneveld,
she obtained an audience of the stern stadholder, fell
on her knees before him, and implored mercy and pardon for her son.[2]

[1] Brandt, Hist. Ref., iv. 959.   [2] Ibid., 1045. Baudartius, xv. 46.

Maurice received her calmly and not discourteously, but held out no hopes of pardon. The criminal was in the hands of justice, he said, and he had no power to interfere. But there can scarcely be a doubt that he had power after the sentence to forgive or to commute, and it will be remembered that, when Barneveldt himself was about to suffer, the prince had asked the clergyman Walaeus with much anxiety whether the prisoner in his message had said nothing of pardon.

Referring to the bitter past, Maurice asked Madame de Barneveldt why she now asked mercy for her son, having refused to do so for her husband.

Her answer was simple and noble:

"My husband was innocent of crime," she said; "my son is guilty." [1]

The idea of pardon in this case was of course preposterous. Certainly if Groeneveld had been forgiven it would have been impossible to punish the thirteen less guilty conspirators, already in the hands of justice, whom he had hired to commit the assassination. The spectacle of the two cowardly ringleaders going free while the meaner criminals were gibbeted would have been a shock to the most rudimentary ideas of justice. It would have been an equal outrage to pardon the younger Barneveldts for intended murder, in which they had almost succeeded, when their great father had already suffered for a constructive lese-majesty, the guilt of which had been stoutly denied. Yet such is the dreary chain of cause and effect that it is certain, had pardon been nobly offered to the statesman whose views of constitutional law varied from those of the

[1] Brandt (ubi sup.) gives the story without citing any authority; also Van der Kemp, iv. 375.

dominant party, the later crime would never have been committed.   But Francis Aertsens, considering his own and other partizans' lives at stake if the states'-right party did not fall, had been able to bear down all thoughts of mercy.   He was successful, was called to the House of Nobles, and regained the embassy of Paris, while the house of Barneveldt was trodden into the dust of dishonor and ruin.   Rarely has an offended politician's revenge been more thorough than his. Never did the mocking fiend betray his victims into the hands of the avenger more sardonically than was done in this somber tragedy.

The trials of the prisoners were rapidly conducted. Van Dyk, cruelly tortured, confessed on the rack all the details of the conspiracy as they were afterward embodied in the sentences and have been stated in the preceding narrative.   Groeneveld was not tortured. His answers to the interrogatories were so vague as to excite amazement at his general ignorance of the foul transaction or at the feebleness of his memory, while there was no attempt on his part to exculpate himself from the damning charge.   That it was he who had furnished funds for the proposed murder and mutiny, knowing the purpose to which they were to be applied, was proved beyond all cavil and fully avowed by him.

On the 28th May, he, Korenwinder, and Van Dyk were notified that they were to appear next day in the court-house to hear their sentence, which would immediately afterward be executed.

That night his mother, wife, and son paid him a long visit of farewell in his prison.   The Gevangen Poort of The Hague, an antique but mean building of brown brick and commonplace aspect, still stands in

one of the most public parts of the city. A gloomy
archway, surmounted by windows grimly guarded by
iron latticework, forms the general thoroughfare from
the aristocratic Plaats and Kneuterdyk and Vyverberg
to the Inner Court of the ancient palace. The cells
within are dark, noisome, and dimly lighted, and even
to this day the very instruments of torture used in the
trials of these and other prisoners may be seen by the
curious. Half a century later the brothers De Witt
were dragged from this prison to be literally torn to
pieces by an infuriated mob.

The misery of that midnight interview between the
widow of Barneveldt, her daughter-in-law, and the
condemned son and husband need not be described.
As the morning approached, the jailer warned the
matrons to take their departure that the prisoner
might sleep.

"What a woeful widow you will be!" said Groeneveld to his wife, as she sank choking with tears upon
the ground. The words suddenly aroused in her the
sense of respect for their name.

"At least for all this misery endured," she said
firmly, "do me enough honor to die like a gentleman." [1]
He promised it. The mother then took leave of the
son, and History drops a decorous veil henceforth over
the grief-stricken form of Mary of Barneveldt.

Next morning the life-guards of the stadholder and
other troops were drawn up in battle array in the
Outer and Inner Courtyard of the supreme tribunal
and palace. At ten o'clock Groeneveld came forth
from the prison. The stadholder had granted as a
boon to the family that he might be neither fettered

[1] Brandt, Hist. Ref., iv. 1047, 1048.

nor guarded as he walked to the tribunal.[1]   The prisoner did not forget his parting promise to his wife.
He appeared full dressed in velvet cloak and plumed
hat, with rapier by his side, walking calmly through
the Inner Courtyard to the great hall.   Observing the
windows of the stadholder's apartments crowded with
spectators, among whom he seemed to recognize the
prince's face, he took off his hat and made a graceful
and dignified salute.[2]   He greeted with courtesy many
acquaintances among the crowd through which he
passed.   He entered the hall and listened in silence to
the sentence condemning him to be immediately executed with the sword.   Van Dyk and Korenwinder
shared the same doom, but were provisionally taken
back to prison.

Groeneveld then walked calmly and gracefully as before from the hall to the scaffold, attended by his own
valet, and preceded by the provost-marshal and assist-
ants.   He was to suffer, not where his father had been
beheaded, but on the "Green Sod."   This public place
of execution for ordinary criminals was, singularly
enough, in the most elegant and frequented quarter of
The Hague.   A few rods from the Gevangen Poort, at
the western end of the Vyverberg, on the edge of the
cheerful triangle called the Plaats, and looking directly
down the broad and stately Kneuterdyk, at the end of
which stood Aremberg House, lately the residence of
the great advocate, was the mean and sordid scaffold.

Groeneveld ascended it with perfect composure.   The
man who had been browbeaten into crime by an overbearing and ferocious brother, who had quailed before
the angry waves of the North Sea, which would have

---

[1] Baudartius, xv. 46.   [2] Ibid.

borne him to a place of entire security, now faced his
fate with a smile upon his lips. He took off his hat,
cloak, and sword, and handed them to his valet. He
calmly undid his ruff and wristbands of point-lace,
and tossed them on the ground. With his own hands
and the assistance of his servant he unbuttoned his
doublet, laying breast and neck open without suffering
the headsman's hands to approach him.

He then walked to the heap of sand and spoke a very
few words to the vast throng of spectators.

"Desire of vengeance and evil counsel," he said,
"have brought me here. If I have wronged any man
among you, I beg him for Christ's sake to forgive me."[1]

Kneeling on the sand, with his face turned toward
his father's house at the end of the Kneuterdyk, he said
his prayers. Then putting a red velvet cap over his
eyes, he was heard to mutter:

"O God, what a man I was once, and what am I
now?"

Calmly folding his hands, he said, "Patience."

The executioner then struck off his head at a blow.
His body, wrapped in a black cloak, was sent to his
house and buried in his father's tomb.

Van Dyk and Korenwinder were executed immediately afterward. They were quartered and their
heads exposed on stakes. The joiner Gerritsen and the
three sailors had already been beheaded. The Blansaerts and William Party, together with the grim Slatius, who was savage and turbulent to the last, had
suffered on the 5th May.

Fourteen in all were executed for this crime, including an unfortunate tailor and two other mechanics of

---

[1] Baudartius, xv. 46. Wagenaer, x. 473–475.

Leyden, who had heard something whispered about the conspiracy, had nothing whatever to do with it, but from ignorance, apathy, or timidity did not denounce it. The ringleader and the equally guilty Van der Dussen had, as has been seen, effected their escape.[1]

Thus ended the long tragedy of the Barneveldts. The result of this foul conspiracy and its failure to effect the crime proposed strengthened immensely the power, popularity, and influence of the stadholder, made the orthodox church triumphant, and nearly ruined the sect of the Remonstrants, the Arminians— most unjustly in reality, although with a pitiful show of reason—being held guilty of the crime of Stoutenburg and Slatius.

The Republic—that magnificent commonwealth which in its infancy had confronted, single-handed, the greatest empire of the earth, and had wrested its independence from the ancient despot after a forty years' struggle—had now been rent in twain, although in very unequal portions, by the fiend of political and religious hatred. Thus crippled, she was to go forth and take her share in that awful conflict now in full blaze, and of which after ages were to speak with a shudder as the Thirty Years' War.

[1] Brandt, Hist. Ref., ubi sup. Wagenaer, x. 473–479.

APPENDIX

APPENDIX

Vol. I. p. 104, note, and Vol. II. p. 187, note.

King James to Cecil (about anno 1608).[1]

MY littil beagle nou that I haue seene youre abstracte, quhairin I can assure you no materiall point is omitted, that is considerable in the letters, I ame to giue you so muche information for youre ansoure to my comissioners thaire as I thinke shall be necessarie for this tyme besydes that quhiche ye uith aduyce of the counsall chaire maye adde in dyuers particulaire pointes quhairwith I neide not to be troublid : the two proiectis are the two maine pointes that are to be considderit upon, of the States proiecte one generall grounde running throuch it all, & one particulaire demaunde, are to be obseruid thairin, in the frenche proiecte one generall grounde runnis throuch it all, without any other particular pointe differing from the reste, firste then, as for the States proiecte thaire generall grounde quhair upon thaire quhole proiecte doth runne is, by this defensiue league uith me & france, to take all the aduantages they can to thaime selfis, makg all the course of the league to serue for thaire particulaire, as in the hudge nombre of shippes, & of all sorte of assistance, quhiche will be most beneficiall to thaime, both by reason of the situation of thaire countreys, as lyke wayes that they haue greattest neide of help, as well because thaye are the weakest, as also because thaye are lykeliest to be first inuadie & begunne withall, but in one pointe aboue all others dois thaire partialitie to thaime

[1] From the Cecil Papers preserved in the Archives at Hatfield House.

selfis appeare in this proiecte, & that is that for the first 4
yeares after the making of this peace, thay will haue all the
prouision of shipping for assistance of any of the confœderatis,
to be made in thaire cuntreys, quhiche is the onlie pointe that
ye have forgottin in youre abstracte, but the best ansoure that
ye can guie to my comissioners anent this generall proiecte of
the league, is, that as ye have ressaved from thaime such á
frame of this league as the States haue deuysed quhairin thaye
have hadde best mynde of thaime selfis, so haue ye in youre
former dispatche, sent thaime suche conditions for a league, as
I thinke moste indifferent, & can best lyke of, and thairfore
after goode debating, lette that frame of á league be agreed
upon, quhiche maye be most indifferent for us all, & I ame
sure the groundis ye sent thaime, will be founde to agree
nearest with reason & indifferencie, & as for thaire particulaire
demande, anent yone hudge somme of money to be advancit,
nay geuin unto thaime in tyme of peace, it is so farre oute of
all squaire, as on my conscience I can not thinke that euer
thaye craued it animo obtinendi, but only by that obiection to
discourage me from any thocht of getting any repayement of
my debtis from thaime quhen thaye shall be in peace, but if
thaye will persiste any longer in this monstruouse demande,
my comissioneris muste renew thaire flatte denyall unto thaime,
as thaye haue allreaddie uerrie uell begunne, shoulde I ruyne
myselfe for maintaning thaime, shoulde I bestowe as muche
upon thaime yearelie, as commeth to the ualew of my quhole
yearelie rente, I looke that by á peace thaye shoulde en-
riche thaime selfis, & be enabled to paye me my debtis, & if
thaye be so weake, as thaye can not subsiste ather in peace or
warre without I ruyne myselfe for upholding thaime, in that
cace surelie minus malum est eligendum, the nearest harme is
to be first eschewid, á man will leape out of a burning shippe
& droune himselfe in the sea, & it is doubtlesse á farrer of
hairme from me, to suffer thaime to fall againe in the handis
of Spaine & lette god prouide for the dainger that maye
thairby with tyme fall upon me or my posteritie, then presentlie

to sterue my selfe & myne, with putting the meate in thaire
mouthe, naye rather, if thaye be so weake, as thay can nather
sustaine thaime selfis in peace nor warre, lette thaime leaue
this uainegloriouse thirsting for the tytle of á free state,
(quhiche no people are worthie, or able to enjoye that can not
stande by thaime selfis lyke substantiues,) & diuidantur inter
nos, I meane lette thaire cuntreys be deuydit betuene france &
me, otherwayes the king of spaine shall be sure to consume
us, by making us waiste our selfis to sustaine his ennemies,
naye of all things I loue not to be lyke the picture of enuye,
that dryes up her owin fleshe to the bones, for the enuye of
others prosperitie, yea the pelicane bestowis her hairte bloode
upon her owin children, but not upon straingers, & as for the
frenshe proiecte, I confesse it is sett doune in uerrie honorable
& ciuill termis, as to the exterioure pairte, but the quhole substance thairof runnes upon that maine grounde of his particulaire aduantage, quhiche is not to be wonderit at, in one of his
nature, quho onlie careth to prouyde for the felicitie of his
present lyfe, uithoute any respecte of his lyfe to come, indeid,
the considderation of his owin aage & the youthe, of his children, the doubte of thaire legitimation, the strenth of competi-
tours, & the uniuersall hatred borne unto him, makes him
seeke all meanes of securitie for preuenting of all daingers, but
the best use that can be made of this, is that presentlie the
league maye be putte to á pointe betuene me & the States, &
betuene him & thaime, & thair after (the first haiste being firste
done) we maye at bettir layser deliberate upon this maitter
betuene oure selfish. . . .

Vol. I. p. 258, note.

P. Pecquius to Archduke Albert, February 2, 1611, Paris.

Extract, Belg. Arch. MS.

Il y a 3 jours le Duc d'Epergnon continue de faire chaude
instance afin que la dite prisonnière soit punie du dernier sup-
plice pour la reparation de son honneur. Le D. de Guise et la

Marq^{se} de Verneuil ne s'en donnent pas beaucoup de peine. On pense que Condé et Soissons tachent de sauver la vie de la d^{te} Demoiselle (Coomans) pour le peu bien qu'ils veuillent au D. d'Epergnon, qui se trouve de sens assez rassis bien qu'elle soit de mauvaise vie.

Same to same, January 28, 1611. *Extract.*

Les comissaires du Parl^{t} de Paris qui sont les prem^{rs} & sec^{ds} Presidens avec deux des plus anciens consillers deputés p^{r} le fait de la Demoiselle prisonnière (Coomans) accusatrice du Duc d'Epergnon, font diligences extraordin^{res} p^{r} sondre la verité ou fausseté de l'accusation—et veult on juger par leur procedures, qu'ils doivent avoir recogneu quelques indices de verité, mesmes pour avoir fait mettre en un cachot le varlet de la Dem^{lle} du Tillet accusé par Coomans d'avoir trempé dans le complot & demain on donnera un adjournement personnel au D. d'Epergnon, ayant, à ce que l'on m'affirme la prisonnière produit une lettre du Ducq escrite à Mlle du Tillet dans laquelle il est renommé d'avoir eu prou de privauté & par la d^{te} lettre l'a qualifié come sa grand amie luy escrivant entre autres choses ce qui ensuyt. Je vous prie d'avoir en recommendation l'homme que savez: traittez le bien: et que rien ne luy manque que la dite prisonnière rapporte à Franc^{s} Ravaillac.

Un personnage des plus intimes du d^{t} Duc m'a dit que cette affaire l'a rendu extremement triste et morne quelque bonne mine qu'il faie devant le monde, mais je ne puis encore croire qu'il il y a du mal. Il est seigneur accort et de grande autorité et qui servit aussi propre à faire un soulevem^{t} par le moyen de son gouvernem^{t} de Metz et aultrem^{t} que grand qui soit en ce Roy^{me}. C'est pourquoy plus^{rs} apprehendent la conseq^{ce} du d^{t} adjournem^{t} personnel, si l'on en vient là. Le Duc de Guise et aultres princes de la maison Lorraine font semblent de ne s'en donner aucune peine, mais ils ne laissent pas de se ressentir de ce rencontre parmy le soupçon qu'ils ont de quelq. pratique du P^{ce} de Condé et du Cte de Soissons—peu de jours nous rendront plus sages.

Vol. I. p. 290, note 2.

King James to Cecil (*about* 1610).

My litle beagle for lakke of any other man heir to ease me
in making of this dispatche I ame forcid to make it with my
owin hande, ye shall thairfore knowe that my ambassadoure
can doe me no bettir seruice then in assisting to the treatie of
this reconciliation, quhairin he maye haue as goode occasion to
emploie his tongue & his pen (& I wishe it maye be with as
goode successe) as generall cecill & his soldiers haue done
thaire swordis & thaire mattokis, as for the place of meeting
that muste be lefte to the pairties to agree upon, I onlie wishe
that I maye handsomelie winde my selfe out of this querrell
quhairin the principall pairties doe so litle for thaim selfis, it is
trewe I think my ambassadouris discourse á litle metaphisicall,
for in my opinion the aduerse pairtie will be the readier to
treate in earniste that juliers is wonne, thogh thay maide shiftes
before for gaining of tyme by delaye, allwayes to conclude, an
honeste appointement nou is the onlie honorable & safe waye
for me, & thairin my ambassadour can not too muche laboure,
nou I longe to heare of balduine quhairof I wonder that he
writtes nothing.   fairwell.

(Signed)   JAMES R.

Vol. I. p. 320, note 1.

Sir R. Winwood to the King, April 7, 1612.

May yt please yor Ma^ty,

Returning from Weesel, where by order from yor Ma^ty I
have concluded the treaty, wth the Commissioners sent from
the Electors, and Princes of th' Union, whereof, at thys tyme, I
doe make a particular accownte, to the Lo: Treasurier, I did
happily meete wth the C^t Maurice at Arneham in Guelderland,
the last of Marche. whom after I had saluted affectuously
from yor Ma^ty, and in yor name, rendred him, many, and harty

thancks, for hys carefull and industrious indeavours for the maintenance of the truthe of religion, lyvely expressed in prosecuting the cawse agaynst Vorstius, and hys adherents, I sayd, I had commandment by express charge from yor Ma^{ty}, to delyver to him, thys message: That yor Ma^{ty}, conferring the present condition of thaffayres of these quartiers of the worlde, with those advrtissem^{ts}, you dayly doe receave from yor Mynisters abroade, together, wth the nature and disposition of thoase men, who have in their hands, the manadging of all busines in thease forrayne parts, can make noe other iudgement then thys, that there ys a generall ligue, and confœderation complotted for the subuersion, and ruyne of religion, upon the subsistance whereof, yor Ma^{ty} dothe iudge, the mayne welfare, as of your realmes, soe of thease provinces solely to consist. Therefore yor Ma^{ty} had geven me charge, out of the knowledge you have of hys greate worthe, and sufficiencye, and the confidence you repose, in hys faythe, and afection freely to treate wth him of thease poynts,: and wthall, to pray him in yor Ma^{tys} name, to delyver hys opinion, what way he did holde the most compendious, and the most assured, to counterquarr thease complotts, and to frustrat the malice of thease mischevous desseigns:　After the C^t had acknowledged wythe very humble respecte, the honor yor Ma^{ty} dothe vouchesafe to doe him, in holding of him soe gracious an opinion, wherein, he sayde, yor Ma^{ty} showlde never be deceaved, and in exchange whereof, he did present to yor Ma^{ty}, hys humble and loyall service:, he answeared that he did concurr in iudgement wth yor Ma^{ty}, that the mayne scope at wch thease plotts, and practizes did ayme, wch he instanced in thalliances between france and spayne, is thys, to roote out religion and by consequence, to bring under th^r yoake, all thoase cowntryes in whiche religion ys professed: the fyrst attempt he sayde, dowbtless was intended, agaynst thease provinces.　The meanes, to countermyne and defeate thease prciected desseigns, he toake to be thease:　The continuance of yor Ma^{tys} constant resolution, for the protection of religion,: then that

yor Ma^{ty} woulde be pleased, to procure a generall confœderation, between the kyngs, princes and common wealthes, professing religion, namely Denmark Sueueland, the Princes of
Grmany, the protestant Cantons of the Suisses and thease
united provinces: and of thys confederation, yor Ma^{ty} to be,
not only the director, but the head, and protector. Lastly,
that by ye favour and countenance you, and yf necessitye so
did requyre yt, by the assistance of thease confederates, the
protestantes of france might be, yf not supported, yet at least
relieved, from that oppression, wch the alliance wth spayne
dothe threaten upon them, and on thys, he long insysted, as
th' only couppe-gorge, of all resultats, whatsoever, between
france and spayne. when he had long, and at larg٬ discoursed
of thease poynts, I asked, what apparance there cou̇ld be, of
thys generall confederation whenas thease provinces, wch here-
tofore have been accounted a principall member of the reformed
churche, beganne to falter in truthe of religion: and that he,
who solely did gouuerne in the metropolitan province of Holland, was reputed generally, as he best knowe, to be the only
Patron of Vorstius, and the protector of the schismes of Arminius. And likewyse, what possibilitye that the protestantes
of france could expect favo^r, from thease provinces, when the
same man ys knowen solely to depend at the devotion of france.
To my fyrst demande, he gave thys answeare, that thoughe
Monsr Barnevelt had cast off all care of religion, and that some
townes in Holland, wherein hys power dothe raigne, were
infected wth the like neglect, yet soe long as soe many good
townes in Holland stand sownd, and all the provinces yf thys
confederacy, were propownded, yt would be at the fyrst motion,
cheerefully accepted: But he confessed, that he fownd diffi-
cultye, to satisfye my second demande, acknowledging, that
Barnevelt wholly ys devoted to the service of france. for
sayde he, during the treaty of truce, upon some differents
between them, the President Jennin came to him, requyring
him in the frenche kyngs name, to treate Monsr Barnevelt well,
whom the king had receaved into hys protection. he added,

thys second reason, that suche letters wch the states Ambassad^r residing in france, hath written to Barnevelt (and to him all Ambassad^{rs}, address th^r dispatches of importance) the very autographa themselves, he sent back into the hands of de villeroy.   And hereupon, he entred into a large discourse, how suspicious the proceedings of thys man are, and how dangerous to their state: when one man who hathe the conducte of all affayres in hys sole power shall holde underhand intelligence, wth the Mynisters of spayne, and the Archduke, and that wthout warrant: whereby, he may have the meanes so to carye the course of affayres, that wyll they nyll they, thease provinces must fall, or stand at the mercy, and discretion of spayne. That therefore, some good resolution may be taken in tyme, to holde up the state from a sodaine downefall, wherein he sayde muche moderation, and discretion ys to be vsed, he tolde me, that he had called hether, agaynst May day, his Cosen the C^t wylliam of Nassau, who ys bothe a wyse, and a religious nobleman, that they bothe together, may resolve of some suche course wch they hope shall preserve, thease cowntryes from confusion, under the protection of yor Ma^{tys} savegard, and thassurance of yor subiects, wch are in thys service, who are, bothe the strengthe, and flower of thys armye.

Thys ys the somme of all that passed between us in thys matter, wherein, when the Ct had soe freely opened himselfe, I made knowen unto him, yor Matys purpose, to bestowe on him the honor of yor Ordre of the garter: and wthall, bothe for my better creditt wth him for thys present, and my future negotiations, prayed him to reade yor Mat^{ys} lettr sent to me: wch when he had done, he sayde, yf yor Ma^{ty} showld holde him worthye of so greate honor, he, and hys familye, showlde ever remayne, as ever they have been, bownd to yor service, and to the service of yor royall posteritye. whye, the states showlde be offended he sawe noe cawse, yet holding the charge he dothe, in their service, aftr he showld have notice of yor gracious favour, he cowld not accept yt, wthowt fyrst acquaynting them, therewth, and receaving therein their approbation.

To wch, I answeared, that yor Ma^{ty} did well understand in what quallitye he lyved wth the states, and therefore he cowld not but thinck, that it was yor intention upon the election of him, into yor Ordre, to be the fyrst that showld aduertyse the States thereof, and to gyve me charge to lett them knowe, that yor Ma^{ty} did iudge, that you did honor the mutuall amytie between your realmes, and their provinces, by honoring the vertues of their Generall, whose services as they have been most faythefull, and affectionnat, so have they been accompanyed with the blessings of happines and prosperous succes. wch yf yor Maty shall vouchesafe to doe, you shall, una fidelia duos dealbare parietes, renverse the desseigns of them, who to facilitat their owne practises do indeavour to alienate yor affections from the good of thease provinces, and oblige to yor service, the well affected people, who doth well knowe, that there is noe surety for themselves, their wyfes, and chyldren, but under the protection of yor Ma^{tys} favour.   Thys perhaps may ensue, that the favourers of Vorstius and Arminius, wyll busse into the eares of their associates, that yor Ma^{ty} would make a party in thease provinces, : fyrst by maintayning and protecting the truthe of religion : then by gayning unto you, the affections of their cheefe Commander, : but yor Ma^{ty} may be pleased to pass forthe : whose worthye ends will take their place, wch is to honor vertue where you fynd yt : and the suspicious surmises of malice, and envye, in one instant, will vanishe into smoake.   what hereaft^r yor Ma^{ty} shalbe pleased to direct, for the continuance of thys negotiation, wch on my part shall duetifully be observed wth secrecy, and faythefulnes, I humbly attend.   And so praying daylye, on the knees, bothe of body, and harte for the preservation of yor royall Ma^{ty}, I rest in humble duetye,

yor Ma^{tyes}

loyall subiect, and obedient
servant.

from the Haghe   (Signed)   RALPHE WINWOOD.
the 7 of April.
stilo vet.

Vol. I. p. 320, note 2.

Sir R. Winwood to Viscount Rochester, April 7, 1612.

Right honorable my very good Lo: I now make answeare to hys Ma^tys letter by thys enclosed: wch I beseeche yor l^p to delyver wth the best conveniency, and to be pleased, to shadowe thimperfections of my wryting, wch are many, wth the cowntenance of yor favo^r. The letter ys long, and tedious, but the negotiation could not be comprysed in fewer words. The C^t Maurice dothe accept wth grateful respect the honor hys Ma^ty doth entend to confer upon him, but being in that qualitye he ys, wth the states, he sayes aft^r notice geven to him of the choice, he fyrst must receave th^r approbation. Perhaps yt may seeme incongruous in thys different, between them and hys Ma^ty in the cawse of Vorstius, that hys Ma^ty should make shewe, that in the bestowing thys honor upon their Generall, he hathe any reference to the esteeme he holdeth of th^r allyance. But yt is not, for the good of thease cowntryes, in whose conservation, his Ma^tys crownes are deeply interessed, that hys Ma^ty showld gyve waye, to the desseigns of them who of purpose by th^r perversenes, doe studye to make, a divorce between hys Ma^tys realmes, and thease provinces, the more easilye to precipitate them, into the armes of spayne. Thys negotiation wth the C^t Maurice, being now on foote, is to be followed, but wth muche secrecye, in regard of the place he holdeth wth the states. therefore, untyll I shall receave other order, I wyll take the boldenes to address my lett^rs to yor l^p:, but whether I shall wryte to hys Ma^ty, or yor lp, I humbly crave yor lps directions.

I have order from hys Ma^ty by hys lett^rs of the $\overline{17}$ of Marche to make knowen to the states of Holland, that the resolution wch they pretend, to have taken, about Vorstius, dothe gyve him noe satisfaction. But they are seperated to their severall townes, neyth^r will they reassemble, before the end of thys monethe. yet sence my returne, from weesel, I have declared to Monsr Barnevelt, what hys Mat^y doth requyre and that noe contentment can be geven him, but by the banishment of Vorstius out of thease cowntryes, he answeared, that yf the towne of Leyden should undrstand soe muche he did feare, that the Magistraty would retayne him styll in their towne; I replyed, that yf the towne of Leyden should retayne Vorstius, to brave or despight hys Mat^y, hys Mat^y had the meanes, yf yt pleased him to use them, and that wthout drawing sworde, to range them to rayson, and to make the Magistrats on their knees demand hys pardon. and the like I sayd of Rottrdam, : At thys speache hys choller was kyndled, : he sayd was borne in lybertye, and therefore could not disgest suche kynde of language, : the kynge of spayne he sayd did never speake in soe highe a style. I replyed, that I did well undrstand that logick; he helde hys argument; to be drawen a Maiori ad Minus : but I prayed him to beleeve, that the kyng of greate brittanye, was payre and campagnon to the kyng of spayne, and that hys Mot ys, Nemo me lacessit impunè. And upon thease termes we parted for that tyme. I fynd thys man extreemely distempered, and whatsoever the matter ys, as extremely distasted wth hys Mat^y: so that I tolde him, at my last being wth him, that whatsoever I propownded in hys Matys name, could fynd wth him, neyther goust, nor grace. Some say, that at hys being in England, when hys Maty fyrst came to the crowne, he conceaved some offence wch ever sence hathe ranckled in hys harte, and now dothe b.. st forthe, wth more violent malice. I holde yt necessarye for hys Matys service, not to conceale thease particularityes, : wch hathe made me the bolder to geve yor Lp thys trowble. for wch I pray to be excused; and soe rest

Yor Lps very humbly
to be commanded
(Signed)   RALPHE WINWOOD.

from ye Haghe
    the 7th of April

Vol. II. p. 174, note 2.

King James to Cecil (about 1606).

My littill beagill I haue nou talked at lenth with Caroun in quhom I fynde that hys englishe education cannot amende his native germane prolixitie, for if I hadde not interruptid him it hadde bene tomorrou morning before I hadde beganne to speake, god perserue me from hearing a cause debatid betwene don diego & him, alluayes he & I are uerrie uell agreed in all things, he will informe his maisters of my inclination in gen- erall, & of this requeste of myne in speciall, that I doe it not as uonne by the importunitie of Spaine, or as blynde of Spaines encrochements upon my fauoure, but upon á seene uell for me & the States both, in tymes to come, upon Spaines promeise neuer to playe any more suche evilles in my harboures, & if thay doe, that I uill allow the States to pursew thaime to my uerrie shoare, I haue ingenuouslie tolde him that I uill thinke my selfe muche obleished to the statis if thay graunte it, but will not quarrell thaim for refusall thairof, if upon á sounde reason, & he hath faithfullie promeist to persuaide thaime to it all he can, & in his owin opinion he thinkis it reasonable, & thairfor the sooner ye make readdie the dispatche for Winuoode, the bettir it is, thus haue I walked in uia regia, uith both the pairties, & I proteste to god I care not allthoch euerie one tolde quhat I saide to the other, qui uadit plané uadit sané, all the particulaire arguments I remitte to the bearar is relation, I haue also spoken unto him anent the trade that some middes micht be founde out in that maitter, quhiche althoch he con- fessis is á uerrie tendir pointe, yett he sayes it is not only á thing reasonable but necessarie, that some meanes maye be agreed upon quhairby the archieduike may ressaue some measure of satisfaction in that pointe, in treuth it is goode dealing with so uyse & honest á man, allthoch he be some quhat longsome, ye maye upon sondaye lett me see the draucht of the lettir to Winuoode, & the lesse that caroun make the frenche

ambassadoure aquainted with this maitter till it be at á pointe,
it will uorke the bettir, fairwell.

(Signed)   JAMES R.

I haue also spokin with the frenshe
ambassadoure anent the matter of
the marchants, he is willinglie con-
tentid to speake uith you in that
maitter before the meiting in france,
& to ende it in substance betuene
you before it goe thaire.

Vol. III. p. 59, note 1.

Letter of Count Louis of Nassau to John of Barneveldt.

WILHELM LUDWIG GRAVE TOE NASSAU etc., Stadhouder in
Frieslandt etc.

Edele, Strenge, Erentveste, Hoochgeleerde ende discrete
besondere goede vrundt, Syner Excellentie hebben wy opt
gevouchelyext voorgestelt, wat U. E. desen voormiddach aen
ons versocht hebben, maer bevinden, dat Syne Excellentie nyet
en sal bewegen syn eenigen anderen voorslach te doen, als 't
Synode Nationael, twelck deselve bij allen Provintien voorge-
slagen ende tot bevorderinge van dien sooveel debvoirs gedaen
heeft, twelck oock alreede by Myneheeren de Staten Generael
uytgeschreven is, Soodat Syn Excellencie anders nyet dan tot
merckelicken ondienst van 't landt ende tsyner eygenen dis-
reputatie en soude konnen gedoen.

Aengaende de wertgelders, vernemen wy een groot misnou-
gen in 't affeyschen van eenen particulieren eedt, insonderheyt
wijl deselve per indirectum soude konnen misbruijckt werden
tot oppressie van die van de religie, emmers in allen gevalle by
deser occasie tot verkleineringe van Syner Excellentie nodigen
respect ende wettelicke authoriteyt soude moeten kommen te
strecken, daerop U. E. nae syne wysheyt konnen letten.

Wy sullen sien by wat gelegenheyt by Syn Excellentie sal willen vallen d' audientie, ende voor sooveel in ons is U. E. by derselver alle goede offitien doen.

Hebbende nyet eer konnen antwoorden omdat de Heeren Ambassadeurs van Vranckrijck desen voormiddach audientie gehadt ende nu nae den middach Syn Excellentie gevisiteert hebben.

Wunschende U. E. eenen goeden avont.

Uyt onse kamer den 4/14 Augusti 1618.

U. E. sehr goede vryndt

(Signed)   WILHELM LUDWIG GRAFF ZU NASSAU.

Same to same.

WILHELM LUDWIG GRAVE TOE NASSOU, CATZENELNBOGEN etc. Stadthouder etc.

Edele, Strenge, Erentveste, Hoochgeleerde ende discrete besundere goede vrundt, Wy hebben d' occasie waergenomen ende Syn Excellencie voorgedragen dat U. E. wel geneycht waeren met deselve te treden in communicatie over d' accommodatie so van de religions differenten als cassatie der waertgelderen; waerop Syn Excellencie ons ter antwoordt heeft gegeven geene veranderinge in 't stuck van 't synode nationael te sullen konnen voorstaen, maer des nyettemin t' U^r E. goede gelegenheyt stellen, wanneer 't derselver believen sal tot haer te komen. Ende also wij vermercken dat Syne Excellencie qualick ende hooch is nemende de proceduren by de Hollandsche Gedeputeerden tot Uytrecht gehouden, seggende expresselick dat het sy eene conspiratie tegens hem ende den staet van 't landt, hebben nijet konnen verbygaen U. E. hiervan te preadviseren, om sich in de communicatie des te beeter daernae te richten.

U. E. sehr goede vrindt

(Signed)   WILHELM LUDWIG GRAFF ZU NASSAU.

Uyt onse camere

den 5/15^n Augusti 1618.

INDEX

INDEX

[The volumes are indicated by Roman numerals.]

A

Aachen, ii. 5, 6.

Aertsens, Cornelis van, iii. 151–153.

Aertsens, Francis, minister of the states in Paris, i. 31, 37, 38, 77, 78, 84, 180, 187, 191, 192, 205, 211, 236, 248, 266, 267, 329–331, 333, 334; his character and position, ii. 19–21; his letter to Maldere, 23; intrigues of the French court against him, 25, 26; interview with Mary de' Medici about the claim of the "Third," 25–28; his recall, 32, 84; remains two years longer in France, 69; derives many advantages from his post, 72, 73; receives unusual presents, 77; objections to his return to France, 81, 82; resides in Zealand, 290; his efforts to excite popular animosity against Barneveldt, 290; his aim to bring about a rupture between the Republic and France, iii. 77, 78; is elevated to the body of nobles, 88; purchases the barony of Sommelsdyk, and is received into the college of knights, 136; appointed special ambassador to Paris, 249, 250.

Agean, M. du, iii. 34, 38.

Albert, Archduke, i. 102, 109, 139, 153, 166, 167, 220, 246; ii. 9, 14.

Amsterdam, reception of Prince Maurice at, iii. 17–19.

Ancre, Marquis d'. *See* Concini.

Angoulême, Duchess of, i. 128, 146.

Anhalt, Prince of, i. 118, 119, 230, 232.

Añover, i. 140.

Arme haenen, or "poor cocks," iii. 47.

Arminians, the, called Remonstrants, ii. 46, 47; pronounced heretics, schismatics, etc., iii. 138.

Arminius, Jacob, appointed professor of theology at Leyden, i. 46; accused of being in correspondence with the Jesuits, ii. 316.

Arnheim, i. 314; yields to the stadholder, iii. 2.

Asti, the peace of, ii. 154.

B

"Balance, The," a stinging and well-merited criticism on Carleton's orations, ii. 274, 275.

Barneveldt, Elias, succeeds his brother John as pensionary of Rotterdam, i. 16; appointed one of the special high commissioners to the King of Great Britain, 192.

Barneveldt, John of, founder of the Dutch Republic, i. 3, 4; advocate and keeper of the great seal of Holland, 12; his genealogy, 13, 14; his studies in the universities, 14; chief pensionary of Rotterdam, 14; head of the embassy to England and France, 15; proposes and carries the appointment of Maurice of Nassau to the stadholdership of Holland, 16; accepts the post of advocate for Holland, 16; makes a compromise between church and state, 19; sent as ambassador to Henry IV., 19; employed by the king on legal and other business, 20; proceeds with Justinus de Nassau to England to have an interview with Queen Elizabeth, 20; sent again to England on James's accession, 21; treaty with Spain, 22; letter to the envoy of France, 24; antagonism between him and Maurice, 26; sounded by the princess dowager as to the feasibility of procuring the sovereignty for Maurice, 28, 29; his majestic presence and fluent eloquence with tongue and pen, 33; his answer to a states ambassador, 34; the consistent and strenuous champion of the civil authority over the church, 51; recognizes the rights of the possessory princes in the duchies, 74–76, 118; urged by the king to go to Paris, 117, 118; his difficult position, 178, 179; extemporizes a system of free international communication, 181, 182; Aertsens remonstrates with him about his son, 190, 191; urged by Sully to come

313